HEIRS OF THE
GREEK CATASTROPHE

On an auspicious
meeting – Colson
lecture 2001 –
with every good wish

Renée.

D1339006

renee.hirschon@
spc.ox.ac.uk

Romantic love was not considered a sound basis for marriage, but through a life devoted to the family the spouses would come to enjoy companionship and affection

HEIRS OF THE GREEK CATASTROPHE

The Social Life of Asia Minor Refugees in Piraeus

RENÉE HIRSCHON

*with a new Preface by the Author
and a Foreword by Michael Herzfeld*

Berghahn Books
NEW YORK • OXFORD

First published in 1989 by
Oxford University Press, New York

Published in 1998 by

Berghahn Books

Editorial offices:
55 John Street, 3rd Floor, New York, NY 10038 USA
3 Newtec Place, Magdalen Road, Oxford, OX4 1RE, UK

© 1989, 1998 Renée Hirschon

All rights reserved.
No part of this publication may be reproduced
in any form or by any means
without the written permission of Berghahn Books.

Library of Congress Cataloging-in-Publication Data

Hirschon, Renee.
    Heirs of the Greek catastrophe : the social life of Asia Minor
refugees in Piraeus / Renée Hirschon ; with a foreword by Michael
Herzfeld ; and a new preface by the author.
        p.   cm.
    Includes bibliographical references and index.
    ISBN 1-57181-730-1 (alk. paper)
    1. Refugees, Political--Greece--Piraeus--Social life and customs.
2. Greco-Turkish War, 1921-1922--Refugees. 3. Piraeus (Greece)-
-Social life and customs.   I. Title.
DF951.P56H57 1998
949.5'1--dc21   98-39616
                                                                   CIP

British Library Cataloguing in Publication Data

A catalogue record for this book is available from the British Library.

Printed in the United States on acid-free paper.

For my father
Barney

69 ႟ငC3

07789⁄600060

078535 39896

ႠႥ ၂ ႖ꝛ

CONTENTS

LIST OF PLATES

Romantic love was not considered a sound basis for marriage, but through a life devoted to the family the spouses would come to enjoy companionship and affection   *frontispiece*

LIST OF ILLUSTRATIONS

LIST OF TABLES

FOREWORD

The basic metaphors of anthropology are strongly grounded in space and building. Home is the fundamental unit through which human beings translate their sociability into material form and in which they invest an enduring significance, perpetuating their social existence either through the creation of lasting monuments or through the reproduction of what space and society share—structure.

Renée Hirschon has written one of the first ethnographic studies to recognise and exploit this relationship. Like myself a student of John Campbell—whose extraordinary talent it has been to nurture a diverse but enthusiastic and mutually appreciative crowd of historians and anthropologists—but also a trained student of the built environment, she has pursued an approach that is no less significant for social anthropology for being so modestly framed. Hers is one of the first ethnographies of any society to be radically attentive to the importance of space.

Greeks, like many others, are attentive to questions of spatial division. Their intense focus on the distinction between exterior appearances and interior intimacies, a cultural theme intensified by the country's all too painfully ambivalent relationship with a "Europe" that alternately shuns it and tries to co-opt it, would make any study of the Greek uses of domestic space interesting. Hirschon's book is much more than that, however, for it brings this central issue together with issues of memory and history, refugee experience, and gender—all of which have played central roles in subsequent anthropological debates. In a sense it was a book before its time, and one that appeared relatively early in the recent explosion of interest in Europeanist anthropology. Its publication now in a paperback edition is ridiculously overdue.

Hirschon was one of the first anthropologists working in an urban setting to question the wisdom of constituting a distinctive category of "urban anthropology." She has been steadfast in her belief that this division of labour within the discipline creates artificial discontinuities. Again, I would argue that she had presciently identified something that has become far more apparent now that anthropologists no longer view "their" communities as cultural and social isolates or confine their fieldwork to single, dehistoricized localities: the persistence of cultural values that are shared by urban and rural dwellers (and that may actually become intensified in an urban context). Her analysis of the relationship between space and religion is particularly significant here, especially given the fact that many of her informants were communists and therefore unlikely to have been warmly disposed to the formal representatives of established religion. Yet, just as one cannot understand the imagery of left-wing European literature without knowing something of the varieties of liturgy and doctrine, it is clear from Hirschon's work that any study of predominantly leftist Greeks would be nonsensical without regard to the deeply ingrained religiosity that others have reported from the rural hinterlands—where, indeed, deep strains of anti-clericalism, albeit in a rather different form, are couched in an idiom clearly shaped by religious values.

But perhaps the greatest achievement of this book is its portrayal of human resilience in the aftermath of catastrophic events. The people of Kokkinia came there as refugees from Asia Minor. They fled hideous cruelties and arrived to a grimly indifferent or even downright hostile reception at the hands of local Greeks they themselves despised as provincial and uncultured. This is a dynamic that we find repeated in many parts of the world where large and violent displacements of population have taken place. Hirschon's study is an extraordinary portrait of social and cultural endurance, of adaptation, of compromise, and of a dignified adherence to deeply treasured identities and convictions. In the decade of Bosnia and Rwanda, of Palestinian resurgence and Albanian hopelessness, and in the face of the nearby and related tragedy of a divided Cyprus, this study provides a perspective of unique chronological depth on the persistence of refugee identity as well as the adaptations that this entails.

In 1989 this book represented a significant departure in method and focus. In the decade since then it has remained unique, and some of its strengths have become more obvious, or perhaps more important. True, others have written about urban Greece, myself included. But that urban focus is, for Hirschon, not a legitimate basis for claiming originality (although this work was indeed the first full ethnography of an urban setting in Greece). Rather, the real originality of the book lies in its transference to a European context of the kind of symbolic analysis of spatial use and meaning that one might have expected to find applied (for example) to the dwellings of the Kabyle or the Purum.

It is thus an important contribution, not to the more self-indulgent variety of reflexive ethnography, but to a kind of *cultural* reflexivity. The ethnographer's own assumptions about the social uses of space are always in question. As we read, we are drawn into the same kind of self-examination as that which she practises—again, not narcissistically, but in the sense of questioning how our unspoken assumptions about our built environment may too blindly determine our understanding of what on the face of it is an extremely familiar-looking society.

If Hirschon rejects the category of "urban anthropology," she is no happier with the facile reduction of socially organised space to the domains of public and private. Rather, she argues, we should see the ideals of gender complementarity that are to be found throughout Greek society as underlying the uses of space in this community. Some may feel today that this is too redolent of structuralist theories about complementary opposition. But Hirschon is no hostage to an outmoded (or even a currently fashionable) theoretical paradigm. Rather, she identifies the patterns that emerge most readily from what her informants have themselves taught her. And if this happens to suggest that Greeks are structuralist at heart, that is a question for others—political historians, perhaps— to try to explain. What she has produced is important in its own right, as a clear demonstration that people translate their socially grounded cosmologies into arrangements and uses of domestic space even when they would disclaim any supernatural foundation for the world they inhabit.

Finally, this is one of the first ethnographies to situate material objects and memory in a common framework. Much has since been written about both memory and material culture. In this ethnography both are present—furniture and icons play an especially dramatic role—in an unobtrusively profound synthesis. Here, perhaps more than in any other respect, Hirschon's sensitivity to the material conditions of everyday life sets a standard of observation and interpretation for contemporary research.

Heirs of the Greek Catastrophe suffered, in its original publication, both from being ahead of its time and for seeming (as it no longer does) to be simply another ethnography of an ethnographically unfashionable place. We can now read it with the distinct advantage of hindsight and can appreciate both its author's remarkable anticipation of intellectual concerns centred on refugee studies and its practical relevance to an understanding of our presently conflict-ridden times. As a few lone voices in the Balkans, in particular, begin to make themselves heard against the stridency of competing chauvinisms, this book will encourage them to persevere. It is a moving but scholarly testament to the capacity of human beings to create, quite literally, a space for hope amidst the hopelessness into which others have tried to cast them. And it is an exemplary demonstration of the powerful and often underappreciated insight that ethnography can bring to bear on the immediate consequences of historical events and global politics.

Michael Herzfeld
Harvard University
June 1998

PREFACE TO THE
PAPERBACK EDITION

Exactly twenty-five years ago, I was sitting on the linoleum floor of the prefabricated shack which had been my home in Kokkinia. It was June in the fiftieth year after the defeat of the Greek Army in Anatolia which had caused the demographic map of the Aegean region to be altered radically and with staggering finality. The Lausanne Convention (30 January 1923) specified the first ever compulsory exchange of populations—'ethnic cleansing' by another name—internationally endorsed in the Treaty of Lausanne (July 1923). This movement involved the reciprocal exchange of most of the Muslims and Orthodox Christians of the countries of Greece and Turkey. It resulted in the uprooting of 350,000 Muslims from Greece, and the settlement of over one million Christians in the Greek state, increasing its population by about 25 per cent in only two years. Many of the people with whom I had been living for over a year were among these refugees. As I was packing up my household goods, books and notebooks, with the summer heat and roadside noises an additional irritant in the disturbing process of ending my fieldwork, I had little indication of what my experience was to yield over time. Besides the obvious professional consequences, I have come to realise in retrospect that it was for me an intensive period of learning. Like many people in an age of increasing mobility and transience, my own life has been one of continual readjustment to new lives in new places. The 'refugee lesson' which I absorbed by living in Kokkinia showed me the importance of engaging with new circumstances in flexible ways, of maintaining continuity and meaningful action, the significance of memory and of values in times of disruption, and it revealed the multiple dimensions of identity.

The Asia Minor refugees, dramatically expelled from their homeland so many decades ago, may well have something valuable to teach us in the contemporary world. Certainly, their experience has direct relevance to the conditions of tens of millions of displaced persons who are forced to abandon their homes every year for fear of their lives, or through development policy decisions. The ever-increasing number of forcibly displaced persons has become a major humanitarian problem in the past two decades (some 25 million in 1997, UNHCR). The now-recognised field of 'refugee studies' did not exist when I first started working in this area, and even now there are few ethnographic studies of refugee groups[1] and fewer which cover a long time-span.[2] The extent of forced migration in many parts of the world over the past few decades has raised international concern and prompted various responses and action, and highlights the need for such studies.

The Asia Minor refugees' experience has particular relevance for current events in the Balkans, as well as for the tragic situation which developed in the post-Second World War period in Cyprus. As the instability and flashpoints of conflict recur, leading to the chopping-up of the former Republic of Yugoslavia into separate 'ethnic' states, and the current volatile situation in the province of Kosovo with its potential for even wider international conflict, lessons from history and from other parts of the region are required. Again we are witnessing the expression of post-Ottoman ethnic problems which have occurred at intervals and in various multi-ethnic locales through the region for over a century. Events in the Balkans were developing while international intervention proved unwilling to, or incapable of, preventing a major human tragedy. The solution, when it did come, entailed the removal of Bosnians, Croats and Serbs from their various homes to 'home-lands' shared by their ethnic brethren. Poignant parallels exist. The Asia Minor refugees' experience in Greece allows us to see what kind of life people have when they become 'strangers at home', in what outsiders sometimes erroneously see as 'repatriation' (how can you be 'repatriated' to a place you do not come from, that is not your home?).

This opportunity to re-introduce the anthropological analysis of my experience in Kokkinia might have provided the ideal time to produce a 'Kokkinia revisited'. This is not my intention, however. The book and the fieldwork upon which it is based are situated in a temporal context, and stand as a representation of a specific moment in the lives of those people, of the place, and of myself. The book marks a finitude of the task, but its reissue gives me the chance to make explicit some of the embedded issues which are not discussed in the work. As I noted in my Preface to the 1989

book, its writing took place over many years. Fieldwork predated
that of the submission of the final manuscript by fifteen years, an
inordinately long period. It did allow a maturation of my thinking
but, on the other hand, by the time it was published, the delay had
diminished some points of innovation.

My interest in the cultural dimension of spatial organisation
arose out of my earlier training and research in urban geography in
Cape Town in the early 1960s. This gave me confidence later in
dealing with the urban morphology of Kokkinia, and certainly
facilitated the analysis of social life in its spatial dimension. I
was interested in perceptual geographical territories, the imbued
meanings attached to 'spaces' which transformed them into
'places'. I was able to plot the informal definition of neighbourhoods in the unbounded setting of the city. I myself became
increasingly involved as a neighbour, and I learned much about
the existence of 'community' in its fullest sense through the vitality of relationships between neighbours, so sadly absent in many
urban localities today. In my work in Kokkinia, I paid special attention to spatial organisation and its symbolism, to reconstructions of
the family cycle in relation to the house and to associated cultural
values. All of this was innovative, and grew out of sensitivity to
architectural issues through my two year association (1968–1970)
with the ACE, the Athens Centre of Ekistics (a multidisciplinary
approach to human settlements created by C. Doxiadis).

My first exploration of Kokkinia in 1969 was through a survey
of spatial use and its relation to cultural values and priorities
while working at the ACE. A joint research project with an Indian
architect, S. Thakurdesai, took place before the publication of
Amos Rapoport's groundbreaking *House Form and Culture* (1969).
This collaboration was in itself an anthropological experience
since our assumptions and expectations were very different.
Thakurdesai was amazed that, under extremely cramped conditions, these Greek housewives insisted on their separate kitchen
space, however minimal, and even though they were usually
blood relatives. By contrast, the joint family residence of his own
experience in Bombay entailed a single kitchen used together by
all co-resident daughters-in-law under the mother-in-law's guidance. I was struck by the impracticality of furnishings, the multi-
functionality of rooms, and the different priorities put upon the

use of space, especially the imperative of providing a dowry 'home' for daughters. Working in an international organisation, one branch of which produced large-scale development plans and housing for many parts of the world, we had already become aware of the unsuitability of some schemes to the local needs, customs and practices of the particular locality (clients were from Ghana, Pakistan, Brazil but the basic design was standard). Our survey in Kokkinia provided even more evidence of the importance of cultural values in planning and development projects. This was the impetus for me to return, after a break from university work, to doctoral research in anthropology which I chose to do in Oxford, starting in 1970.

And so I embarked on what turned out to be one of the first full length urban ethnographies in Europe. Besides the challenge to fieldwork methods posed by the city as an unbounded metropolitan complex (and here my geographical training stood me in good stead), another was the dimension of the past. History had to be dealt with. It was clear that I needed to examine both macro- and micro-scale historical factors in order to understand the lives of refugees in Kokkinia in the 1970s. The incorporation of an explicit historical dimension was necessary not only for epistemological reasons, but also at the level of people's lives. It was not possible to understand the '*Mikrasiates*' sense of identity without knowing about the events which had brought about their settlement in this urban locality. Clearly, it was indefensible to neglect the previous fifty years of the refugees' experience in the modern Greek state. Even less could I have ignored their memories of life in the homeland in Asia Minor. I was challenged into analysing the role of memory in social life and its significance in the context of cultural values and practices. Memory—now a buzz word in contemporary anthropology—was at that time a somewhat novel focus of attention; little reference material was at hand.

This was where the real test of an interpretative anthropological approach was made. My intention to study the lives of city dwellers assumed that I was dealing with people who were 'Greek'. Although I knew that they were of refugee origin, I did not anticipate that the issue of identity was to play a major part in an interpretation of life in Kokkinia. But I was soon shaken into a sharp awareness of the fine lines of separation and identification which the people living in this locality used, the ways in which they referred to themselves and to others. 'We *Mikrasiates*', they used to say, differentiating themselves in various ways from the 'locals' or 'Greeks'. From the outsider's point of view, actual differences appear to be non-existent or minimal, and the issue, therefore, is one of definition and boundaries. The existence of a sense of separate identity among Asia Minor Greeks might have been expected, but to encounter it based upon perceived differences amongst their descendants into the third and fourth generation deserved attention. This finding has been borne out by other studies of Asia Minor groups in Greece. Was this a limiting case of 'ethnicity'? If so, what does it tell us about 'ethnic' phenomena, and about ways of marking identity more generally? The persistent salience of cultural notions and perceptions, their transformation into different social circumstances, struck me forcibly. Again this feature might be instructively included in contemporary assessments of the consequences of forced displacement and resettlement for people in other parts of the Balkan and Aegean region, as well as in the Middle East, those areas where the Ottoman legacy is strong, and where such disruption to human lives is an ongoing process.

My approach to theory can be stated here, since little was said in the book. Theory is not absent: for me, theory is embedded in the nature of the task. It informs the structure of the text, the selection of the material that is presented and analysed, as well as the ways in which that analysis takes place, and the kind of interpretation which results. It is difficult to classify oneself, and I am especially aware of a kind of theoretical fluidity. I think of theory and concepts as tools in a tool box, chosen for their suitability to do a certain job. They are a means to an end, not the end in themselves, for the end is to make sense of one's lived experience among a people, to arrive at an understanding of the quality of their social life, and to be able to transmit this and the meanings (which are salient for those people) in textual form. Anthropology and ethnography are ultimately acts of communication within and across cultural divides. My primary commitment as an anthropologist is to an interpretative task, one which I acknowledge to be both subjective and relational. It is a creative endeavour in which sensitivity and intuitive insights ideally play a large part, as does intellectual acuity. It has an analytical component as well as an expressive one.

This book was written at a particular time: it reflects a reality which is both temporally and biographically unique and unrepeatable. The locality and its inhabitants have changed, and so have I. It could not be written the same way today. My tool box at that time held a variety of concepts: in places functionalism and structural-functionalism inform the interpretation; elsewhere, French structuralism, and American symbolic anthropology. I was much impressed by Weber's writings on sociological analysis, which deeply influenced my approach to the practice of anthropology. Overall, my aim is to provide an interpretation of the themes which I felt were of central importance, the particular quality and nuance of relationships, the significance and meaning which were imbued in action and object, in environment and belief. Eclecticism, a way to achieve this end, sits easily with me, probably because of my background and earlier training in other disciplines (geography, archaeology), as well as my exposure to diverse schools of anthropology, both in the British and American traditions (Universities of Cape Town, Chicago, Oxford).

At the time of writing my book, the constraints on expression were tighter than they are today, and conventional forms prevailed. The current interest in reflexivity and narrative in anthropology reminds me of an early inclination I had towards life history and biography. Even then it seemed to me that the most vivid way of conveying the quality of social life in the locality would be by presenting material in a personal form, related to specific figures. I had been so impressed by the life histories of people that first drafts of the wealth of material in my field notes took the form of biographies. People like Eliso, Prodromos, Marika, Avraam, Margaro had shared with me stories about their previous homeland and, revealing how their lives had been shaken subsequently through the decades of Greece's turbulent history—by the depression, the German occupation, the Civil War—they illustrated the depths of the 'refugee experience' and the possibilities for survival with integrity. In their vivid narratives, the ways in which they had met these upheavals showed the resilience of belief and practice, the persistence as well as the shedding of cultural patterns, and the modifications which took place in response to altered conditions.

I am immensely grateful to the many colleagues and friends who have read my work, provided useful and critical comments, and helped sharpen my own understanding of what I do, and my ways of expressing it. John Campbell has been a constant support. It is with gratitude that I acknowledge his strong encouragement for my work in an urban locality at a time when this was a highly unusual site for anthropological fieldwork. His perspicacity and guidance set me on a path through a far richer field of discovery than I could have imagined at the time, one that has been the source of a lifetime's inspiration.

The republication of this book occurs in the seventy-fifth anniversary year of events referred to in Greece as the 'Asia Minor Catastrophe' and which celebrate, on the other side of the Aegean, the birth of the Turkish Republic through its War of Independence. The asymmetry in views is striking. An encouraging sign is that, in the past few years, Turkish and Greek academics, businessmen and journalists have increasingly engaged in dialogue in order to develop a forum for the exchange of ideas and collaboration. This can only be for the good. Many of us share the view that a clearer understanding of this region can best be achieved through approaches which include both sides of the Aegean, and which transcend national divisions. The timely reissue of this book bears witness to life in Kokkinia in the 1970s. It is a memorial to the place, to those who had grown up there, and to the older generation whose own lives not only bridged the Aegean, but also the disintegration of the Ottoman world, and their incorporation into the nation-state of Greece. Their memory should be preserved for the many insights of value which they impart to us in these critical times in which we live.

Renée Hirschon, 1998

NOTES

1. But note the important contributions by Loizos 1981, Salamone 1987, Hitch-
    cock 1990 and Malkki 1995.
2. In the wider field of forced migration notable exceptions are the work of
    Scudder and Colson 1982, Hansen 1982, and Clark et al. 1995.

REFERENCES

Clark, S., Colson, E., Lee, J. and Scudder, T., 'Ten Thousand Tongans: a Longitudi-
    nal Anthropological Study from Southern Zambia, 1956-1991', *Population
    Studies*, Vol. 49, 1995, pp. 91-109
Hansen, Art, 'Self-Settled Rural Refugees in Africa: the Case of Angolans in Zam-
    bian Villages' in Art Hansen and Oliver Smith (eds), *Involuntary Migration*,
    Westview Press, 1982, pp. 13-35
Hitchcock, Linda, *Vietnamese Refugees in South East Asian Camps*, Macmillan, 1990
Loizos, Peter, *The Heart Grown Bitter: a Chronicle of Cypriot War Refugees*, Cambridge
    University Press, 1981
Malkki, Liisa, *Purity and Exile: Violence, Memory and National Cosmology among Hutu
    Refugees in Tanzania*, University of Chicago Press, 1995
Salamone, Stephen D., *In the Shadow of the Holy Mountain: the Genesis of a Rural Greek
    Community and its Refugee Heritage*, East European Monographs, Boulder, 1987
Scudder, Thayer and Colson, Elizabeth, 'From Welfare to Development: a Concep-
    tual Framework for the Analysis of Dislocated People,' in Art Hansen and
    Oliver Smith (eds), *Involuntary Migration*, Westview Press, 1982, pp. 267-87

PREFACE

Anthropologists are sometimes asked how they create relationships with the people they study. This question is crucial in determining the depth of understanding and insight which can be gained about the lives of other people. A commonly experienced difficulty is explaining the purpose of one's presence to local people: why is the anthropologist there at all? Naturally enough, some suspicion about motives is often encountered.

When I first attempted to rent a room in the area of prefabricated houses in the poor locality of Yerania, a district in Kokkinia, near Piraeus harbour, I was taken around and introduced by a well-known, elderly resident, Eliso. Even so, I was refused by several families, who gave feeble excuses. Later, Eliso explained apologetically that people couldn't be sure, since I was a foreigner, whether I was a 'good girl' (καλό κορίτσι). This was my first indication that real acceptance would mean conformity to their notions of good conduct and that this would determine the degree of trust I would have with local families in the area. Being in the city might potentially confer a greater degree of freedom than life in a small village, but as a committed field-worker I chose to ignore it since my purpose was to achieve a close understanding of the quality of life these people shared.

A few months after moving in and renting a front room with a dug-out basement kitchen in the prefab house of Prodromos and Marika, an elderly couple whose four sons had all married and moved away into dowry houses provided by their wives, an incident occurred which brought this home again. While out visiting in the home of a friend, Koula, a few blocks from home, I heard my name called. The messenger's curiosity was palpable: a man was looking for me at home. Who could it be? My landlady, similarly agitated, was waiting at the corner, full of questions. In the yard was a young man in eye-catching garb, inappropriate for this neighbourhood—a long Afghan leather coat, red shirt, and open sandals—with a camera and extra lenses. Surely a foreign spy—or a tourist? What had he to do with Rena? These thoughts, my landlady confessed later, were going through her head with much consternation. In fact he was an architect from India who had been told of my research in a planning office in Athens. My landlady, anxious to chaperone me, invited us both into her room, gave us coffee, and answered his questions about housing in the locality. After the brief visit, she and other neighbours who had seen him arrive and heard him asking for me expressed concern: such events could easily be misunderstood and should be avoided at all costs. 'Don't let it happen again, Rena. We know you're a good girl but others might misinterpret (παρεξηγίσουν) ...'

I was indeed aware of the fact that 'women of ill repute' lived in the locality. They were not acknowledged by my friends, since I had become involved with the 'respectable' section of the population. Consequently, I did not get to know the few prostitutes, or the women of dubious reputation who were pointed out on occasion, usually during the afternoon, when pavement gatherings take place and passers-by are discussed. Younger women are warned not to keep company with these women who lead scandalous lives; the stories told are clearly moral tales for the benefit of the innocent and unwary. I frequently visited an elderly woman whose youngest daughter, still unmarried at 35, was known to have a lover. She was both pitied and criticized, and even her relatives warned me that she was unsuitable company: 'She's got a kind heart, but avoid her ... people would start speaking about you too ...'

This solicitous concern was associated with another feature of social relationships between women in this area, one which caused logistic problems for me. Women's friendships involved exclusive loyalty and a degree of possessiveness. I had to balance my visits to friends and not show partiality to anyone. But each one wanted to know, every time we met, where I had been and where I was going next. I adopted various strategies used by other women, including evasive answers and taking indirect routes with detours to visit people, instead of just going, for example, straight to a house two streets from my home. The intensity of social exchange in the neighbourhood and the cyclical nature of friendships (Chapter 8) were part of my own experience with women in the locality.

As a single woman, I was bound to observe the appropriate conduct and my direct association with men was limited. I never entered a coffee shop, for instance, since none of my women friends did. This does not mean, however, that I had no contact with men: in this respect, single women field-workers in Greece do have an advantage over their male counterparts. I was fortunate in developing very close relationships with a number of families, where I was accepted as a family member ('like a sister/ daughter'). With access to people's homes, I got to know husbands, brothers, and sons and could converse with them in the home on most topics. It has not been possible, though, to devote as much attention to men's activities in this book, given that I was more naturally involved in the social lives of the women.

I have concentrated on the quality of social life associated with women and have adopted an interpretative emphasis preferring a kind of Weberian *verstehen* approach. I attempt to cover structural, together with cultural, dimensions and to elucidate the relationship between various kinds of data and different levels of abstraction. The analysis deals with social conduct, values, linguistic expressions, analytically distinct institutions, and the overall cosmology or world-view. Since Greece has a long literate tradition, anthropological naïvety is inadequate and unacceptable. I did not, however, deal with the rich historical sources on Asia Minor Greeks, but recourse to aspects of Christian doctrinal theology was fruitful; it provided an explanatory framework for the interpretation of several puzzling and apparently contradictory patterns in the ethnography. This attention to the religious dimension in social life reflects the experience of my field-work; it is also a conscious attempt to give greater emphasis to an area of social life not always dealt with fully in the existing anthropological literature.

One noticeable omission—the analysis of political life—was an inevitable and sad consequence of the national political climate at the time of the field-work. This covered fourteen months in 1971-2, a period of severe repression during the military dictatorship (1967–74). An effective network of police informers operated in Kokkinia as in all residential districts. My presence as a foreigner in a poor, neglected part of the city with its left-wing reputation was disquieting to the authorities. I was aware that my movements were being checked. During this period I was visited by security police on two occasions, and a full-scale household survey had to be abandoned when official displeasure was conveyed to me. Even photographing in this locality could be construed as politically dangerous: it was suggested that I wished to publish denigrating information abroad to damage the junta's reputation.

Under these conditions, the political orientation and history of the locality had to be neglected. Contemporary political life was part of the centrally controlled administration: any other activity was illegal and dangerous. In one or two encounters I realized that my position was being protected: people would say 'It's better for you not to know more about that.' With the establishment of democracy in 1974 the situation has now changed. Kokkinia has an active, popular Communist Party mayor and municipal council, and the vitality of political life is striking even on a brief visit, contrasting with the tense political atmosphere which prevailed in the 1970s when I first lived there. My account of life in the locality is, therefore, historically placed in a particular period, and records conditions as I experienced them at that time and stage of my life.

My experience with these people was marked by their warm concern for me, expressed in open hospitality and offers of help at any moment of need. People here had a strongly developed ethic of neighbourly aid, in part a response to the long periods of deprivation they had endured. My presence alone, as a student and far from my family, was seen by them to reflect a determination to improve my lot in the world, aims of which they approved. With empathy they projected on to me their own experience of loss and destitution. I lived in the same inadequate housing with a basement which flooded at every rainstorm, with peeling walls and holes in the panels. I had explained to everyone that I was a student writing about their present lives in Greece and their experiences in Asia Minor. Most people understood this to mean history, though I kept reiterating that it was to do with social customs (τα ήθη και έθιμα, a way of conveying the anthropologist's concern with social life). But clearly many were puzzled that I was away from my family, unmarried though in my late twenties, and living in poverty-bound conditions.

One day, after I had spent three months in Yerania, a neighbour stopped me while I was assiduously sweeping the pavement. 'I know, Rena,' she said, 'You've come here to study the lesson of being a refugee' (. . . . να κάνεις το μάθημα της προσφυγιάς) . The word she used, προσφυγιά, can only be translated as the 'state of being a refugee', 'refugeeness'. I had come to take the lesson of 'refugeeness'. For them this experience had been a lifetime one, and the word προσφυγιά has different levels of meaning. This book is an attempt to present the experience and to expose, in the analysis, the rich quality of life which had been generated despite great material hardship. It is a tribute to the people of Kokkinia, who taught me much about life and its meaning, and I cannot repay my debts to them in any like manner.

ACKNOWLEDGEMENTS

In 1972, during my field-work in Kokkinia, the fiftieth anniversary of the Asia Minor catastrophe was commemorated. As the years passed and various texts on that experience evolved, the ethnography gained a historical dimension of its own. Writing this book has involved a slow process of deepening insights. Although based largely on material presented in my D.Phil. thesis, the book also draws on wider personal experience in Greece. The debts I have incurred, too, have multiplied. Both before and after my life in Kokkinia, many have aided me through their intellectual guidance, encouragement, friendship, and practical help, or critical appraisal of numerous drafts. I take this opportunity to express my deep gratitude to all, located in many places at different times, some by name, many others unnamed but not forgotten:

In Cape Town, to the late Monica Wilson, Ray and Adi Inskeep, Peter Carstens, Graham Watson, David Hywel Davies, Brett Hendey, David Seddon, and James Moulder.

In Chicago, to the Faculty of the Department of Anthropology at the University of Chicago, to Ronald Singer, Jerry Hyman, and Sally Duncan.

In Athens, to the late C. A. Doxiadis, the late Jackie Tyrwhitt, Panayis Psomopoulos, John Papaioannou, S. Thakurdesai, Dora Anagnostopoulou, Myrto Bogdanou, Thalia and Yannis Dodopoulos, Stella Vrana, Lilian Hadzidaki, Alex Freme, Alex Courpa, and staff at the Centre for Social Policy, Piraeus.

In Oxford, to the late Maurice Freedman, Rodney Needham, Kenneth Kirkwood, Helen Callaway, Renée Paton, Barbara Harrell-Bond, Julie Marcus, Biff Shore, Charles Stewart, Andrew Schuller, Rachel and Sinclair Hood, Joanna and Maurice Pope, Stephen and Matty Mitchell, Deborah Honoré, Vassiliki Chryssanthopoulou, Steve Page, Jenny Davidson, as well as members of the Women's Anthropology Seminar.

A special debt of gratitude is due to John Campbell, my supervisor. For his constant interest and guidance, both intellectual and personal, over many years, I express my sincere thanks and appre-

XXX ACKNOWLEDGEMENTS

ciation. I am grateful as well to my thesis examiners, Peter Loizos and Juliet du Boulay, for constructive comments.

I wish also to thank the Warden and Fellows of St Antony's College, Oxford, for a studentship which funded the early period of my research, and the Bertha Johnson Loan Fund, Oxford University. The Nuffield Foundation and the SSRC provided funds which allowed me to return to Kokkinia in 1983. Thanks are due to the Directorate of Oxford Polytechnic and to colleagues who have supported my periods of absence for research, and to Julie and Rory Williams for stimulating discussions at times when this endeavour was grinding to a halt.

Without doubt the greatest burden of support was carried by members of my family. Although most often at long distance, Barney and Del Hirschson, in Cape Town, gave continuing encouragement and support of all kinds, and George and Desirée Dracoulis, in Athens, provided much practical help; to them my warm appreciation and thanks. I would like to express here my deepest gratitude to Manolis Philippakis, whose determination fuelled this effort, to Nicolas, whose patience and understanding far exceeded his years, and to Yannis, whose recent arrival brought great joy and only slight delay in the production of this book.

Oxford, May 1987
R. H.

GLOSSARY

Apókreas	carnival season
badzanákis (s.), *badzanákides* (pl.)	reciprocal term for men married to sisters
egoismós	self-regard
iconostásti	icon-shelf in the home
kandíli	oil-lamp
kérasma	customary offering of sweets and liqueurs
kóllyva	wheat-based dish prepared for memorial services
koumbára (f. s.), *koumbároi* (pl.)	spiritual kin
koumbariá	spiritual kinship, bond contracted through marriage or baptismal sponsorship
Mikrasiátes	people from Asia Minor
noikokýris (m.), *noikokyrá* (f.)	master, mistress of the house: the latter is not the equivalent of 'housewife', though commonly translated thus
nýphi	daughter-in-law
Panayía	appellation of Mary,. All Holy Mother of God
petherá	mother-in-law
prósphygas (s.), *prósphyges* (pl.)	refugee(s)
prosphygiá	state of being a refugee
proxenió	arranged match/marriage
seirá	rank, series, level
symphéron	family or self-interest
yeitoniá (s.), *yeitoniés* (pl.)	neighbourhood(s)

Asia Minor towns are referred to by the Greek usage.

1

REFUGEES FOR FIFTY YEARS

The journey from Piraeus harbour to Athens, a route taken by many who visit the islands of Greece or the antiquities of the capital, has never been a breath-taking panorama of scenic views. Yet through the colourless and dusty trip the observer in the 1970s might have noticed certain residential areas which had a distinct atmosphere. In contrast with the ubiquitous modernity of angular cement, marble, and glass structures which increasingly suffocate the city, low houses appeared with tiled roofs and walls painted in pastel shades of blue, deep ochres, greens, and pink. Jasmine and honeysuckle twined around gates and walls, pots of geranium and sweet basil lined wooden balconies. Streets were clean and pavements marked with fresh lines of whitewash.

A morning's view would reveal housewives returning from the local bakery with armfuls of bread, hanging washing in one another's yards, airing bed-linen on lines hung between lamp-posts. On certain mornings a bustle of activity at street corners showed women carrying bins of rubbish to the dustman's cart which moved ponderously down the main road, a hand-bell ringing out. While passing through in the late afternoon, you could see people sitting on pavements with a small coffee-cup beside them, chatting as strollers paused to exchange greetings.

These districts, known as 'the refugee quarters' (τα προσφυγικά), provoke many questions, opening a fascinating but little-known chapter in modern Greek life. Refugee quarters settled over fifty years ago are found in Piraeus, Athens, Salonika, and many provincial Greek towns. In these localities uprooted people were settled, forced to adapt and make the best of their conditions through the decades of turbulent history which followed. For that period the immense scale of the disruption was unique, so great that, even in the 1970s, the Greek Red Cross broadcast daily messages for relatives seeking those with

whom contact had been lost fifty years before. This disruption
also involved a neglected event in international history. The
existence of these 'refugee quarters' bears witness to the first
compulsory exchange of minority populations negotiated
internationally, ratified and executed by the League of Nations
in accordance with the Treaty of Lausanne (1923). The relevance of these events to the present is highlighted not only by
the continuing political deadlock in Cyprus, involving thousands of refugee families—a situation which has strong
parallels with the subject of this study (cf. Loizos 1975a,
1981)—but also by the critical problems of displaced populations in many parts of the world today. The experience of the
Asia Minor Greeks merits special attention, since it provides a
unique long-term case-study of adjustment and settlement in
both rural and urban areas. Understanding social life in such
localities may provide insights into some ways in which
uprooted people cope with the challenges of survival, with
material deprivation, with social and personal disruption, and
with the issue of identity.

The present study, conducted over seventeen months early in
the 1970s through intensive field-work mainly by participant
observation, attempts to describe the quality of social life in the
urban district of Kokkinia. This was one of the largest refugee
quarters established near Piraeus in 1923, with a population of
40,000 a decade later, and some 86,000 people in its municipal
area in 1971 (census figure). Kokkinia was the locus of my
observations, but more detailed investigation centred on Yerania, one of its districts, where I lived. Some refugee quarters
of the metropolis—particulary Kaisariani, Vyrona, and Nea
Ionia—have a similar character and history; others differ, possibly because the original housing provisions, population composition, and conditions varied (e.g., Nea Philadelphia, Nea
Smyrni).[1] This is the study of a well-established urban locality,
its focus shifting from specific conditions in one district of the
orginal refugee quarter to that of the wider locality. The interpretation of social life takes account of events in Greek society
over a period of five to six decades in political and economic
spheres, while the social and cultural affiliations of Asia Minor
Greek society provide a key to resolving some of the puzzles
presented by the character of Kokkinia life.

Spotless Slums

As one travelled through the old refugee quarters of Athens and Piraeus, the attractive impression produced by well-kept, colourful dwellings and an atmosphere of lively sociability soon gave way to questions (see Plates). The washing hanging between lamp-posts and children playing in the streets were signs of high population densities and overcrowding; street surfaces, although clean, were unpaved and rutted; the pungent odour and insistent hum of a pump revealed that a household's cesspool had filled and was being drained by a private contractor's lorry. Even in 1983 there was no central sewerage system in Kokkinia. Every winter many basement rooms (where aged couples resided) flooded in storms, causing drowning in the worst incidents. Casual conversation revealed that few houses belonged to single families; most had been subdivided between several households, often totally unrelated to and in conflict with one another. Overcrowding, together with the inadequate provision of basic facilities, had been a chronic problem for decades.

Under such circumstances why had these areas not degenerated into ugly slums? In the district of Yerania, a spotless, pleasant appearance and well-developed sense of decoration concealed the flimsiness of the houses and the low standard of public facilities. Houses, themselves of prefabricated temporary material, were painted in pastel colour combinations; tiny gardens on balconies and pot-plants abounded. Under adverse conditions which arose within a few years of settlement, with overcrowding in insubstantial buildings and the lack of public provisions, this locality could rapidly have become uninhabitable and a major problem area.

That it had not reflected the efforts and commitment of its residents (particularly the women) and their intensive expenditure of time and care to maintain passable living standards. This is all the more remarkable because many dwellings in this district were not owned but simply occupied under rights of tenure specific to refugees (see Chapter 4). Despite legal ambiguities and contesting claims among co-resident households, people had maintained a conscious effort to preserve the quality of living conditions. 'If we didn't look after the houses, they'd fall down around our ears,' people explained, adding, 'We Asia Minor Greeks have a reputation for this, we are known for being house-proud' (. . . νοικοκύρηδες).

This statement reveals several themes explored in the following chapters: the emphasis on the home as the centre of individual commitment and the important role of cultural values in the upkeep of the environment and in the treatment of housing. It demonstrates, too, the conscious evaluation of the Asia Minor Greeks' own sense of their distinctive tradition. In this lies a further paradox.

Strangers at Home

The inhabitants of Kokkinia had a clearly developed sense of identity, separate from that of metropolitan Greek society. This was conveyed early on in my acquaintanceship by two terms, used interchangeably. Referring to themselves, people would say 'We are refugees' (prósphyges) or 'We are Mikrasiátes' (Asia Minor people). Significantly, not only the original refugees, survivors of the exodus, used these terms, but also younger people of the second and even third generation, born in the locality or elsewhere in Greece.

The force of the self-designation is clear: it was used to distinguish themselves from local Greeks, whom they variously called 'locals' ((ε)ντόπιοι), 'Vlachs' (βλάχοι), meaning shepherds, 'old Greeks' (Παλιοελλαδίτες), or simply Greeks (Έλληνες).[2] In Greek, as in English, the term 'refugee' (πρόσφυγας) denotes a particular mode of migration, forced exodus from the homeland. Clearly then, since the event had occurred over fifty years before, something more was being conveyed in the retention of this label for decades and across generations. It had become shorthand for a sense of separate identity compounded of various elements, with two main components. On the one hand, their long-term marginal and disadvantaged position in Greek society gave them a specific political cause. In this respect their identity as 'refugees' arose from claims for compensation which made them act as a vested-interest group. On the other, their well-developed sense of identity, reflecting their former position in Ottoman society, endowed them with a psychological and cultural predisposition to marking boundaries. Thus, Asia

Minor Greeks in this locality responded to their changed circumstances by consciously and unconsciously emphasizing their cultural distinctiveness.

The existence of a separate sense of identity through five to six decades is notable since the original refugees and the host population, metropolitan Greeks, shared most social and cultural characteristics. The refugees were all Orthodox Christians, culturally and physically identifiable as Greeks, and the overwhelming majority were Greek-speaking. Any overt markers such as physical differences, language or religious barriers, factors often employed to explain separate ethnic identity, were absent. Thus, one might reasonably have expected that the two populations would have merged quite smoothly over this long period.[3] By preserving a sense of separate identity in the face of close similarity, however, the residents of Kokkinia had worked continually at constructing a 'boundary'; in this way they came to constitute a group distinguishable in conceptual terms but not by readily observable criteria. This aspect of life in the locality of Kokkinia was one of its many interesting features. In the conscious retention of a separate identity through five decades, they can be seen as a minority group of Greeks within Greek society, a phenomenon of considerable interest for studies of 'ethnicity' and 'ethnic identity'.

Religious Radicals

The informed observer was also struck by other contradictory features: Kokkinia was renowned as a centre of left-wing political support, and it achieved a certain notoriety among bourgeois Athenians as a communist stronghold during and after the Second World War. My field-work took place, however, in the period of the military junta (1967–74), when political life was strangled, so that I was unable to learn much about it. Instead, I found quite unexpectedly that local people gave considerable attention to religious observances. Since these chiefly involved the women, I was soon drawn into such activities and began to see how deeply the religious dimension pervaded social life. This finding challenged the preconceptions in my own attitude to urban life which derived, as can be seen with hindsight, from an ethnocentric bias. Urban living is too often assumed to be 'modern' and to preclude the 'traditional'; in this view, urban life involves secularization, individual alienation, and fragmented social institutions.[4] None of these characteristics applied to Kokkinia.

Entrepreneurial Stereotypes

Finally, the character of this urban refugee quarter, together with others of similar status, challenged the common Greek stereotype of the Asia Minor refugee as successful and shrewd in business. The contribution of Asia Minor refugees to the development of modern Greece has indeed been striking, particularly in relation to economic growth, since the sheer size of the population influx increased the labour force and the internal market. Specific skills and expertise were introduced and new industries were established (carpet-making, tobacco production). The expansion and diversification of the Greek economy from the 1920s is directly attributable to the influx of these refugees, and many well-known entrepreneurial figures came from Asia Minor. It is also true, however, that large numbers of urban Asia Minor refugees failed to improve their position, so that over fifty years after settlement they continued to constitute a disadvantaged section of the population.

These, then, are some of the striking and paradoxical features of Asia Minor Greek life in the locality of Kokkinia half a century after the settlement. This study touches on some of the factors which led to this situation and shows too how people created an integrated and vital community in the face of economic deprivation and political marginality.

The Uprooting

Understanding the separate identity and social life of these urban dwellers is impossible without reference to their history. The presence of refugees in mainland Greece was the result of international pressures and political upheavals in the eastern Mediterranean in the first two decades of the twentieth century.

The people in this study were originally Asia Minor Greeks, a population long established in that part of the Ottoman Empire now known as Turkey. They were uprooted because of the collision of Greek and Turkish policies at a time when each country was being reshaped in the aftermath of the First World War and was establishing its present political boundaries. Modern Turkey is a new nation, established in 1923, just one hundred years after the struggle leading to national independence for Greece. Under the leadership of Kemal Atatürk, the establishment of the modern Turkish state ended an era in the eastern Mediterranean. Until that time the Aegean Sea was bordered on the east by the immense heterogeneous Ottoman Empire, a medieval state in decline under a decadent sultanate, and on the west by the small kingdom of Greece (population 4.5 million, established in 1830). In modern Greek history, 1922 was a watershed, a more catastrophic date, it has been said, than the Fall of Constantinople in 1453. With finality it marked the end of the Hellenic presence in Asia Minor, where Greek settlement and activity had existed over a period of three millennia.

Asia Minor or Anatolia, particularly the western coastal region, had been an important centre of Greek civilization throughout the historical period. The Ionian coast and islands were renowned in antiquity for the achievements of Greek writers, philosophers, and scientists (Homer and Sappho, Heraclitus, Thales, Hippocrates, and Hippodamus are among them). In the early Christian period the Apostolic journeys covered this region, focusing on important Greek towns such as Ephesus, Philadelphia, Pergamos, and Smyrna, and the converts were Greeks as well as Jews. Major figures in church history, the early Fathers, Saints Basil, Gregory of Nyssa, and Gregory of Nazianzus, were from this region of the Byzantine Empire. Early Christian doctrine was thrashed out in the debates and Councils held in Anatolian towns.[5] Deep in the interior of Asia Minor, too, the presence of Greek culture and Christianity for about two thousand years is evidenced in the monuments and churches still to be seen there. Even the modern Turkish name for Greece, Yunanistan, is derived from the word Ionia, the western coastal region of Asia Minor where Greek settlement was rooted for centuries.

The Asia Minor Greeks had a rich background, therefore, a

long-established heritage in which the threads of continuity were strong. Before the expulsion from their homeland, their social milieu was varied and diverse. Despite its political decline and its ineffective leadership, the Ottoman Empire continued to be a vital society in the early decades of this century. Its heartland in Asia Minor was productive and its population large and varied in linguistic, cultural, and ethnic terms. Among the more important minorities were Armenians, Jews, Bulgarians, Levantines and Gypsies, while the Greeks, the largest, probably numbered about 1.5 million.[6] Today, however, the Turkish state projects a public image of national homogeneity (with the notable exception of the Kurds), and the presence of minorities tends to be underplayed. It was the events of the period following the First World War which brought about the transformation of the social, political, and demographic characteristics of Greece and Asia Minor, and a radical change in the societies on both sides of the Aegean Sea.

Since the political history of this period cannot be adequately covered here, a brief survey must suffice.[7] Following the terms of the ill-fated Treaty of Sèvres (1920), the Greek army disembarked in Smyrna with a mandate to take charge of the region to which Greece had long-standing claims, both historically and demographically, and which had been ceded to her as one of the victorious allies. Following an election and change of government in Greece, however, the allies reconsidered their support for the Greek claims to territory. Rashly, in view of the withdrawal of support and shifting international alliances, the Greek army in 1921 began a campaign of conquest into the Asia Minor interior. But by that time Kemal Atatürk at the head of a nationalist movement was busy in the interior reorganizing the Turkish army. Considerable headway was made by the Greeks until Atatürk initiated his counter-offensive. After some limited victories, the Turkish army gained the upper hand, resulting in the total rout of the Greek army in the summer of 1922. As the Turkish army pursued fleeing Greek forces, the minority populations of the region, particularly the Christians, were subjected to violent reprisals. These countered earlier atrocities perpetrated by Greek soldiers against Turkish civilians (a view corroborated by the original Greek refugees who had themselves suffered at the hands of the Turks). Widespread massacres of unprotected civilians occurred and a mass exodus followed as people desperately fled from towns and villages to the coast in the hope of escaping to the islands or to mainland Greece. The military disaster culminated in the total destruction of the thriving city of Smyrna, razed by fire in September 1922. Thousands of civilians—mainly Greeks and Armenians—were wounded, maimed, or killed, women were assaulted, houses looted and burnt; many who succeeded in reaching Smyrna harbour drowned in their attempts to escape (Housepian 1966; Llewellyn Smith 1973). The fortunate were finally evacuated by Greek, Italian, and American ships. Most men aged between 18 and 45 were detained forcibly by the Turks for service in the notorious 'labour battalions', where inhuman conditions resulted in very high mortality rates. Survivors from this period provide harrowing accounts of physical and emotional suffering (e.g., Venezis 1931; Sotiriou 1963; Centre for Asia Minor Studies 1980, 1982).

The influx of destitute persons into Greece reached several hundred thousand within a few weeks, and raised tremendous problems of shelter and sustenance. As the autumn passed and the refugees huddled in warehouses, sheds, and tents in Greek ports and towns, hopes for a speedy return were uppermost in their minds and at this time there was little reason to suspect that repatriation would not be possible. The first indication of the permanent and irreversible nature of the migration came in the peace negotiations of January 1923, when the new Turkish leadership made its conditions known. The new nation-state of Turkey was to have a secular legal system, applying to all Turkish citizens: there was no place for religious minorities and the Christian population had to be removed. Turkish conditions for peace were unyielding: an agreement signed between Greece and Turkey preliminary to the Treaty of Lausanne (1923) stipulated, in an unprecedented move, the compulsory exchange of populations. Thus, over the next two years a further 200,000 Christians moved from Asia Minor and Thrace to settle in Greece, joining the destitute refugees who had escaped earlier in the hostilities, and who numbered many hundreds of thousands. At the same time about 350,000 Muslims were compelled to leave Greece to settle in Turkey; exempted from the exchange were the Muslims of Thrace and

the Greeks of Istanbul. (See Pentzopoulos 1962 for a compre-
hensive discussion of this exchange.)

The Bond with Byzantium

The experience of Asia Minor Greek refugees in the Greek state,
like that of all forcibly uprooted peoples, was one of dispossess-
sion, fear, poverty, and readjustment. An influential factor in
this process was their historical experience and position as a
minority group in the final phase of the Ottoman Empire. In
this, a significant and formative divergence of experience
existed for the refugee and the host Greek populations.

The Asia Minor Greeks had lived in Ottoman society, which
preserved a line of continuity with its predecessor, the Byzantine Empire. Right into the twentieth century the Ottoman
Empire was a loosely structured imperial state with a cosmopolitan and heterogeneous population. The diverse ethnic
groups were grouped by religious affiliation (e.g., as Orthodox
Christians, Jews), granted legal status, and administered as separate 'nations' in the *millet* system (Gibb and Bowen 1957;
Lewis 1968; Shaw and Shaw 1976–7). This policy effectively
allowed the survival and coexistence of ethnic minorities, and
promoted their sense of cultural and civil autonomy in a varied
social environment.

The historical experience of mainland Greeks over the previous hundred years stood in sharp contrast. From the early
nineteenth century political developments in Greece (emanat-
ing from European influences) had caused this section of the
Greek-speaking population to follow a different path. Through
the establishment of the modern Greek state following the War
of Independence (1821–9), mainland Greece was increasingly
shaped by Western European ideas and institutions. Among
these were the establishment of the monarchy, the presence of a
Bavarian king with his court and later the Danish king, the
return of Western-educated expatriates, and the activities of the
Philhellenes. Soon the new Greek state was organized as a parliamentary democracy, with foreign business interests taking
over economic life. The capital was moved from Nafplion to
Athens. Classical scholars and the romantic movement encouraged the revival of the pre-Christian past and devalued the

people's more recent heritage in Byzantium, gradually relegating it to antiquarian obscurity. Indeed, the War of Independence itself can be seen as a response to the spirit of liberalism and the ideals of the Enlightenment which flourished in the West at that time. The modern Greek state, then, was created, cradled, and nurtured in Western arms, and Western influence pervaded all aspects of life, political philosophy, art, and education. This process of course was not uniform throughout Greece. These influences hardly touched life in rural communities, especially those remote from the metropolitan centres, and urban dwellers were differently affected depending on their social stratum. The Greek state was, however, based on Western prototypes (Campbell and Sherrard 1968: 30–43, 71 ff.; Clogg 1979: 60 ff.; Herzfeld 1982).

In broad contrast, the mass of Asia Minor Greeks in the Ottoman Empire were relatively isolated from the Western reassessment of their cultural heritage and identity. Although close contacts and increasing intervention by Westerners took place during the late nineteenth and early twentieth centuries, in the main these occurred at higher levels of administration. Overall, Greeks in the Ottoman Empire were exposed neither to the negative comparisons with classical antiquity nor to the controversy regarding purity of descent which so marked the mainlanders' image of themselves, their society, and its supposed shortcomings. For the Asia Minor Greeks the bond with Byzantium remained vital, and their first point of reference was Constantinople, not Athens. They saw themselves as witnesses and bearers of tradition—a rich linguistic, cultural, and ideological heritage—entrusted to them through their Orthodox Christian faith. It can be argued that Asia Minor Greeks escaped the sense of national inferiority which even today plagues modern Greece's self-image in its relationship with Western Europe.

This facet of their previous experience undoubtedly affected the Anatolian Greeks' responses to their exile and resettlement. Their attitudes to life in the Greek state were bound to be influenced by these perceptions and their different historical experience. From this point of view alone, a smooth process of integration between the two groups could be seen as unlikely. Furthermore, objective differences were apparent to the newcomers. In the 1920s the Greek state could offer little to compare favourably with the wealth and diversity of their homeland. Athens and Salonika, where many refugees had their first view of Greece, were small towns; they seemed provincial and the country as a whole appeared disorganized, backward, and poor. Indeed, Greece's resources had been drastically depleted; it had been at war for over ten years, from the Balkan Wars (1910–13) onwards. Athens was of little importance as a commercial centre; at that time the major trading centres of the region were in the Ottoman Empire—Smyrna was the leading port of the eastern Mediterranean. Towns in Asia Minor were cosmopolitan and lively. Consequently, once the first relief at survival had passed, the refugees soon became disappointed with the lack of sophistication of local society. At this early stage of contact they began to formulate derogatory opinions about local Greeks (reciprocated by the locals, but on the basis of other criteria). The newcomers perceived locals as narrow-minded, ignorant, and uncouth, a view which became entrenched as time passed and disillusionment grew. This early sense of disappointment was undoubtedly significant in the process of adjustment and in the development of their separate identity.

Superior Subordinates

When people in Kokkinia in the 1970s identified themselves as *prósphyges* (refugees) or *Mikrasiátes* to outsiders, they were conveying in two shorthand terms a complex process of adjustment and cumulative experience. As *prósphyges* (lit. 'fugitives'), they indicated both a mode of migration and a subsequent state of dependence; this term has political and economic overtones. By calling themselves *Mikrasiátes*, they conveyed a particular cultural endowment associated with place of origin and their unique heritage. Though its diacritical features were not apparent to an outsider, this provided a basis for their enduring sense of separate identity.

The interaction of two sets of factors was responsible for this. On the one hand, their historical experience as Orthodox Christians in Ottoman society provided the basis for differentiation, with its emphasis on a specific cultural heritage, perceived and preserved through memory and recollection. On the other, after their settlement, the inability of successive Greek governments—during years of national, political, and economic instability—to alleviate their particular problems meant that the cumulative effect of years of economic hardship and of social and political marginality reinforced this sense of separation.

The end result of this combined experience is of special interest: a remarkable structural replication had taken place. In Ottoman society the Asia Minor Greeks saw themselves as a group subordinated to an alien administration; yet, paradoxically for a subject people, rather than developing feelings of collective inferiority they had a pronounced sense of superiority in relation to others in the Ottoman community. This cannot be explained simply as the defence-reaction of a threatened minority group. Structurally it was based on an overall identification with the many influential Greeks employed in the Ottoman administration and culturally on the conviction of the preeminence of their Christian tradition.

The administrative and social emphasis on religious affiliation in Ottoman society meant that social cleavages were more readily seen as vertical or ethnic, and not horizontal and class-based. In their relations with other groups, therefore, rich and poor Greeks could perceive themselves as sharing a single collective identity. Since many Greeks had become influential and wealthy, their less successful fellows were able to bask in reflected glory, as it were, reinforcing the conviction of their overall superiority as a group. Later, in the Greek state, despite their rapid entrenchment at the bottom of the social and economic ladder and their political impotence, this sense of cultural and moral superiority was maintained. Conviction of the excellence of their ways did not waver and bolstered their self-esteem through many hardships. In the face of almost total disruption, a coherent and vital social life developed in the urban quarters, where despite tremendous difficulties a society with a defined sense of identity and clearly articulated values came into being.

In the process of settlement, social and cultural continuity was a source of strength and gave coherence to the lives of these people. Social organization developed in the urban quarters around the family and the neighbourhood, and with them two contrasting modes of orientation, one tending to exclusive bonds and closure, the other to inclusive, communal, and open interaction. Patterns of interaction in everyday life reflected fundamental symbolic categories, the opposition between 'open' and 'closed' states. Expressed in numerous verbal metaphors and apparent in various rituals as well as in daily mundane activities, this symbolic opposition can be explained by reference to the religious tenets which constitute the basis of their world-view. The separation and complementarity of male and female roles and the marked contrast in philosophy and life-style of elderly and younger adults were notable features of social life. In all these respects, the similarities with other Greek communities are evident. Continuity is both geographical, stretching across the Greek world, and temporal, since social institutions were reconstituted after settlement. We should not be surprised that 'traditional' patterns existed in this urban locality among people who were townsfolk. Rather, this suggests that core elements in social and cultural organization were reinstated in the new environment. Moreover, social life in Kokkinia demonstrated that the values and perceptions which people hold about themselves and the world around them, the ways in which their relationships are organized, may be far more adaptable and durable in changing situations, even the most disruptive and traumatic, than we are prepared to credit. My experience of life in Kokkinia in 1972 suggested that Asia Minor Greeks' culture and social organization had a resilience and flexibility, even a dominating power, which allowed them to transcend the undeniably deprived conditions of their material existence.

The next two chapters examine the forces which combined to produce a sense of separate identity among refugees in urban quarters. Their collective self-perception already contained a marked awareness of group boundaries and a consciousness of their distinctive history. This cultural element is discussed in Chapter 2, while in Chapter 3 the economic, political, and educational disadvantages which they suffered are shown to have reinforced the predisposition conferred by their Ottoman heritage to maintain an identity separate from the rest of Greek society.

2

THE OTTOMAN PAST IN
THE REFUGEE PRESENT

The Bridge of Memory

The importance of shared memories for any uprooted group is obvious: in order to reconstitute their lives memory becomes a critical link, the means of a cultural survival, a kind of capital without which their identity would be lost. Indeed, the connection between identity and memory as a social and collective fact deserves some consideration, especially in the case of displaced peoples.

The importance of oral tradition and, consequently, of the exercise of memory in non-literate cultures is self-evident; literacy, its effects, and various techniques of oratory have been explored cross-culturally (Goody 1968, 1977; Finnegan 1973; Bloch 1975; see also Yates 1966, Ong 1982). As Street (1984) argues cogently, a clear-cut distinction between literate and non-literate cultures has little analytical value. None the less, among people whose literate tradition is more fully developed, memory is not the sole repository of knowledge, nor is identity dependent upon its exercise: other means of retaining the past exist. It seems probable, therefore, that a people's experience as refugees will be deeply influenced by the particular characteristics of literacy which they have as a group. I suggest that forced displacement may be more devastating for those people for whom literacy is peripheral, where oral skills predominate, and where past and present are bridged through the active exercise of memory in a familiar environment. Similarly, individual differences in literacy may help to explain different rates of adjustment and assimilation within a displaced group.

For the Asia Minor refugees as a whole, memories and the use of memory were undoubtedly important, though probably to a different degree in each individual. Certainly, for many it came to constitute their most valuable property, since they had managed to bring little else in the way of possessions. In constructing a new way of life from the chaos around them many responded by reliving aspects of their past and by emphasizing continuity.

But besides this adaptive function, memory had another dimension in this group of people. As my familiarity with their way of life grew, I began to see that the religious background specifically reinforced the way in which identity was being maintained. The Eastern Church emphasizes the authority of tradition as a tenet (see Ware 1964: 203 ff.), and memory itself is institutionalized. Tradition and memory are linked elements relating to the deeply conservative nature of this branch of Christianity. In the broadest sense, then, the effect of religion was to increase the potency of these collective memories of the past, providing a framework in which the process of recollection was enhanced. This is because memory is endowed with an intrinsic value and provides the explicit foundation for many ritual acts. For example, it is the basis of the Eucharist or Liturgy (Communion Service), in which Christ's sacrifice is re-enacted, his words are repeated, and the injunction to 'Do this in remembrance of me' is explicit and emphatic. In the Liturgy, commemorative litanies are said, past generations of Orthodox faithful are recalled, and the day's dedication to a particular holy figure is announced. Thus the past and the present are brought together and the divisive aspect of time is abolished. The act of memory brings grace through the participatory role of all Christians who celebrate the Liturgy together.

Furthermore, it is every family's obligation to commemorate its deceased. Rituals for the dead recur throughout the year and are ordained at set times for the newly deceased (see Chapter 9). The tombstone (μνήμα, μνημείο) erected for the fortieth-day memorial service (μνημόσυνο) is also the physical manifestation of memory. In Orthodox Christian practice, memory (ανάμνηση) is appreciated consciously, it confers grace, is a linguistically explicit category, and is embodied in numerous ritual acts. The socially recognized power of memory for these people may thus explain something which puzzled me: often an elderly person would give me a small present (a cloth, a doily, or piece of crocheted lace) for no particular reason, but always with the words, 'So that you will remember me' (για να με θυμάσαι). This power may also explain the intensity of images depicting the quality and character of life in the towns and countryside of Asia Minor in a past era which were transmitted so vividly to me, a stranger to the eastern Mediterranean, some fifty years after their expulsion. It was this past, containing the lost but meaningful patterns of life, which impressed me with its vital images. The older refugees, people in their late sixties and over, preserved their parents' tales together with their own memories, and the recital of these constituted, as it were, continuing memorial, a μνημόσυνο, of that life now dead. They presented these tales with such clarity that they conveyed to me long afterwards a colourful picture of places and people and of another epoch: life in the final period of the Ottoman Empire.

Filtered through the subjective recall of many individuals, accounts of life in the homeland came to constitute a collective memory, a central aspect of the culture of Kokkinia. While not representing a historical record, its importance in social and cultural terms lay in providing a wide frame of reference against which all subsequent experiences, even those of their descendants, could be interpreted. This collective memory also provided a template for identity, since it specified those cultural markers, the critical points which differentiated them from others. When people of the urban quarters, even those born and raised there, referred to themselves as *Mikrasiátes* in distinction from local Greeks or *Palioelladítes* (lit. 'Old Greeks'), they were conveying this sense of cultural distinctiveness derived from a background and experience, a tradition and heritage, perceived as essentially different despite (to the outsider) its objective similarities.

In this chapter we examine the cultural dimension of identity, which had its basis in the collective memory of Asia Minor refugees now settled in Kokkinia. After the traumatic break caused by their expulsion, memory became a rescuing bridge; it re-created the meaningful past and provided them with the guidelines for a coherent adjustment to a new way of life.

Religion and Regions: The Basis for Identity

The sense of identity of the Asia Minor refugees was rooted in a shared heritage which centred on their religious affiliation.

Although sharp differences in wealth, education, and life-style did exist for Greeks, particularly in the major cities, class differences were less important than common cultural bonds, for in the *millet* system, Ottoman society was itself structured on this basis. Vertical rather than horizontal cleavages predominated in this diverse and cosmopolitan society, yet with the Greek population regional divisions were also important, as the frequent reference to Asia Minor regional stereotypes amongst all generations of Kokkiniots showed.

Before the expulsion, Greek settlements were both numerous and widespread throughout Asia Minor, indeed throughout most of today's Turkey. The greatest concentration was in the province of Pontus, on the Black Sea, where the Greek presence goes back for millennia (see Kitromilides and Alexandris 1984–5: 15–18 n. 17). The western coastal regions and northwestern area of Asia Minor were also densely settled with numerous Greek communities in coastal and inland cities and in the countryside. Generally, fewer Greek communities existed in central and southern Asia Minor, but the provinces of Kappadokia and Lykaonia had large numbers of Greek settlements and substantial populations in urban centres such as Kaisaria, Nigde, and Ikonion (see Merlier 1974). Linguistic and dialectal diversity, as well as distinctive social features, marked this settlement pattern, and regional differentiation provided the basis for cultural stereotyping. The Greek population of Asia Minor, unevenly spread over various regions, was differentiated by popular perceptions of localized cultural traits and character. Economic criteria were also employed in this differentiation. But in their relations with other groups in Ottoman society, Greeks tended to ignore regional divisions and those based on wealth and livelihood. Far more important was the common bond based on religious identity, the feature of Ottoman social organization and administration which reflected and reinforced their own cultural conceptions.

Religious Identity under Ottoman Rule

From the first period of Ottoman rule, administration of the Empire was based on the religious affiliations of its diverse population. Like the Byzantine Empire which it replaced, it was a theocratic state. Ethnic, linguistic, and economic divisions were subordinated to religious identification, and a considerable degree of autonomy was granted to the *dhimmi* groups, 'people of the Book' (Jews, Christians) (Gibb and Bowen 1957 İnalcık 1978). Orthodox Christians were administered as the *Rum millet*, a single religious community (*millet*, lit. 'nation') under the Patriarch of Constantinople, who was responsible for all civil matters pertaining to the Orthodox. Thus, all Orthodox Christians, whatever language they spoke, whether rich or poor, from whatever region, owed allegiance to him and were identified as a group by their common religious affiliation. One point must be stressed. Religion in Ottoman society was not a separate aspect of social life: it provided a total cultural milieu. For the Greeks, besides defining their identity, religion had preserved their language, and for the vast majority it also set a framework for everyday life in which the ritual and spiritual dimension penetrated all other spheres. This absence of separation between the 'sacred' or 'spiritual' and the 'mundane' or 'secular' is still characteristic of much contemporary Greek life (see Chapters 9 and 10) and was a pronounced feature of life in Asia Minor communities. Older people in the urban refugee quarters demonstrated the close identification of religion with other aspects of identity by their reluctance, almost inability, to distinguish between contemporary religious, national, and linguistic affiliations (cf. Lewis 1963: 102). They were surprised, for example, that I spoke Greek but was neither Orthodox nor had Greek parents. When the Indian architect who visited me (see Preface) gave his name as Hussein, my landlady began talking Turkish to him, and found it hard to believe that since he was a Muslim he was not also a Turk.

For the Asia Minor Greeks, Christianity was strictly defined by the rite of baptism and by the veneration of the Cross. For them, Christians are those who 'venerate the Cross' (προσκυνάνε το Σταυρό) (and they consequently have difficulty classifying Low-Church Protestant denominations where this symbol is not central). Through baptism an Orthodox child becomes a full member of the Christian community (able to take Communion), receives a name, and hence becomes a person. Older Asia Minor Greeks would assert that 'Europeans' (i.e. non-Orthodox Westerners) are 'like Turks and Jews', since they give names without the rite of baptism. This emphasis on visible symbols and specific rituals is interesting and probably reflects how outward signs were used in Ottoman times to identify people's ethnic affiliations in a diverse population. At certain periods items of clothing, even modes of transport, were specified for different groups. While Turks and Jews practised male circumcision, the Orthodox emphasized baptism as the basis for membership of the group.

The emphasis on baptism as the prime mark of Christianity is significant from another aspect. Baptism in dogmatic terms is the rite of rebirth and redemption; it is the new covenant established by Christ and, in Orthodox thought, it is the foundation of Christian belief (Schmemann 1974a). In this respect, as in others, Asia Minor Greek culture had many elements which corresponded closely with the precepts of Orthodoxy. I was struck by the matter-of-fact awareness of points of dogma, particularly among the elderly. Without this being consciously pious, their life-style was marked by a level of theological consistency. I gained little evidence of witchcraft, sorcery, 'folklore', or superstitious beliefs, but direct references to Christian precepts were common. For example, after eating yet another meal in the basement room of an elderly, impoverished, but endlessly hospitable couple, my thanks were countered by their gesture to the icon over the table, that of the Last Supper. 'As Christ did, so do we', Eliso said (Ὅπως ο Χριστός έτσι και 'μεις). This icon was noticeably present in nearly every home, and the sacramental character of the meal was evident in other practices (see pp. 136–8).

The close correspondence between dogmatic precepts enshrined in formal theology and the everyday understanding of religion has, I suggest, a historical explanation. Early missionary journeys in Asia Minor led to well-established Christian communities in towns such as Ephesus, Miletus, and Pergamos; the flourishing theological tradition of the early Church Fathers, many of whom lived in the region; the Ecumenical Synods which took place in this part of the world—all helped to create a climate in which Christian thinking predominated. Christianity became public, overt, recognized—the dominant culture—from the earliest centuries of the Byzantine Empire, and western Asia Minor was its heartland (see Staniforth

1968: 135). Thus, at the popular level and subsequently under Ottoman rule, the practice of Christianity in this region tended to correspond closely with the high tradition of the Eastern Church.

Another effect of religious adherence for the Asia Minor Greeks in the Ottoman period was that, as they were convinced of its excellence, they claimed cultural pre-eminence and a more elevated position in society. This may explain why apostasy appears to have been rare through four hundred years of sub-jugation and periods of intense persecution (Campbell and Sherrard 1968: 51). When recollecting life in Asia Minor older people often told me that 'The Turks were envious of us—our religion is beautiful' (Οι Τούρκοι μας ζηλεύανε· η θρησκεία μας είναι ωραία). This allusion to the dramaturgical dimension and aesthetic elaboration of Orthodoxy indicates a contrast with what they saw as the starker practices of Islam (cf. Lewis 1963: 106–8). Orthodox ritual stimulates the senses—sight, sound, touch, taste, and smell. Indeed the unity of the spiritual and material worlds is a fundamental tenet of Orthodox Christianity, expressed in ritual through the use of material substances (water, bread, oil, wine, incense, icons, amulets) and outward bodily signs (crossing oneself, kissing icons). The interpenetration of these two realms also pervades the nature and use of household items and space (see Chapters 6 and 7).

Travellers' accounts of life in Asia Minor provide some independent evidence that Turks actually emulated certain Christian practices (cf. Ramsay 1917; Hasluck 1929). These reports corroborate the refugees' stories that some Turkish mothers, believing in the beneficial effects of baptism, would have their children baptized in secret. Turks were averse neither to using Christian crosses as protective amulets, nor to visiting the shrines of various Christian saints (Hadjinicolaou-Marava 1953: 37–41). St John the Russian, a saint of Kappadokia, was particularly renowned and both Christians and Turks bore witness to his miraculous powers (Hasluck 1929: 30–3). The knowledge that their Turkish neighbours were willing to imitate certain Christian practices helped to reinforce the pride which Asia Minor Greeks felt for their religion.

Furthermore, older refugees said that the Turks' belief in the power and efficacy of Christianity made them desire marriage with Christians. To illustrate, an elderly woman from Broussa told me the story of a Greek girl who, after persistent courting by a Turk, decided to accept his proposal of marriage. Attempts to dissuade her failed and finally an old woman warned her that she would be able to see the unfortunate consequences of her action. She instructed the girl to place two small plates of water at their heads on the night of the wedding. The bride did so. The next morning she noticed drops of oil in the water at her husband's head. She went to the old woman, who explained what had happened: the chrism of her baptism had left her and gone to her husband, the Turk (*Της έφυγε το μύρο και πήγε στον Τούρκο*). 'Turks believed that they gained grace by taking Christian brides' (*Το 'χανε ψυχικό να πάρουνε γυναίκες χριστιανές*) my informant commented. This story illustrates several points: the closeness of contact between Turks and Greeks (I heard from others about marriages which had taken place between these communities); the Asia Minor Greeks' conviction of the excellence of their religion, a view they believed others shared; and the importance of baptism as the criterion of Christianity.

Our understanding of the social position, the cultural percep-tions, and the reactions of the Asia Minor refugees must, there-fore, take account of the central role taken by religion in their former homeland. In the Ottoman Empire it was the basis of individual identity and also defined membership of adminis-tratively discrete ethnic and cultural groups. In addition to pro-viding a bond of solidarity among those of common religious affiliation, it conferred on the Greeks a sense of superiority over the non-Orthodox population. For them, religious identity was thus also a basis for stratification. Although this was not necess-arily reflected objectively in any recognized social hierarchy, none the less it was a significant element in the people's self-image and certainly affected their relations with mainland Greeks in the period after settlement, though the criteria for perceiving rank differences had to change.

Regional Identity and its Persistence

All the same, despite the sense of common identity based on religion, sharp distinctions existed within the Greek population

of Asia Minor which depended on place of origin. In the Ottoman period, regional divisions had been marked, for local communities had developed differently their own culture, dialect,
cuisine, and manners over a long time. Added to this is the
strong attachment to place of origin (τοπικισμός) which characterizes Greek social life wherever it is found. Regional origin for
the uprooted Asia Minor Greeks was clearly of profound significance, since they transposed it to their new home, and
maintained its associations through several decades. Older
people who actually remembered the homeland would refer to
someone from the same town or village as a 'fellow country
(wo)man' (πατριώτης/πατριώτισσα), and the term would be
extended to the child or even grandchild of their contemporaries.

In this way regional identification provided a means of orientation and adjustment, a way of creating a familiar geography
out of an uncharted expanse. Its strength and persistence into
successive generations is impressive. Even fifty years after the
expulsion, people born and raised in Kokkinia who had never
visited Asia Minor were none the less familiar with and used
the stereotypes of regional origin in their discourse with one
another.

One incident which illustrates this was a joking exchange
between a man of forty (born in Kokkinia of refugee parents)
and an elderly woman, who was chatting in his shop. Dis-
tracted by her gossip and bantering, he shooed her out. Her
voice full of innuendo, she turned to appeal to the other customers as she left, 'Ask him where he's from.' Since his parents
were from the interior region of Asia Minor near Ankara, this
was a snide reference to their supposed lack of manners and
boorishness. She herself was from Krini in the Smyrna region
and the shopkeeper commented drily, 'These Smyrnaians think
that they are somewhat above the rest' (Νομίζουν οι Σμυρναίοι ότι
είναι κάτι παραπάνω).

A most interesting feature of social life in the urban refugee
quarters of Athens and Piraeus, therefore, was the way regional
stereotypes in Greek society of Asia Minor were employed in
common parlance decades after settlement. In Kokkinia I often
heard them being invoked to explain conduct, life-style, and
individual qualities and also to characterize residential districts

(see pp. 25, 68). As with all stereotypes both positive and negative features co-existed, so that their invocation depended on
the speaker's own regional affiliation and intentions.

People from the Ionian coastal communities, for example,
epitomized by Smyrnaians, were said to be gregarious and fun-
loving, with progressive ideas. At the same time, they were
characterized as frivolous, quarrelsome, and prone to gossip,
with loose moral standards (the women in particular). People
from other parts of Asia Minor held that areas settled by
Smyrnaians were inevitably noisy and turbulent.

In contrast, people from the interior of Asia Minor, called
Tourkomerítes (from the Turkish side), *Anatolítes* (lit. 'orien-
tals'), or *Karamalídes*, were generally considered to be serious,
peace-loving (*φιλήσυχοι*), and devoted to their families; yet
they were also said to be slow-witted, plodding, and uncouth
(*χοντροί*). Inhabitants of the Pontus region on the Black Sea
coast, speakers of an archaic dialect with distinctive traditions
in music, song and dance, were regarded as conservative,
hard-working and proud. Nicknamed *aoútides* (from their pro-
nunciation of the demonstrative pronoun as '*a-oútos*', not the
usual '*aftós*'), they were also held to be innately stubborn: to
have an *aoútiko kepháli*, a Pontic head, is an idiom for extreme
stubbornness.

In most assessments, however, people from Constantinople
were regarded as somehow better than all others, irrespective of
their affluence or status in the community. That venerable city
with its sacred associations for Greeks apparently conferred an
aura on its inhabitants so that people from the 'City' (*Πόλη*)
could have an air of assurance unrelated to their present conditions of life. But they were also stigmatized by others as being
'conceited' and 'stuck up' (*φαντασμένοι, ψηλομύτες*).

Unlike the organized phase of rural refugee settlement in
Northern Greece, where almost entire communities were reconstituted, the settlement of Kokkinia occurred without regard to
place of origin. It is all the more interesting, therefore, that residential districts in the locality became associated with regional
stereotypes and continued to be characterized by these attributes. Any concentration of people by regional origin had in
fact come about by chance or by informal arrangement. For one
district only, that of Yerania (see Chapter 4), an unpublished

household survey of 1930 revealed that over a third of its population was from the wider region of Smyrna. It is interesting to
note that years later Yerania continued to be characterized as a
noisy, quarrelsome district. In contrast, the district of Osia Xeni
was reputed to be quiet and orderly because, people said, the
residents were from Pontus and parts of central Asia Minor,
characteristically peace-loving. The only objective evidence for
this attribution was the sizeable two-storey building, the Pontic
Shelter (Ποντιακή Στέγη), located here. Built in the 1950s entirely
through voluntary labour and private contributions (money
and materials), it contained a library, entertainment hall,
canteen, and offices, and stood as tangible proof of the noted
communal dedication of Pontic people. Near by, the most pres-
tigious district in the old part of Kokkinia, Ai Nikola, centred
on the church of St Nicolas. People told me that 'the aristocrats of Kokkinia live there' (εκεί μένουν οι αριστοκράτες της
Κοκκινιάς), adding that most people from Constantinople had
houses there. Others explained that this district had the best
dwellings, the first available for habitation when the settlement
started, and consequently they were obtained only by people
who 'had influence' (είχαν μέσο).

The significance of attaching regional stereotypes to districts
within Kokkinia has another, equally interesting, dimension. In
the process of creating a spatial environment, of making
'spaces' into 'places', the refugees appear to have used regional
mapping as a means of orientation. Through assigning a particular character to areas within the new settlement, they began
to re-create a familiar mental landscape out of an unknown,
uncharted expanse. They apparently imbued the new environment with meaningful attributes, based on regional stereotypes, reinstating the social characteristics of their homeland
areas. In the process of adjustment to radically changed circumstances, the refugees constructed a kind of social landscape
geography in the new settlement. In this way, Kokkinia's residential districts came to revive and to represent the regional
divisions of Asia Minor Greek society. Besides the stereotyping
of districts in the urban landscape, other socially significant
landmarks were created. Place-names, churches enshrining
icons, even stones transported from the homeland: all were
elements aiding in reconstructing a meaningful environment.

Here again, memory was obviously the crucial factor, the means of mapping out their past conceptual geography.

The process of attributing character and meaning to the physical environment, of creating significant 'places', is recognized as a vital element in social life (see Lynch 1960; Tuan 1974; Relph 1976). In the experience of the urban refugees, this may well have been a critical step in adjusting to their changed circumstances and in establishing a basis for their social life. Certainly, in view of the length of time since their expulsion, the persistence of regional attributes and the tenacity of cultural perceptions are significant sociological factors; these had constituted one criterion of differentiation within Asia Minor Greek society. Economic distinctions were another.

Economic Differentiation: Rich and Poor

The inevitable tendency of expatriates to romanticize their former way of life might at first seem to explain the descriptions commonly given of the elevated position of Greeks in Ottoman society. Typically, the older people would say, 'We Greeks were more advanced, we had the Turks as servants' (. . . τους είχαμε δούλους). Chauvinistic claims aside, numerous historical accounts do attest to the relative affluence of the Greek population of Asia Minor. Their commercial success was well known. They flourished in trading and business sectors of the economy. In addition, many diplomatic and administrative posts went to Greeks of the Phanariot group, an influential section of Constantinople society. One consequence of the *millet* system of organization was that in their dealings with others in this heterogeneous society even the poorest Greeks could identify their position with that of the richer and more influential. Notwithstanding economic differences, they were first and foremost Greeks.

Yet, undoubtedly, the Greek population varied widely in mode of livelihood, skills, and wealth. After their arrival in Greece as refugees, the differences in economic status were soon apparent. An early report describes three categories of refugee: those few who had established themselves rapidly in the forefront of trade, industry, and banking; a more numerous group who had become self-supporting and were reasonably

adjusted to their new conditions; and a third who were described as 'living from hand to mouth', barely able to support
themselves (League of Nations 1928, quoted in Pentzopoulos
1962: 114–15). These differences most probably reflected their
status before the expulsion, though other factors (personal, psychological, chance) must also have played a part. Fifty years
later evidence of the economic diversity of the original refugee
population still existed. For example, though Yerania was one
of the poorest areas in Kokkinia, some of these dilapidated prefab houses displayed signs of former affluence. My landlady,
Marika, still had some porcelain coffee-cups and crystal
liqueur-glasses which she used for guests on special occasions,
and the remnants of a fine large *kelim* carpet had become bed-
side mats. She had brought these with her in the second phase
of the expulsion, the exchange of populations. Before that she
had lived as a young bride in her mother-in-law's house in
Constantinople with its two reception rooms, a piano, and furnishings whose covers were changed from yellow silk in summer to red velvet in winter. On the wall of Antonis's small
barber shop across the road hung a picture of Nigde, his home
town, and in a drawer he kept the titles, in Arabic script, to the
large properties which his family had owned in the district.

Others in Yerania, however, recalled their own former
poverty without hesitation and verified that Greeks in the
homeland had not enjoyed equal affluence. An elderly woman
from Pergamos was critical of a neighbour who had been put-
ting on airs since her daughter's successful marriage: 'It's no
use pretending. I know—we were poor in our homeland; we
had mudbrick houses, and what did we own? Rags' (Φτωχοί
ήμασταν στην πατρίδα μας, πλίθινα τα σπίτια μας, και τι είχαμε;
Πατσαβούρες). In the larger towns wealth and social distinctions
appear to have been precisely marked. Seventy-year-old
Margaro's comments on a photograph of Greeks attending a
festival in Smyrna in 1920 were revealing. 'These people are all
gentlefolk', she pointed out, 'There's not one without a hat', and
added, 'It would have been shameful for us to wear hats—
after all we worked in their houses' (Είναι όλοι κύριοι. Δεν
υπάρχει ένας χωρίς καπέλο. Για μας ήταν ντροπή, εμείς δουλεύαμε στα
σπίτια τους). Among the collective memories of the homeland,
then, distinctions of wealth and life-style within the Greek

population had had a place, and they were not forgotten by the survivors.[1]

The Cosmopolitan Heritage

The rich diversity of population and the close contact between people of different groups were vividly presented in the stories and recollections of people from Asia Minor. Ottoman life was essentially cosmopolitan; even in the provinces of central Anatolia settlements of all sizes contained various ethnic, religious, and cultural groups. Familiarity with cultural diversity was, therefore, part and parcel of daily life in the homeland, a major contrast with the experience of these people after their uprooting.

Many of the older people I got to know were barely literate yet most were familiar with at least one other language, and some were bilingual in Turkish and Greek. In the 1970s Turkish was still used as the first language of the older generation in some families, so that the children and even the grandchildren became familiar with it to different degrees.[2] Cinemas in Kokkinia regularly showed Turkish films, which were especially popular among the elderly women, who praised them for their high moral tone (σεμνότητα). Outings to the cinema provoked nostalgic reminiscences, providing glimpses of the countryside and landmarks of their former homes. I heard Turkish proverbs quoted, and in some families naughty children were threatened with the 'stick of Sultan Mehmet'.

If they had come from cities or coastal towns where Levantines and Europeans lived (e.g. Constantinople, Smyrna, Menemeni, or Kaisaria), the older people might have had a smattering of French, Italian, or English. My landlord, who had known British troops in the Dardanelles during the First World War, used to tease me about thinly sliced bread, saying that we ate 'mere cigarette papers' (τσιγαρόχαρτα). Since few towns or even villages in Asia Minor were ethnically homogeneous, all the older refugees were familiar with the culture of at least one other community. Conversations in Kokkinia frequently included references to the customs or beliefs of Turks, Armenians, Jews, Bulgarians, Gypsies, or Europeans, depending on their place of origin. The accounts may not have been accurate but were significant in showing awareness and appreciation of cultural diversity, an experience which distinguished them from most metropolitan Greeks and led to a heightened consciousness of their own identity.

Particularly at times of festivity in Kokkinia these references abounded. Women reminisced about life in the neighbourhoods of their homeland towns and recalled their relationships with those of other communities. I was told many times how food was exchanged between Turks and Greeks at the major festivals of Ramazan and Easter, and about Muslim customs of marriage and circumcision. Tales of the pilgrimages made to the Holy Places of Islam by Turkish neighbours were recounted. Indeed, Christians of these mixed communities also aspired to visit the shrines in the Holy Land in Jerusalem, Bethlehem, and Nazareth, and to be baptized in the River Jordan. On their return these Christian pilgrims were called *Hadzi* (m.), *Hadzienna* (f.), after the Arabic *ḥajj*, 'pilgrimage', or prefixed it to their names, a clear example of cultural borrowing (see pp.224–5).

Although Christian, the customs of the Armenians were usually contrasted unfavourably with Orthodox practices. For example, Armenians were criticized for emphasizing the Epiphany rather than Easter as the major religious festival. They did not have particularly close relationships with the Orthodox, it seems, since I heard fewer stories about contacts between these groups or exchanges of food between the women. Possibly the Armenian quarters in Asia Minor towns were highly segregated and inward-looking; the social distance may also reflect the doctrinal differences between forms of Christianity.[3] The Jewish communities of the Ottoman Empire were usually prosperous and well established. Their customs and religious practices were familiar to refugees from the towns. In Kokkinia a noisy or rowdy gathering was jokingly described as being 'like a Jewish Quarter' (σαν Εβραίικο μαχαλά).

Generally, when talking about their relationships with others goodwill and harmony were emphasized; rancour, hatred, and bitterness were noticeably absent. People often mentioned how they had lived peacefully with their Turkish neighbours. They noted that for long periods an atmosphere of mutual respect existed in the urban centres, for people knew how to get on with one another. Older people were quite categorical that the disturbances and military confrontation which finally resulted in their flight were not the responsibility of the ordinary Turk. They attributed the hostilities between their communities to interference by 'the Great Powers' (οι Μεγάλες Δυνάμεις). Again and again the conclusion was 'The politicians made us hate one another' (. . . μας φέρανε το μίσος). These views reflect a degree of insight all the more remarkable considering the extent of their suffering and losses, and that they were themselves the immediate victims of those political struggles. This contrasted with the more chauvinistic views of their contemporaries among metropolitan Greeks. Those who did not have the close experience of life in mixed communities were more likely to express animosity towards Turks in general. Such negative sentiments were also more common in the younger generation of Greeks, whatever their origin, in Kokkinia and elsewhere. One must conclude that enmity towards the Turks is a product of life in the nation-state of Greece, of exposure to political rhetoric reinforced by the media, and of an educational system which espouses a narrow nationalistic teaching of history. The saddest aspect of this narrowing of people's attitudes, no doubt also present on the other side of the Aegean, is that the actual victims of that most bitter conflict did not express the supposed 'atavistic hatred' of Turks and Greeks for one another. It is also sad to reflect that the compulsory exchange of populations between Greece and Turkey in the 1920s did not bring harmony or peace to these countries' relations. The continuing crisis in Cyprus as well as current tensions in NATO reveal only too well how, as the refugees said, 'It's the politicians and the Great Powers who bring the hatred.'

Greek Meets Greek

The Asia Minor Greeks I knew in Kokkinia were characteristically disparaging of metropolitan Greeks. Their opinion of local people was summed up in the commonly heard and scathing statement, 'They know nothing' (Δεν ξέρουν τίποτα). Various widely expressed views were: 'They don't know how to behave', 'They don't know how to speak', 'They have no manners' (Δεν ξέρουν να φερθούνε. Δεν ξέρουν να μιλάνε. Δεν έχουν τρόπους). They repeatedly told me that most of the advances made in Greek life were introduced by the refugees, a view corroborated by mainlanders themselves. One elderly refugee woman expressed the common opinion succinctly: 'Before we came here what were they? We opened their eyes. They didn't know how to eat or dress. They used to eat salt fish and wild vegetables. It was we who taught them everything' (Πριν έρθουμε εμείς, τι ήταν αυτοί; Εμείς τους ανοίξαμε τα μάτια. Δεν ξέρανε να φάνε ούτε να ντυθούνε. Τρώγανε μπακαλιάρο και χόρτα. Εμείς τους μάθαμε τα πάντα).

Here in a nutshell are attitudes on which the separate identity of the refugees was initially founded. Their initial impressions of mainland Greek life were disappointing. By contrast with the towns and villages of their homeland, metropolitan Greece could not be viewed in a favourable light. This small country was backward, and parochial, and its people unsophisticated. This disappointment promoted a curious replication of social position. Although the mass of urban refugees in the large settlements soon became entrenched at the bottom of the social and economic scale, they re-established their claims to cultural superiority, based now on the minutiae of conduct. Whereas before in the homeland claims to superiority were rooted in religious and cultural differences, now they were defined by minute distinctions in life-style. Religion continued to play a part in this even though they were settled in an official Orthodox country: now the refugees proudly noted that they were more observant, more devout than the locals. Their perception of difference also included manners, comportment, and especially cuisine, a tradition held to most tenaciously by many minority groups. These features were usually stressed by the older refugee women, while the men tended to criticize the country's lack of skills and enterprise, its poverty and feeble economy. These different areas of men's and women's concern closely reflected the gender dichotomy which so characterized social life in Kokkinia (cf. Chapters 5–7).

Patterns of discrimination and animosity which had arisen in the early phase of settlement were reinforced through subsequent experiences (cf. Chapter 3). Although the signs of assimilation were evident, changes in Kokkinia's population from the mid-1960s revived the confrontation between refugees and locals. At that time Kokkinia began to accommodate increasing numbers of rural migrant families and the oldest part of the settlement was no longer exclusively of refugee origin. Owing to changes in tenure (see Chapter 4), villagers from the Greek countryside moved into the original refugee districts and bought or rented the old houses or the new flats which were beginning to replace them. For the old refugees at least, the proximity of these two sections of the population revived the sense of difference, refinement, and superiority. They would emphasize with pride how they had maintained their own ways, typically saying, 'That's the way the refugees/*Mikrasiátes* do it' (*Έτσι κάνουν οι πρόσφυγες/Μικρασιάτες*). Stung into awareness of the condescension of their neighbours, the rural migrants would react with pejorative references to the refugees.

In the early 1970s a competitive spirit existed between refugees and rural Greeks in this locality. One small incident illustrates the form this rivalry took. After selling their land in Kalamata, a village family settled in Kokkinia, where they rented an old refugee house. The wife's father died after several months of illness during which her refugee neighbours had called regularly and helped on many occasions. Preparing for the three-month memorial service after his death, the woman purchased a full dinner service, an expensive item, in order to avoid borrowing anything for the anticipated number of callers. She proudly displayed it to everyone, announcing how much it cost (about £40 when average monthly earnings were £65). Most revealing was her accompanying retort, 'Is it only the refugees who have money?' (*Μόνο οι πρόσφυγες έχουν λεφτά;*).

Indeed, money was a recurrent theme in the rivalry between local Greeks and refugees. The older refugees remembered barter transactions when they had searched for food in villages near Athens during the German Occupation and they characterized it as primitive economic conduct. They would recall that money was an unfamiliar item in the countryside and they mocked the villagers' financial incompetence. One refugee woman remarked scathingly, 'They collect eggs from the hens' backsides to exchange for a handful of rice at the grocer. Only here in the city are they learning about money' (*Μαζεύουν τ'αυγα απ'της κότας τον κώλο για να πάρουν μια φούχτα ρύζι απ'το μπακάλικο. Μόνο εδώ στην πόλη μάθανε τα λεφτά*).

In Kokkinia the refugees were quick to notice any attempt to assume city airs and mocked those who adopted pretentious ways. A young woman walking past a basement window in new high heels with a noticeably unsteady gait was immediately picked out by two women in the room. Chuckling at her effort to appear sophisticated, they laughed, 'Anyone can see that she's just a peasant' (*Φαίνεται πως είναι χωριάτισσα*). I heard refugee residents recall the days when many households in Kokkinia kept a few chickens, pigeons, and even a goat or sheep. But once the villagers arrived in the district all that had to change. It was the villagers, they said, whose continual complaints about disturbances caused trouble until it was forbidden to keep animals. An elderly woman from Smyrna remarked drily, 'The peasants come to town and become aristocrats' (*Έρχονται οι χωριάτες στην πόλη και γίνονται αριστοκράτες*).

These statements were employed to define the boundaries between 'us' and 'them' and expressed markers of perceived difference which upheld their sense of separate identity. Though this section of the urban refugee population and the local Greeks had few identifiable differences—their historical experience apart—their interaction generated boundaries, a recognized characteristic of ethnic groups (cf. Barth 1969: 15–16). This constitutes an instance where separate identity developed within a fundamentally similar population, a suggestive limiting case of 'ethnicity'. The subjective and perceptual nature of distinctions maintained by the refugees is further revealed by their reference to symbolic categories.

Open and Closed: The Symbolism of Separate Identity

Refugees referred to local Greeks as uncultured, rough, and boorish, commonly calling them 'Vlachs' (*Βλάχοι*), shepherds or 'country bumpkins'. They would also refer to them as 'mountain people (*βουνίσιοι*) or say that they were 'from the mountains' (*απ' τα βουνά*). Criticism of local Greeks' behaviour typically concluded, 'What can you expect? They're from the mountains' (*Τί περιμένεις; Απ' τα βουνά είναι*). This topographical image is significant. Since the refugees were not ignorant of Greece's geography, and they knew that not all rural Greeks were shepherds nor were they all from mountainous regions, the choice

of image is suggestive. It relates to a set of symbolic oppositions, pervasive in the cultural vocabulary of Asia Minor
Greeks (and probably in all Greek culture). This is the spatial
metaphor of 'open' and 'closed' states, expressed with explicit
linguistic referents in many diverse contexts. Briefly, 'open'
(ανοιχτός) is a positive state, denoting a communal mode of
orientation, sociability, new life, continuity, luck, light, and the
divine realm. 'Closed' (κλειστός) is a negative state and denotes
isolation, confinement, deprivation. The symbolic opposition of
these states ramified into many aspects of social life and belief,
and understanding it helped elucidate patterns of interaction
and values.

In characterizing all local Greeks as 'mountain people', an
association contained also in the term 'Vlach', the refugees were
drawing a metaphorical contrast by place of origin: between the
towns of Asia Minor and the villages of rural Greece, the former
seen as bustling, cosmopolitan centres, the latter as small,
remote, and isolated. The image of the mountain settlement was
also expressed as being 'far from the world' (μακριά απ' τον
κόσμο). These small communities were thought of, then, as
inward-looking and 'closed'. By contrast, Asia Minor towns
were centres of contact, exchange, and variety, and by implication they represented the 'open' world. This contrast, associated as it was with central values and modes of orientation in
social life (cf. Chapters 8–10), highlighted the conceptual boundaries which the refugees had constructed between themselves
and the local Greek population, and added a symbolic referent
to other social and cultural markers.

The sense of separate identity which continued for more than
fifty years after settlement was one of the fascinating aspects of
social life in this locality. The collective memory of the refugees
had been a major force in creating and perpetuating this separation, building it upon recollections of the Ottoman past. The
role of memory was a predisposing factor, since Orthodox
Christianity, in which their way of life was rooted, itself
emphasized the active use of memory to live with the past in
the present. The sense of separate identity had, therefore, a dis-
tinctly cultural dimension. The conviction of their cultural pre-
eminence in a diverse, cosmopolitan society, their attachment
to regional character and place of origin, their sense of identity

based on religious affiliation were all contained in these memories. Continuity was maintained. Some of these elements can be seen to have helped, others to have hindered their adjustment to the new environment. Besides these cultural factors, however, others of a structural kind relating to conditions in the wider society contributed to the construction and preservation of refugee identity. These must be sought in historical developments, in the economic and political conditions which marked the urban refugees' experience after their settlement.

3

IDENTITY AND HARDSHIP
The Urban Refugee Experience

The catastrophic defeat of the Greek army during the summer of 1922 resulted in a mass exodus of the Christian population from their homes as the Turkish army advanced on the western coastal region. This culminated in the sack of Smyrna, razed by fire in early September. Hundreds of thousands of refugees fled and were evacuated to Greece.

Mass Exodus

That summer, thousands of shocked and destitute people arrived daily at harbours of the Greek islands and mainland. Makeshift arrangements sought to provide minimal shelter, food, and some degree of medical care. In emergency conditions, much of the early work was undertaken by international voluntary relief organizations, such as the Red Cross and Save the Children Fund, while the Greek Government designated an *ad hoc* body, the Refugee Relief Fund (RRF, *Ταμείον Προστασίας Προσφύγων*) to deal with the emergency. In Athens, Piraeus, and Salonika, many public buildings were converted into dormitories: several hundred families occupied the Athens Opera House; others sheltered in school buildings and public baths, or camped in railway sheds near the harbours, in factory store-rooms, warehouses, and in tents. Those who initially escaped to the Aegean islands gradually made their way to the cities, seeking relatives or fellow-townsmen from whom they had been separated. The winter of 1922–3 was harrowing; hundreds of thousands of incapacitated people helplessly awaited events, and for many, only the hope of their imminent return sustained them. That hope of return ended with the signing of the Treaty of Lausanne in 1923, which specified an unprecedented compulsory exchange of populations.[1] At the most elementary level, the size of the incoming population was a serious handicap to their absorption. For the new Turkish state the influx of 350,000 exchanged Muslims presented fewer problems since the country was large, sparsely populated, and the departing Christians had left sizeable properties in the towns and countryside. But for the Greek state, politically disarrayed and economically weak, an acute emergency resulted. Indeed the problems of dealing with so many refugees and exchanged persons were practically insoluble.

Although reliable statistical records do not exist, it is possible to come to an estimate which indicates the overall scale of the problem. The earliest official figure (April 1923) records over 785,000 refugees with numbers increasing on a daily basis. The death-rate at the time was very high following extreme deprivation and a bitter winter, and it continued at this rate for several years. One estimate mentions about 6,000 deaths per month in the first nine months after the influx. From 1923 to 1925 the proportion of deaths to births was 3 to 1; in some parts of the country about 20 per cent of the refugees died within a year (League of Nations 1926, Pentzopoulos 1962: 96–9).

The first official figure of the total number of refugees in the 1928 population census records 1,221,849 persons (1,104,217 were from Asia Minor, Pontus, and eastern Thrace). There can be no doubt, however, that this is lower than the number of people who actually entered Greece and received aid. The census figures do not take account of high mortality rates or the emigration of thousands who left Greece after a few months or years to settle in other countries. One report estimated that about 50,000 persons left between 1923 and 1928 (cited in Pentzopoulos 1962: 98 n. 7); another that 66,000 Greek refugees finally settled in Western Europe, the United States, or Egypt; another that about 75,000 persons died in Greece between 1922 and 1928 (cited in Kitromilides and Alexandris 1984–5: 34). It is impossible to know the actual number of refugees who entered Greece but certainly it was considerably higher than the census figure of 1928, and was probably in the order of 1.25–1.4 million. Since the total population of Greece was under 5 million at this time, provision had to be made for a sudden population increase representing something like a quarter of the total. In terms of contemporary British conditions, this would be

TABLE 1. *Population of Four Urban Refugee Quarters*

	Under 16		Over 16		Total population
	Males	Females	Males	Females	
Nea Kokkinia	5,685	5,292	7,240	11,068	29,285
Kaisariani	1,977	1,938	2,367	4,268	10,550
Nea Ionia	3,031	3,039	4,030	6,360	16,460
Vyrona	1,478	1,580	2,392	4,479	9,929
TOTAL	12,171	11,849	16,029	26,175	

Source: Census of the Urban Quarters June 1926, in League of Nations 1926: 176.

equivalent to absorbing over 12 or 13 million refugees in a couple of years.

In addition to the sheer size of the refugee population, its demographic composition was a problematic factor in the history of their settlement. Even before their arrival in Greece, the Asia Minor people had suffered severe casualties as a consequence of war and their precipitate flight. Civilian losses were then exacerbated through the Turks' forced conscription of all Christian men into 'labour battalions' after the defeat of the Greek army. Losses in the adult male group were particularly marked, therefore, and this was shown in the demographic imbalance of the incoming refugee population. The proportion of widows, for example, was extremely high: nearly 25 per cent of the female refugee population, and almost 8 per cent higher than the equivalent figure for Greece at that time (Pentzopoulos 1962: 100–1). For the refugee population as a whole, the proportion of women was considerably higher than that of men in the productive age-group, and women constituted 60.5 per cent in the age group 20 to 24 years. In four urban refugee quarters of Athens for which statistics are available, there was an even greater disproportion: here, women comprised 62 per cent of the adult age-group (persons over 16 years) and only 38 per cent were men (see Table 1).

The social and economic consequences of this imbalance were undoubtedly serious, and probably had two immediate effects. A shortage of men in the critical age-groups affected marriage prospects and this, I suggest, was instrumental in changing the nature of dowry provision (see Chapter 6).

Furthermore, the successful economic adjustment of families was handicapped by the absence of able-bodied working men. Women and children were forced into the labour market, unskilled jobs were in demand, exploitation was rife, and wages were very low. The Refugee Settlement Commission (RSC) noted that there was no protection for the worker (League of Nations 1926: 188). The long-term prospects for improving their position were prejudiced in many families (in Kokkinia right up to the period of my field-work), as children were sent out to work and their education was neglected. This strategy for coping with the needs for survival is an immediate response to emergency conditions. When these pressures continue as they did in quarters such as Kokkinia right into the 1960s, long-standing patterns are established which affect people's perception of their disadvantages in social, economic, and political terms, as well as their overall integration into the host society.

The sheer size of the refugee population in relation to that of Greece was thus a factor of tremendous significance in the history of their settlement. But early in 1923 when the permanent and irreversible nature of the population influx was only just becoming clear, the immediate problems of dealing with destitute, psychologically shocked people in rapidly deteriorating health were foremost. Efforts had to be directed to the short-term emergency relief as well as to long-term solutions for their settlement.

Urban Refugee Settlement: Economic Limitations

In recognition of the acute crisis in Greece, the League of Nations authorized an independent international body, the Refugee Settlement Commission (RSC), to take over from the Greek government relief organization (RRF) under whose auspices the first refugee quarters were already being established on the outskirts of the main cities as well as in small urban centres such as Volos, Edessa, and Eleusis. The RSC was made up of four members, two being appointees of the Greek government, one of the League of Nations and the fourth member, the chairman, was an American citizen, representative of those relief organizations which had already contributed greatly to the care of the refugees. For the next six years, until 1930, the

RSC was responsible for the settlement of refugees throughout the country. It was funded on an international basis, mainly through loans totalling some £19 million provided in two rounds (see Pentzopoulos 1962: 89 ff.).

Under the immediate pressures of the time there was an understandable emphasis on establishing the refugee population as self-sufficient and productive. Thus rural settlement was given priority over the provisions for refugees in the towns.[2] Over 2,000 new villages were created, chiefly in the North where international territorial disputes were long-standing. Their establishment—a major achievement in sheer physical terms—acted also to establish finally the claims of the Greek state to this region.[3] But the emphasis on agricultural settlement took place despite official recognition that 'the notable feature of the national community was the large proportion of the urban element compared with the purely agricultural element' (League of Nations 1926: 15). Many town-dwelling families were settled in villages, inevitably a temporary measure for, sooner or later, they moved to the towns, particularly to refugee quarters, even though provisions were minimal and economic opportunities limited.

In the cities the RSC concentrated on immediate problems of shelter rather than those of economic subsistence. It therefore provided low-cost permanent housing and some community facilities in the urban settlements but had no co-ordinated plan for the economic integration of urban refugees: it neither assessed employment possibilities in local industries, nor settled the refugees in relation to their particular skills. Sources of livelihood were left to the individual's own enterprise and chance. For those with no capital or entrepreneurial talents, the situation was critical. In 1926 the RSC noted that unskilled workers comprised about 45 per cent of the working population in these areas (League of Nations 1926: 177) and that persons engaged in 'minor commercial activities' and in 'small-scale artisan jobs' were concentrated in the urban settlements. Dispersed throughout Anatolia, as they had been previously, people who practised similar trades could flourish; but their concentration in a few urban centres created a situation of extreme economic competition.

Clearly at the national level too, the absorption of so great a

TABLE 2. *Population Increase in Refugee Settlements of Athens and Piraeus*

	1920	1928
Athens		
Kaisariani	11	15,357
Vyrona	0	7,723
Nea Ionia	79	16,382
Nea Philadelphia	110	6,337
Kallithea	4,940	29,446
Piraeus		
Nea Kokkinia	0	33,201
Drapetsona	0	17,652
Keratsini	0	10,827
Peristeri	123	7,268

Source: Kayser and Thompson 1964: 2.07.

number of urban refugees in relative as well as absolute terms posed serious problems, given the economic and political disarray of the country at the time. Greece had been at war for almost a decade (from the Balkan Wars to the First World War and the Anatolian campaign). Following the débâcle, those allegedly responsible were executed, the king went into exile, several governments were formed and failed and Greece was declared a Republic in 1924. In view of these unstable conditions, the poverty of the country, and the fact that the policy of the RSC concentrated attention on the rural settlements, it is hardly surprising that long-term problems of integration were experienced in the urban refugee quarters. Indeed, when the major work of settlement ended in 1930 with the dissolution of the RSC, only one-fifth of its total budget had been spent on the urban localities (Pentzopoulos 1962: 114). Despite the emphasis on rural settlement, however, the record in the urban areas was impressive. In the vicinity of Athens, for example, areas entirely uninhabited in 1920 had become by 1928 large residential quarters housing thousands of families (Table 2). Some already established communities were turned into refugee settlement areas: Kallithea, for instance, with a population of about 5,000 in 1920 grew into a suburb of 30,000 in only eight years. In the vicinity of the harbour of Piraeus, provision was made for the settlement of 60,000 persons in three new quarters and the largest of these, Kokkinia, the locality of this study, had a population of 33,000 by 1928 and 40,000 by 1934.

Contemporary reports on the first urban refugee quarters draw an auspicious early picture. The RSC took pride in the fact that, despite the shortage of money and time, additional facilities were provided so that by 1926 each refugee quarter in the Athens area was equipped with a dispensary, schools, crèches, and the beginnings of a water supply. The funding for these projects was almost exhausted, however, so that a second round of loans had to be raised internationally. This allowed the RSC to continue its work for the next three years but, unfortunately, after 1930 in localities such as Kokkinia, where large-scale public investment was still required to complete the provision of basic services, little improvement had taken place and these minimal facilities gradually began to deteriorate.

Given the enormity of the refugee influx, its demographic imbalance, and the internal state of the country, the immense contribution of the RSC to the early phase of the settlement programme is patently clear. The constraints on public investment over the ensuing decades in the urban refugee quarters were, however, a crucial factor determining the subsequent experience of this section of the refugee population.

The Political Factor

In the decade following the Asia Minor débâcle, the country was weakened by a series of civilian and military governments (Veremis 1977). Perennial political instability was aggravated by a severe economic crisis; the international funding for the RSC, considered to be a vital boost of foreign capital, had taken the form of loans contracted at rates of interest unusually high in view of their humanitarian purpose (Pentzopoulos 1962: 89–91). As world-wide economic depression set in, this contributed to the country's bankruptcy.

In 1930 the Ministry of Social Welfare took over from the RSC, but there were still over 30,000 urban families in need of permanent housing and over 12,000 housing units required in agricultural settlements. In the 1930s the government made limited attempts to aid refugee families through self-help projects and the construction of three- and four-storey blocks of flats, but this was nothing to compare with the scale of the earlier effort. In March 1940 the programme of urban refugee housing was still incomplete; an estimate at this time suggested that a further 16,000 dwellings were required (Vasiliou 1944: 84). The turbulent decade of the 1940s with widespread famine and huge population losses in Athens during the German Occupation, and the subsequent turmoil of the Civil War, meant that the needs of urban refugees continued to be neglected.

Only after 1950 was the serious plight of thousands of families again officially recognized; it provided the impetus in 1952 for another programme of 'Urban Refugee Housing' (Στέγασις Αστών Προσφύγων). By this time, conditions in the urban centres had further deteriorated through bombing, war damage, and civil strife. The problem was aggravated by the influx of new refugees from Balkan countries as well as from many rural villages destroyed during the Civil War. In 1952 over 32,000 families were recognized as being in critical need of housing throughout the country, a number which did not reflect those whose housing conditions were simply inadequate. After a seven-year programme, 6,000 families had been rescued from the most squalid conditions, so that the number of officially recorded needy families was reduced to 26,000. Thus, even after the post-war housing programme, nearly 7,000 families were still living in 'sheds' (prefabricated, temporary housing) in the Athens–Piraeus area alone (Pentzopoulos 1962: 227). It is clear, therefore, that public investment in housing consistently failed to meet the needs of a sizeable section of the urban refugee population.

Government policy undoubtedly played a significant role in the perpetuation of the refugees' sense of 'separate identity'. Their grievances were ignored by successive governments and they failed to become a pressure group. In short, the mass of urban refugees lived in a state of long-term political marginality and, for Greece as a whole, in spite of their substantial numbers, the refugees were never represented in Parliament in proportion to their population strength. Early attempts to organize politically were not successful. From 1923 to 1934, a period of political instability with a number of elections, refugee deputies in the Greek Parliament achieved their highest proportion, 15.2 per cent, only in 1932 (Legg 1969: 211) but fell a year later to 12 per cent and never rose beyond that. Nor were they ever able, as a disaffected group, to mobilize effectively in order to rectify these basic grievances (cf. Pentzopoulos 1962: 186–7).

Several factors contributed to the political ineffectiveness of the refugees. Their voting strength was limited at the outset by the settlement policy which dispersed them throughout the country and, in addition, it appears that electoral districts were gerrymandered to prevent refugee majorities (Legg 1969: 210). The country's political structure, polarized at the time between 'royalists' and 'Venizelists', was organized around patron–client relationships and did not easily accommodate this new element on the political scene. The disaffection resulting from the refugees' exclusion from patronage links in the established parties may help to account for the rapid growth of the Communist Party in urban refugee quarters in the 1930s. Its egalitarian rhetoric and ideological emphasis must have appealed all the more in the absence of the political links of clientage.[4]

Certainly, the well-established network of clientage hampered the refugees' ability to organize themselves as a pressure group. Since clientage creates 'vertical cleavages' based on individual transactions, it was the wealthier refugees with some influence who were recruited to the political establishment. In the process they soon dissociated themselves from the concerns of the poor mass of refugees. As conditions in the urban quarters deteriorated further with increasing population pressure and lack of further government investment, these localities began to epitomize a situation of endemic poverty and misery, aggravated by physical and social isolation. Successful refugees, who alone might have felt bonds of sympathy based on a common experience, even those who had improved their lot from simple beginnings in the urban quarters, appear to have dissociated themselves from the less fortunate. They apparently felt that little would be gained by identifying with this group of people who were rapidly becoming entrenched at the lowest level of urban society. Thus, as the successful refugees gradually adjusted to their new circumstances, stratification and class distinctions began to prevail over place of origin or ethnic affiliation for a section of the Asia Minor population. Indications also exist that discriminatory treatment depending on the refugees' means was meted out by the settlement authorities (Pentzopoulos 1962: 184).

Refugees as an Interest Group

At first, many refugees were obviously in a state of shock and disbelief following their uprooting. They were reluctant to adjust to the changed conditions of life and hoped that they would soon return to their homeland. The persistence of refugee identity in Greece had not, however, centred on any irredentist purpose. The Ankara Convention of 1930, a watershed in Graeco-Turkish relations, put an end to any dreams of the refugees regaining their homeland. Attempting international reconciliation with Turkey, Venizelos led the Greek government in a final settlement to resolve the issue of property of the exchanged minorities. The value of Greek properties in Asia Minor was accepted as somewhat less than that of the Muslim properties in Greece and outstanding debts were cancelled. Up to that time many promises had been made for various kinds of compensation against loss of property and livelihood, to be returned in cash, bonds, lands, or houses, but few had received what was due to them. The refugees' reaction was therefore understandably negative: this treatment exacerbated their growing sense of alienation from the Greek state, their feelings of dissatisfaction, of injustice, even betrayal. With very real grievances regarding living conditions and unfulfilled expectations for rehabilitation, a section of the refugee population began to perceive itself as an 'interest group' *vis-à-vis* successive Greek governments. The status of 'refugee' conferred certain rights to monetary indemnification, to housing, to social services. The unfulfilled expectations regarding compensation must have become a focal point for a section of the refugee population in entrenching their sense of a 'separate identity'. In their self-designation as 'refugees' even fifty years after their arrival, people expressed political disaffection, economic deprivation, and social marginality, an additional dimension to the cultural elements conveyed by the term (cf. Chapter 2).

Obviously this situation did not affect the more fortunate

refugees who had brought capital with them, and those who by skill and luck had improved their position in society; what they stood to gain by way of government compensation was negligible and in any case those with influence had been the first to be recompensed with the early offerings. Therefore it was the less fortunate, the poor, the uneducated, or those who were psychologically disorientated by the traumatic changes who began at this stage to have a vested interest in their status as 'refugees'. These people began to emphasize their right to compensation, and to build upon it a sense of their own position in society.

The seventh Pan-Refugee Congress held in 1956 some thirty years after the influx provided an opportunity to air the accumulated grievances of past decades. It revealed clearly the role of policy. In particular, a major complaint centred on the serious inadequacies in the refugees' housing situation. The complicated laws which had been promulgated regarding the acquisition of titles to refugee housing were a specific cause for complaint: payment for titles to what they regarded as their minimal rights to shelter, and what amounted to grossly inadequate compensation was deemed totally unacceptable; understandably many refugees simply refused to pay the nominal sum for titles to their houses (cf. Chapter 4) since for most urban refugees the houses provided by the RSC or the state constituted the only compensation for everything they had lost in the exodus. Another severe criticism centred on the mishandling of the Muslim properties which the Greek Government had been authorized to liquidate in 1930. The proceeds were to have been used as compensation and for the settlement of the refugee population but the money had been so inefficiently and irresponsibly managed that little benefit had actually accrued to them in twenty-five years. The explicit aim of the 1956 Congress was to rectify these sources of dissatisfaction, and it appealed explicitly to the refugees on the grounds of their common interest in material claims.[5]

Political Orientations

It is hardly surprising that long-term neglect and indifferent treatment by those in the established political structure resulted in political disaffection. Initially the Republican Party (liberal) of Venizelos gained the most support from the refugee vote in the country, but as time passed, and especially after the 1930 Convention with Turkey, refugees swung to the left. The Greek Communist Party was founded in 1918 but at the time did not have much impact on the political scene. Significantly, its slogan was soon modified to include 'workers, peasants and refugees' in recognition of the disadvantages of this section of the population. From the late 1920s up to 1936 when it was banned,[6] the Communist Party recruited increasing support, notably in the urban localities of Athens, Piraeus, and Salonika. Localities such as Kokkinia became known as Communist strongholds, a reputation which was later used to stigmatize them.

Results of two elections in the 1930s give an indication of the political orientation of Kokkinia at that period.[7] The 1932 elections showed the popularity of the Republican Party of Venizelos: it gained 77 per cent of the vote in Kokkinia but only 50 per cent in the municipality of Piraeus, while the Communist Party got 7.5 per cent in Kokkinia and 6 per cent in Piraeus. The right-wing Laïkón Party of Tsaldaris gained only 4.7 per cent of the votes in Kokkinia, but 33 per cent in Piraeus. The 1935 elections, the last before Metaxas' coup and the dictatorship of 1936, was marked by the abstention of Venizelos' party. While the centre-right governing coalition gained 45 per cent of the vote in Kokkinia, 63 per cent in an adjacent locality, and 55 per cent in the Piraeus area, a marked difference was recorded for the party of the far right: this party—under Metaxas and two others—received only 7.5 per cent of the votes in Kokkinia, 19.5 per cent in the adjacent area, and 20.7 per cent in Piraeus.

Within five years Greece was caught up in the tribulations of the Second World War, the invasion by Italy, Germany and the Occupation, events which might have ended the refugees' separation in the face of a common enemy. But divisions in the country were deep-rooted and enduring. Initially reflected in the resistance movement, these later took full expression in the bitter Civil War between left-wing forces and the returned government-in-exile. The already disreputable public image of some urban refugee quarters was exacerbated when certain localities, including Kokkinia, became known as centres of extreme left-wing activity. In reality, the urban quarters were divided and the Civil War raged there as it did in the rest of the country. I was told of betrayals in the locality and occasionally former Nazi collaborators were pointed out to me. Electoral results in the post-war period show a strong preference for left-wing parties though the right did not lack support: the left, represented under various names, consistently gained over 40 per cent of the vote in Kokkinia, peaking at 66 per cent in 1958. The right-wing parties (also under various names) gained increasing support during the 1950s with 7 per cent of the vote in 1950, 11 per cent in 1951, growing to 18 per cent in 1956 and reaching a peak of 23 per cent in 1961. In the early 1960s the centre party also recruited successfully (26 per cent in 1961, 38 per cent in 1963, and 47 per cent in 1964). Nevertheless, the image of left-wing fanaticism left its imprint. In the 1970s Kokkinia was characterized on the one hand as a bastion of democratic ideals and on other, as a hotbed of Communism. When I went to live there in 1972, some middle-class Athenians expressed concern about my residence in such a 'notorious' area and, quite unjustifiably, about my safety.

Instead of unity being generated by their suffering during the German Occupation it seems that the urban refugees' sense of separate identity was further reinforced by wartime events. Its continuity was assured as yet another generation of people, the youth of the post-war period was affected by the stigma attached to their home districts. This was deeply impressed upon them in various ways. For example, just after the Civil War ended in the 1950s a right-wing headmaster was appointed to the only high school in Kokkinia. Serving a population of 70,000, the school consisted of some prefabricated huts, hopelessly crowded with classes of 120. Some of those who were pupils at the time told me how he and other teachers had berated them as 'dirty communists' (βρωμοκομμουνιστές) and 'wretched refugees' (παλιοπρόσφυγες). In this way, awareness of the obvious and continuing neglect of their locality and the deprivations suffered by their parents was imprinted on the next generation, those born in the 1940s. Their identity clearly began to convey a long-term status, an almost hereditary condition. Despite the passage of thirty years, the sense of a separate 'refugee identity' was not being eroded but was alive for the younger as for the older generation.[8]

The Urban Refugee Quarters

In the history of the urban refugees after the settlement, housing and employment problems were sources of long-standing
and deeply felt grievance. They acted as a focus of collective
self-definition in a situation of continuing political helpless-
ness. Kokkinia illustrates well the experience of settlement and
the social, economic, and political position of the mass of urban
refugees and provides a reasonably typical picture of some of
the processes which contributed to the separation of these refugees from the wider society, a structural dimension which coexisted with the cultural features discussed in Chapter 2.

In 1922 Piraeus consisted only of the port, a small commercial
centre, and a few industrial establishments on the edge of a
limited residential area, surrounded by open land and fields. It
was deemed eminently suitable for the siting of new residential
quarters with employment available at the harbour and in local
factories. One area demarcated for refugee settlement lay to the
north of the industrial section, today the southernmost portion
of Kokkinia. At the time it was used as a rubbish dump while
the surrounding area offered seasonal grazing to shepherds
from villages in the region. Early in 1923 the government relief
agency (RRF) carried out a hasty survey of this area and construction started. Temporary shelter in tents was given to
several hundred refugees. These first houses were on extremely
small plots, only about 20 to 25 sq. m. (measuring 5 m. × 4 m.,
5 m. × 5 m., or 6 m. × 4 m.), and were low, single-roomed, and
made of a kind of wattle and daub (μπαγδατί).

Kokkinia began, therefore, as a wattle-and-daub village. The
RSC then took over the systematic planning of Kokkinia, with
the housing programme of successive phases over the following
five years. The initial phase of housing (1924–6) covered an area
of about fifteen blocks, one square kilometre, extending north-
wards for over a kilometre.[9] These areas became known as Ai
Nikola and Osia Xeni after churches built in two parts of the
district. Houses were solidly constructed in a variety of styles
and sizes (Plate 1). But the organization broke down when the
houses came to be allocated. People today recall that it was a
matter of luck, good management, or influence which decided
the house one was allocated. In 1924, for instance, shortly before

the first houses were completed, about 1,000 refugees were transferred from the public baths at the coastal resort of Phaliron to large hospital tents in the vicinity. They were reluctant to move from the warm building with its abundant water to Kokkinia, which they had heard was a desolate rubbish dump. The houses were soon completed but the committee delayed making allocations. As winter approached agitated refugees who were sheltering in flimsy tents sent delegations, but to no avail. One night during a heavy storm they took matters into their own hands, broke into the houses and occupied them. This also occurred in at least one other quarter, Kaisariani, where frustrated families forced their way into a large area of housing before allocations were officially made.

In the following two years, 1925 and 1926, the housing programme was at its peak and the settlement expanded impressively so that by the end of 1926 Kokkinia was a substantial settlement of nearly 30,000 persons. With the second international loan in 1927 the RSC continued its activities: another survey was carried out on open land extending further north where the cemetery was located at that time. However, housing in this new area was quite unlike that in other parts of Kokkinia, reflecting, perhaps, the financial pressures and the priority given to rural settlements. This district, known as Yerania, our main focus in the following chapters, was provided with uniform prefabricated buildings of panel-board. These houses were the last provision made in Kokkinia by the RSC, allocated in December 1927 to people who had been sheltering for almost six years in the warehouses and factory basements of Piraeus (Plate 2).

Kokkinia continued to expand for the next few years but without a housing programme. Plots of land were allocated to refugee families by the government, but housing was the responsibility of the recipients, who were aided by small loans to be repaid at low rates of interest. The district of Karava, lying to the west of the settled area, and the eastern 'arm' extending along the main highway were developed through the allocation of plots in this way. The last public provision for refugee settlement in the area was the construction of several blocks of flats by the Ministry of Social Welfare in 1934 and 1935.

Kokkinia was finally incorporated as a municipality (δῆμος) of

Piraeus in 1934 with a population of about 40,000 refugees and exchanged persons from Asia Minor and Thrace. It was roughly rectangular, 2 sq. km. in area, with ribbon development extending a short distance along the main road to the east. An extensive wedge of open land, fields, and olive groves separated the built-up centre of Athens from that of Piraeus. For almost two decades Kokkinia remained physically distinct, a separate residential quarter. Its isolation decreased with improved communication networks, however, as the growth of the urban area in the post-war period (which took on massive proportions, cf. Kayser and Thompson 1964) created new residential areas surrounding and linking the refugee quarters (see Map).

But the physical integration of Kokkinia did not result in overall social absorption. In the post-war period the divisions in the urban population did not disappear but on the contrary may even have become accentuated as living conditions could be compared in adjacent areas. In the newer districts surrounding Kokkinia, for example, public funds were made available; street lighting, piped water, and tarred roads were provided, yet municipal funds due to Kokkinia were consistently docked so that local government could do little to improve conditions in the old locality. Former municipal councillors commented to me that the long-term deprivation was not fortuitous; they saw it as the obvious penalty exacted by higher authorities in central government for the left-wing political orientation of the area.

Indeed, results of elections in the post-war period (1950–65, see pp. 47–8) showed that the left had considerable support in Kokkinia and in similar refugee quarters, while the right had solid backing in the surrounding districts settled by rural migrants. The low standard of public facilities in Kokkinia became clearer as the newer areas were established. It was evident that public funds for investment in these areas were not lacking, unlike the situation in Kokkinia. As time passed, it seems that a sense of political impotence overwhelmed many residents, and though open discussion of these issues was almost impossible in the climate of 1972, many remarks indicated how bitter people felt. People saw themselves as victims in an unjust world where the rich get all the benefits and the poor are unprotected. In discussions about living conditions in Kokkinia people would say, 'It's the poor who pay' (Ο φτωχός τα πλερώνει όλα),

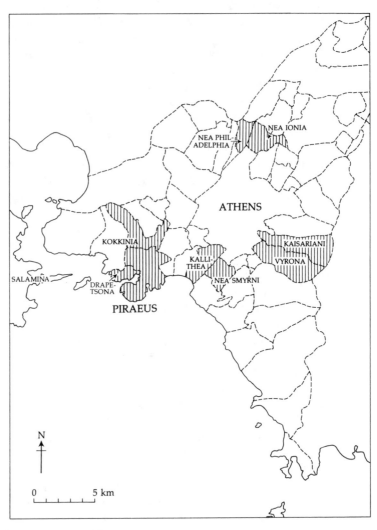

Main Areas of Asia Minor Refugee Settlement in Athens

'Where can you find justice?' (Πού να βρεις το δίκιο σου;) and they often concluded, 'They exploit us' (Μας εκμεταλλεύονται), remarks which convey a deep sense of bitterness about their past treatment.

In 1972, however, a much-publicized programme of improvements was undertaken in an effort to popularize the municipal officers appointed by the junta. The task which they faced indicates something of the neglect to which the quarter had been subjected for years. Roads which had been levelled in the 1920s were still unpaved—in the mid-1960s only a quarter (in extent) of Kokkinia's road surfaces had been tarred (Plate 10). Extensive road-surfacing work took place to provide full tarring at this time. Street lighting was poor, with sparse lamp-posts and unlit side-streets, and there was no central sewerage system. The municipality undertook improvement of these basic requirements as well as the infilling of a notorious gully in the southern part of the area which had become an exposed rubbish dump and a hazard to children and traffic. Among other planned improvements were several parks and a badly needed high school building. The fact that funds for public works were at last made available during a period of military dictatorship was an irony not lost on the residents who felt that they had suffered much in support of democracy. When I returned to Kokkinia in 1983, the mayor, a Communist Party candidate, had been returned for a second term with 75 per cent of the vote. His popularity directly reflected the energetic attention directed to providing facilities in the locality, improving roads and parks, planting trees, and organizing the long-overdue central sewerage network.

The Educational Factor

The inadequate educational facilities of Kokkinia reveal yet another of the handicaps under which people of many urban refugee quarters lived and which undoubtedly affected their development and experience in Greek society.

For purposes of primary education, the metropolitan area (Athens–Piraeus) is divided into administrative 'neighbourhoods', ideally each having its own state-funded school. In Kokkinia, however, most of the twenty primary school buildings served two neighbourhoods and were used in a rotation system, with alternate morning and afternoon staff. In Yerania, for example, a district of Kokkinia, one primary school building served both Yerania and the adjacent district of Karava (Plate 3). Class size averaged 45 pupils, but this was considerably better than the average for the municipality as a whole, which was 65 pupils per class.[10]

The facilities for secondary education were even less satisfactory. The high school built in the mid-1950s, to replace the huts which had been in use during the previous decades, served a population of 86,000 in the early 1970s. The building was being used for three sessions a day, a boys' high school, a girls' high school, and an evening high school for working youths. In 1972 the boys' and girls' schools had alternate morning and afternoon sessions with over 3,500 pupils. Classrooms seldom had less than 60 to 70 pupils, and each year was subdivided into three or four sections. Inevitably teaching standards as well as discipline were compromised, the more so since there were insufficient desks and textbooks, and few teaching resources such as laboratories, equipment, or maps.

However, low educational achievement also reflected the economic pressure on families in this locality since more than one member of the family was required to earn money and this was often one of the children (see Chapter 5). Even with increasing affluence in the 1960s, 20 per cent of children in Kokkinia who completed primary school did not go on to high school or technical school. Of those who did, about 60 per cent completed only two years. Finally, an additional barrier to secondary schooling was created when the junta reversed previous policy and reduced the years of compulsory education to primary school only, while entrance to the high school depended upon passing an examination. Some children therefore had no choice but to study at home or enter employment illegally since the statutory age for wage earning was 14 (in 1972). Some parents were also hesitant about sending their children, particularly girls, to the state high school, where there was inadequate supervision and many opportunities for misconduct. It is true that there were two privately owned high schools in Kokkinia, but fees were above the means of most families.

In addition to the economic and demographic disadvantages

which marked a large section of the urban population of Asia Minor refugees, certain urban refugee quarters acquired a cumulative social and political stigma. This stigma was both created and reinforced by physical separation, by competition with the established urban population for scarce resources, by the Civil War, and by discriminatory public provision of residential and educational facilities. In this chapter some of the forces which affected the urban quarters, both at the time of their establishment and during subsequent decades, have been outlined. These provided the reinforcing structural context in which the sense of separate identity, already an integral element in the cultural heritage of the group, was further shaped. The way of life and thinking, impressive in its coherence and vitality, can best be understood through exploring a particular district, Yerania. For a variety of reasons this densely populated, poorly endowed section of Kokkinia reveals most clearly the central themes and responses in the urban refugee experience.

4

YERANIA
Place and Space

Cityscape

Kokkinia, with a population of over 86,000 in 1971, can in no sense be regarded as a closed community, nor are there any visible boundaries 'on the ground' which could serve to designate the area as a discrete unit. Unlike the situation at an earlier period in its history, Kokkinia is fully integrated into the metropolitan Athens–Piraeus area, an urban complex of about three million in 1972, its residents involved in the life of the city—indeed the whole country—through politics, economic and religious pursuits, education, and recreation. The limits of its municipal area, which encompasses 4 sq. km. and includes areas settled by migrants in the post-war period, are impossible to define by observation; nowadays it is totally integrated in the unbroken expanse of buildings, crosscut by highways and roads, and interspersed by some green areas and open squares. But Kokkinia remains chiefly residential in character and, despite extensive changes through time, several sections exist where the original refugee housing is still discernible and where the vast majority of the people are of Asia Minor descent.

Despite Kokkinia's overall integration into the life of the city, in 1972 a degree of operative self-sufficiency existed on a day-to-day basis, for the area was endowed with most public facilities and all varieties of consumer goods and services were available. The heart of the oldest section lay at the junction of two main roads, one leading to the harbour of Piraeus, the other joining up with the main arterial route between the shipyard and commercial port of Keratsini and the city of Athens. In this commercial and administrative centre were the recently constructed municipal offices, which housed all local government functions, as well as the Post Office, the Telecommunications Centre (*OTE*), and the Public Bath (*Λουτρό*). Modern buildings of two to four storeys with ground-floor shops have replaced the original houses. Financial, legal, and other professional offices tended to be concentrated in this area although every square in the locality also had several such small enterprises. Commercial activity also extended along about half a dozen main roads where many of the old refugee houses had been replaced. Elsewhere, scattered throughout Kokkinia in side-streets were the small grocery stores, bakeries, and dairies which served the daily needs of the neighbourhood as well as providing meeting places for the women's informal daily contacts. In addition, the city-wide guild organization of street markets operated three days a week in the central section of Kokkinia alone. There good quality, fresh produce was sold cheaply, so that the street market (λαϊκή αγορά) was the most important source of most households' provisions.

Other important facilities which intensified social life within the locality were the public squares lined with small shops, taverns, cafés (patronized only by men), and confectioners (ζαχαροπλαστεία), where couples and family groups would go. The parish churches (each serving an area of roughly 10,000 inhabitants) played an important role in the life of this locality both at family rituals (baptism, marriage, funerals) and at major festivals celebrated by the community (Easter and particular saints' days). But Kokkinia had few recreational facilities, playgrounds, parks, or cinemas. Many children's games and adult social life, too, took place mainly on the streets and pavements for at least eight months of the year, particularly on the rough, unpaved streets which carried little traffic until the municipal improvement programme of 1972. Excursions out of the area by Pullman buses were frequent and very popular throughout the year. During the winter months these were mainly to religious shrines in various parts of the country, usually visited by women, or to particular sporting events and football matches, popular among men. During the summer months buses would leave two or three times daily from various parts of Kokkinia for sea-bathing, usually about a half hour's drive away.

For its inhabitants Kokkinia is further differentiated into residential districts having no clearly defined boundaries but ranked by common consensus in order of reputation and desirability. The parish churches provide orientation points in the landscape and the names by which informally distinguished neighbourhoods are known. Ai Nikola, where in 1924 the first solidly built houses of the original settlement were established, ranks highest. An area composed of many different types of house, this district centres on the church and square of St Nicolas where official commemorative services are held, and extends several blocks around it. Near by to the north-west is a respectable district called Osia Xeni after the small church which housed a famous miraculous icon of this saint brought from Smyrna in the exodus. The main arterial road of Petrou Ralli runs through a district known as Chalkidona, an ill-defined area of mixed residential and commercial use, and north of this is Ai Yorgi, the largest district in size encompassing about fifty blocks on all sides of the parish church and square. Finally in the north of the original quarter is Yerania, the only district with definite boundaries owing to its distinctive housing. Established six years after the influx, it used to abut on the former cemetery on the northernmost edge of the settlement, beyond which was open land, but today Yerania is simply a district within the large parish of Evangelismos (15,000 in 1972), which includes a vast residential area developed by rural migrants in the years following the Second World War.

Despite its general underendowment, poverty, high densities, and the appalling lack of public utilities, the oldest part of Kokkinia was not unattractive, monotonous, or dull. Even on overcast wintry days, its appearance was one of pleasing visual variety. At least five distinct types of structure could still be identified when I lived there, for settlement provisions over a period of about eight years had taken various forms, styles, and sizes of dwelling (see pp. 49–51). Subsequent modifications and additions, often showing great ingenuity with limited resources, enhanced the impression of individuality throughout the area. Variety was increased too by the imaginative use of colour, of pot-plants and greenery, and because of the different degrees of affluence (and hence of modernity) displayed by the houses (Plates 1–8).

Why Yerania?

While these remarks apply to any part of Kokkinia, the district of Yerania, the last for which the RSC provided housing, differed in one important respect. Unlike that of earlier phases of settlement, housing was uniform in this district, and was not solidly constructed but made of prefabricated panel-board structures. Indeed, some residents maintained that these structures had been intended as temporary shelters only, which is remarkable since 83 per cent of the original dwellings were still standing and inhabited in 1972 (Plates 2, 3, 7). Even by 1983 when the ambiguities of ownership rights had been resolved at last, only 40 per cent of the original prefab houses had been replaced.

The uniform housing and the easy modification of the prefabricated structures make Yerania a particularly revealing case study: the past conditions of refugee settlement were still evident and living problems and the solutions which evolved were most clearly shown. The original provision of standardized housing provides a basis for comparative observations, and the combined effect of many factors common throughout the district—pressures on space, poverty, claims to compensation, and the changing needs of the family—reveals clear patterns in the organization and use of space. Under severe economic pressure individual choices are limited, and it can be argued that those changes which do occur reflect culturally defined priorities as they are individually executed. Even in stigmatized refugee quarters distinctions of reputation existed. Yerania laboured under a bad reputation not only among refugees from other parts of Kokkinia but also among its own residents. These views reflected the hardships which resulted from the inadequate housing in this district, and its subsequent social history. The fact that deprivation was possibly more acute than in other districts of Kokkinia highlights central issues encountered by the urban refugees in their adjustment to a new way of life. Yerania houses provide fascinating insights into the crucial concerns of the urban refugees, their social relationships, and into the symbolic categories which lie behind more obvious manifestations of social life.

Yerania's Prefabs: Provisions and Modifications

In 1927 a roughly rectangular site of over 400 m. × 200 m. on rising ground to the north of Kokkinia was surveyed and an area of over 80,000 sq. m. subdivided into 32 standard-sized blocks measuring 50 m. × 35 m. These were separated by strips 10 m. wide which provided the street pattern and linked up with roads to the south in the already established area of settlement. Each block was subdivided into 20 plots and 10 prefabricated structures were erected there. Thus each structure of panel-board comprised twin dwelling units under a single roof strad-dling two plots. Ideally each family was to occupy one half of the structure and be provided with an open inner courtyard, the dimensions of which depended on position in the block. The largest plots, those in the centre, were 20 m. long, four others were 17 m., while the remaining eight, the corner plots, measured only 12 m. (see Fig. 1).

While the amount of open courtyard space varied consider-ably, each family was to have the same amount of interior space since the structure was a standard size, 8 m. × 9.5 m. The family dwelling therefore measured 4 m. × 9.5 m., subdivided into three rooms, two of 3.25 m. × 4 m. each, a third intended as a kitchen, 2 m. × 3 m., and a small lavatory (see Fig. 2). The pre-fabricated structures were of wooden frame construction with two-inch panel walls (including a cavity) made of a type of asbestos, while the interior walls were merely single partitions. Water was a problem in several urban refugee quarters: in Yerania for many years it was supplied through a few public taps in the district. A common cesspool was excavated for every four houses and most of these were still in use in 1972 since there was no public sewerage network in this area (as indeed in many other parts of the capital).

The 276 prefabricated structures erected here and allocated at the end of 1927 provided dwelling units for 552 families. (A few plots were left open and only built on through private initiative several years later.) People recalled that from the start some of the dwellings were given to more than one family because of pressing need—there were thousands of unhoused refugees still sheltering in warehouses and sheds. The 1930 survey records 588 households: thus in the first two years 36 of the 552 dwellings were already occupied by more than one family. As time passed, subdivision of houses became a regular feature (see p. 63). Although full statistical data were not available, two recent census returns provided some evidence of this

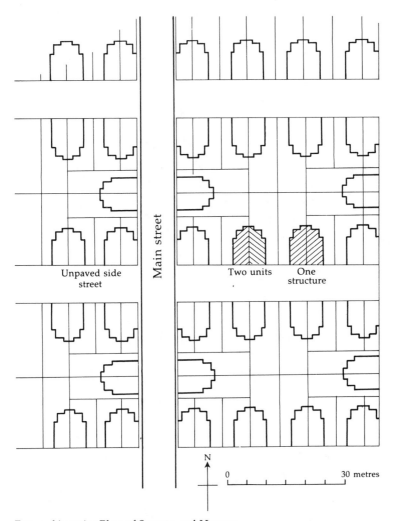

FIG. 1. Yerania: Plan of Streets and Houses

pattern: in 1961 the number of households had increased to 997 and even further to 1,071 in 1971. Over the same period household size had decreased from 3.99 in 1930, to 3.77 in 1961, and 3.28 in 1971. In absolute terms Yerania's population increased from 2,346 in 1930 to 3,763 in 1961 and decreased by 1971 to 3,518 persons (Table 3).

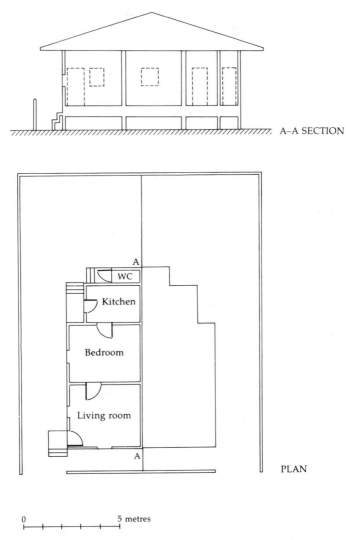

A–A SECTION

PLAN

0   5 metres

FIG. 2. Yerania Dwelling: Original Provision on Central Plot

TABLE 3. *Population, Households, and Densities in Yerania, 1930–1971*

	1930	1961	1971
Total population	2,346	3,763	3,518
Total households	588	977	1,071
Persons per household	3.99	3.77	3.28
Persons per hectare (ha)	290	448	418

Sources: Unpublished Census Data: Ministry of Social Welfare, and Greek Statistical Service.

From the very earliest days, therefore, pressure on space in Yerania has been acute with overcrowding reaching a peak during the 1950s (both of population and density). In Yerania in 1930 population density compared with that in other parts of the quarter at around 300 persons per ha. but over the next three decades to 1961 it rose to nearly 450 persons per ha. (see Table 3). In 1971 it was still higher than other parts of the old quarter at 418 persons per ha., considerably more than the 250 persons per ha. in newer areas around Kokkinia. The adaptability of Yerania's prefabricated houses which could accommodate a growing population and changing family needs on the same site allowed this remarkable increase in population. Indeed pressure on space was visibly evident to any passer-by: rickety wooden balconies extended over pavement areas, room extensions annexed pavement space, and in many parts of the district small windows at ground level and ventilation grilles revealed the existence of underground living-rooms and kitchens (Plates 5, 6, and 8). The use of different colours on walls and doors indicated the presence of several households in one dwelling and expressed the sense of 'territoriality' as each household asserted its individual claims to living space (Hirschon and Gold 1982).

The need for more living space resulted in two kinds of modification: the adaptation of existing rooms to other uses, and the creation of new living areas. Since the prefabricated buildings had been erected in rows on wooden plinths with the land sloping southwards, the buildings were slightly raised off the ground and rested on a rubble infill. A simple solution requiring little expense or effort was to excavate under the building to the required depth, creating one or two basement rooms without the addition of structural members. The raised floor of the prefab provided a ceiling, the gap at ground level could be bricked in to leave spaces for windows which were fitted and shuttered. This ingenious solution to the need for more space is widespread throughout the district. In fact, about three-quarters of Yerania houses have these basement additions; some are pleasant living areas, more comfortable and better insulated than those of the prefab itself, but others have problems of damp, seepage or flooding since the roads lack proper drainage and gutters. Together with the creation of additional rooms in courtyards, the estimated overall increase in living space was 117 per cent (Hirschon and Thakurdesai 1970). In the main, additional space was required for accommodating more households on the plot and not because of an increase in family size. Originally intended as single-family semi-detached houses, the vast majority were shared between several households (an estimated 88 per cent in 1972). One reason was the provision of dowry which in this district resulted in the house being divided into separate households of related families (cf. Chapter 6). House division also occurred through the wartime bombing of Piraeus when unrelated families were given shelter, with complications arising from subsequent legislation regarding tenurial rights (see Appendix I).

One of the most striking findings of the research was the emphasis on providing extra kitchen space since the original kitchen, a small room (2 m. × 3 m.) was of necessity converted into a living or sleeping area (in none of the houses studied was it used solely for cooking). The additional kitchens were built in nooks and crannies, in basement alcoves, stairways, and even partially excavated under the pavements. They were notably small in size: around 2 sq. m. on average, with several being only 1 sq. m. and very few reaching 5–6 sq. m.

Kitchen spaces were primarily for cooking, not for family activity or for communal or shared use. In fact each nuclear family had its own separate cooking area, regardless of pressure on space or of the closeness of kinship ties (co-resident housewives were often related as mothers, daughters, sisters, grandmothers, or aunts). Indeed the number of kitchens accurately reflected the number of households present on a plot. Since most of the houses were subdivided, two or three kitchens per

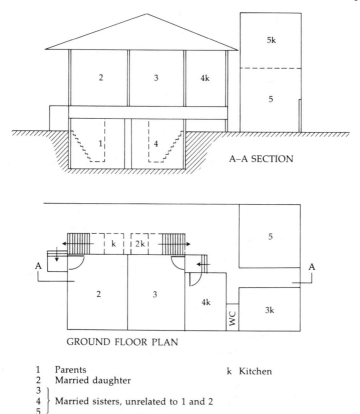

1   Parents   k Kitchen
2   Married daughter
3
4 } Married sisters, unrelated to 1 and 2
5

FIG. 3. Five Households, Five Kitchens

plot were common. In my survey of 62 households occupying 42 dwellings, there were 60 kitchens. Only two households did not have separate kitchens, one being an elderly widow who cooked on a primus stove in her room. The single case of a shared kitchen known to me involved a mother and two married sisters living under extraordinarily cramped conditions (see Appendix I). The autonomy of each household was marked physically and symbolically by the provision of a separate kitchen for its sole use.

The importance of separate kitchens was clearly shown in one house occupied by five separate households. The front part of the dwelling was shared between an elderly couple who lived in one basement room and their married daughter's family who lived in the ground-floor front room. Mother and daughter had entirely separate kitchen nooks in the stairway leading to the basement. Three married sisters unrelated to the front occupants occupied the back of the house and plot, and again each woman had her own kitchen space, however small. The dwelling housed 17 persons, in five separate households with five kitchens—and only one lavatory (see Fig. 3).

In contrast with the emphasis given to each household's separate facilities for food preparation, the lavatory was characteristically unchanged in Yerania and was shared by all those living on the plot. The density of use was remarkable: in the sample surveyed, the average was 9 persons per lavatory, few being used by under 5 persons and many shared between 12 and 18 persons. The level of cleanliness was uniformly of a very high standard, again a feature associated with the domestic values of Asia Minor culture. But inevitably sharing at this level led to tension and conflict between co-resident families. It is doubly interesting, therefore, that each household marked its existence by the creation of a kitchen space, however small, but did not provide for separate lavatory or toilet facilities. Certainly greater expertise and expense would have been required, and on the smaller plots shared between a few households space was simply not available.

The provision of dowries for daughters also led to the construction of additional rooms in the open courtyard, a solution which calls for more skill in construction and greater financial outlay, so that such rooms tend to have been created in the period from the mid-fifties. The reduction in open space, resulting from building additional rooms, is another notable feature of present-day Yerania: when averaged out, it amounts to an overall reduction of 70 per cent of the original provision. Additional building meant that most corner plots were left with no courtyard space at all: even some of the larger plots had been built over almost totally (depending on size of family, number of daughters, and other factors). For housewives who needed space to dry laundry and air linen, and for children needing play areas, problems resulted since the use of streets and pavements carried the danger of prosecution by police in the former case and the risk of accidents in the latter.

Finally it is worth emphasizing once again that, in spite of the utterly inadequate public services, extreme crowding, the insubstantial prefabricated buildings, and the chronic poverty of Yerania's inhabitants, this district presented an attractive and clean appearance. Upkeep and care of dwellings were of a consistently high standard (Plates 7 and 8). Although the houses were not of solid construction they have endured continuous occupation for over fifty years; clearly any neglect by their occupants would soon have resulted in abject slum conditions. This can be explained only by the strength of cultural values, particularly the central importance of house and family, the power of neighbourhood opinion, and the housewife's role in maintaining the home environment. Considerable time and energy was expended on maintenance, particularly by the woman, whose reputation was assessed in terms of her housekeeping abilities. Walls and shutters were painted twice a year before the major religious festivals of Easter and Christmas, while details such as steps, flower pots, even lamp-posts and pavement edges, were whitewashed by the more diligent every few weeks (Hirschon 1985). Despite the refugees' uncertainty about their future in the early days, the dashing of their hopes for a return to their homeland, and their disillusionment at their subsequent treatment, and despite their later sense of dependence and impotence in Greek society, they did not neglect the areas of primary concern—the house, the family, their immediate community. The strength of these three major elements in the cultural heritage of the disadvantaged urban refugees provided the basis for building a new way of life from the old.

A Handicapped Area: Poverty and Reputation

It is quite clear that, in part, Yerania's later problems resulted from some specific conditions at the time of settlement. One of these was that the housing had very poor insulation. Besides the extremes of temperature to which the rooms were subject, this led to privacy being difficult to achieve. Even ordinary conversations were audible from room to room, and sometimes from house to house. This was a common source of stress as in most cases several households occupied one structure. Not surprisingly therefore, co-resident families often admitted having strained relationships with one another or to open conflict. Indeed one of the things often said about Yerania was that its residents were 'quarrelsome' (καυγατζῆδες). It was undeniably a noisy district, owing to a combination of factors: to poorly insulated houses, to high densities and overcrowding, and to the traffic, especially buses and many three-wheeled vehicles with their high-pitched rasping engines, passing along the four main roads which ran through the area.

In addition to its being quarrelsome, the reputation of the district derived from several other perceived social characteristics. Residents and outsiders alike said that there were few good families (Λίγες είναι οι καλές οικογένειες), a statement which indicates that family problems were thought to be more prevalent than elsewhere in Kokkinia. Besides attributing social problems to the crowded living conditions and insubstantial structures, specific cultural notions regarding regional origin were invoked to explain the prevalence of gossip, quarrels, and frivolity. All these features are associated with the negative stereotype of people from the Smyrna region (see p. 24). The unpublished 1930 household survey provides interesting information. Yerania houses were allocated late in 1927, without reference to place of origin, to families who were still in several different Piraeus warehouses where they had taken shelter. The 1930 survey shows a regionally heterogeneous population, but there was a marked preponderance of refugees from the Ionian coastal area, totalling almost one-third of all household heads. More precisely, 21 per cent of household heads came from the city of Smyrna itself and another 10 per cent from nearby towns such as Menemeni, Magnisia, Pergamos, Chesme (Krini), Aivali. The others were from all over Asia Minor—Dardanelles, Constantinople, Broussa, Nicomedia as well as from interior regions, the Ankara area, Kaisaria, Ikonion, even Adana and the Caucasus. The Smyrnaian stereotype did not, therefore, apply to the majority of Yerania's original inhabitants, yet it does show how durable were these notions of regionally specific characteristics.

One thing which all the older Yerania people shared, however, was an acute experience of poverty. The most striking evidence for this exists in the 1930 household survey which records the occupations of household heads. Both the composition of the working population and the types of jobs show the precarious economic position of the vast majority of families two years after being housed. Clear evidence of the disruption of family life exists: nearly 20 per cent of Yerania households were headed by women and only 5 out of 105 were recorded as employed (2 as cleaners, 3 as 'employees'). The remaining 100 were occupied with 'housework' (οικιακά). Although the survey provides no indication, it is reasonable to assume that many of these households comprised widows and young children, given the high mortality rate for men during and after the exodus (see Table 1 for the disproportion between adult men and women in the refugee quarters).

Since no state welfare provisions existed, many of the 'housewives' undoubtedly worked whenever the opportunity was presented. Regular employment was difficult to find, however, given cultural attitudes to women earning money (see pp. 99–101) and the deepening economic depression in Greece in the late 1920s–30s. The proportion of non-earning heads of household was even higher: 10 per cent of the men were recorded as 'unemployed' (άεργος) and another 2 per cent were 'disabled' (ανάπηρος, ανίκανος). Thus, about one-third of Yerania household heads were not gainfully employed. Obviously, a variety of strategies must have developed to make ends meet, including irregular and multiple jobs, and contributions by children. The original refugees certainly recalled the extreme hardship of that period and recount how all family members were expected to bring in money regardless of age or sex.

The low level of earnings and the precarious nature of employment is also clear from this early survey. Two years after settlement 40 per cent of family heads who had jobs were classified as 'labourers' (εργάτες). Only 12 per cent were in skilled occupations as carpenters, barbers, tailors, shoemakers, cooks, typographers; another 7 per cent were engaged in commercial activities, most of them as itinerant hawkers and pedlars, and also as greengrocers, coffee-sellers, and grocers. A few were employed as seamen, and some as 'employees' (υπάλληλοι). This latter term designates security of earnings rather than type of job for in contrast with others the 'employee', whether rubbish collector or office clerk, is paid on a regular monthly basis, a huge benefit under contemporary conditions.

Yerania's 1930 household survey is valuable in revealing clearly the handicaps which were common to the mass of urban refugees—overcrowding, inadequate housing, the high proportion of female household heads, and of disabled or unemployed men. Perhaps more acute in Yerania, these characteristics provided grounds for distinctions of reputation within the refugee population in Kokkinia, reinforcing the unflattering stereotypes associated with people from Smyrna. An additional factor associated with the continuing disadvantage of Yerania, was that its inhabitants had had to shelter in makeshift arrangements in school buildings, warehouses, and factory basements, for up to five years before being housed. It is fair to conclude that these people lacked the social expertise, initiative or influential connections which could have led to an earlier alleviation of their plight. Accounts of settlement procedures suggest that contact with appropriate officials was crucial for the early allocation of houses and also for the type of house obtained. Those refugees who in 1928 were already well established elsewhere in Kokkinia may have scorned these late recipients of somewhat inferior housing in Yerania. The fatalistic attitudes of Yerania residents and the continuing legal confusion over ownership of their houses reflected their continuing lack of influential contacts.

Claims for Compensation: The Legal Basis of Identity

The disadvantaged position of Yerania is further evidenced in the legal complications regarding ownership which continued unresolved into the mid-1970s. By then a tangled web of contradictory claims to housing had developed which were closely bound up with the consolidation of refugee identity around their rights to compensation. The problematic question of the Yerania refugees' legal status and tenure rights in relation to housing explains also the subdivision of many houses, particularly between unrelated families, and hence the extreme overcrowding (see Appendix I). Since the laws defining refugee rights are complicated and constitute a specialist legal topic, having undergone numerous revisions, only those points bearing directly on the analysis of Yerania are discussed here.

Full ownership titles (conferring legal rights to disposal

through sale, by demolition and rebuilding, or by renting) were available to the residents of Yerania houses, in the form of a concession (παραχωρητήριον). The sum of 5,000 drs. was required by the Ministry of Social Welfare in exchange for the concession. In the past, however, many Yerania people, like refugees in other areas, objected to the payment since they felt entitled to housing without cost to themselves. Others trusted in the promises made at the time of settlement, that the pre-fabricated housing was a temporary measure and that permanent dwellings would be provided, and so would not commit themselves to purchase. Some families also could not afford to pay this amount which, in the early days, constituted a considerable sum. In any case, refugees were assured of permanent rights of occupancy (δικαιώματα) without cost, as long as they remained in the houses, regardless of obtaining concession rights. For several decades therefore, the legal situation remained unresolved. But by the 1970s there was a real incentive to settle for the concession. While the original refugee occupant was alive, the cost of the concession was 5,000 drs., but after the death of the original claimant under conditions of 'inherited rights' the amount required was twelve times higher. Rather than pay 60,000 drs. for a property which was becoming increasingly valuable as urban land values rocketed, many second generation people decided to avoid further expense by paying for the concession in the name of an aged parent (cf. Appendix I).

If only one household occupied a dwelling, this could be done easily. In Yerania, however, subdivision of dwellings between several households was extremely common: indeed, 88 per cent of the houses in my sample were occupied by more than one household (usually two or three, but sometimes four or even five). In these cases payment for the concession was complicated since it entailed agreement by all parties on two key issues—the name of the title holder, i.e. the original occupant, and the future disposal of the property. Conflicting interests in the vast majority of shared houses precluded the possibility of obtaining the concession. In such cases, families were assured of 'occupancy rights' which were also inheritable. Thus children of the original refugee occupant could not be dispossessed without replacement housing or compensation.

If, however, the refugee family moved out of the dwelling without having obtained the concession, these occupancy rights and any other benefits which might be attached to them were entirely lost. There were two direct consequences of this legal bind. First, the tenacity with which some families endured appalling conditions of overcrowding, sharing a house with others despite extreme conflict, is explained. Their apparent lack of initiative was not simply the result of poverty and the absence of alternative solutions, but revealed the vested interest in their status as 'refugees' in relation to the Greek state. Secondly, the low incidence of rebuilding in this district reflected the unresolved issue of full legal entitlement, for the securing of concession rights was a pre-condition for demolishing the original structure. Since the majority of houses were subdivided between different households, the concession had not been obtained. Thus, even those families who had the financial means to rebuild or pay rent and live under better conditions remained in crowded prefabricated houses, awaiting long-promised arbitration by the Ministry of Social Welfare (cf. Appendix I).

The widespread subdivision of Yerania houses, a most characteristic feature, highlighted the refugees' plight and their continuing disadvantaged position. Many factors had operated together here: the effects of dowry provision through the years had resulted in the co-residence of several households related through women (see Chapters 6 and 7), while some dwellings had been allocated to two families at the outset. Subdivision had also taken place through individual transactions in which a room would be 'sold' to a homeless party for a small cash sum. In addition the bombing of Piraeus in 1942 destroyed large areas of refugee housing near the harbour. Those who escaped were sheltered by refugee families in other districts and were given the use of one or two rooms on what was seen initially as a temporary basis by both parties. In 1946, however, the Government effectively froze the situation by passing a 'moratorium law' (ενοικιοστάσιο), a tenancy law which protected the rights of occupants whether they paid rent or not. Thereafter residence in a dwelling which had begun before 1946 whether by gift (i.e. without titles) or by rent, was assured permanence and could not be cancelled.

Although this may have alleviated distress for some in the short term, it constituted a delaying tactic in the face of other government priorities in the post-war period. For the refugees, greater complications resulted as time passed and the families jointly occupying a house increased in size. After some years and the death of the old people, it was no longer easy to establish the original claims since most refugee housing was occupied without titles. The 1946 tenurial legislation had several consequences. It perpetuated a situation in which refugee families were unable to clarify their legal rights to property. It also promoted an attitude of helpless dependence upon outside agencies to solve the problems of living, exacerbating a response now recognized as common among displaced persons. The expectation of an external solution to their housing problems clearly had a profound effect on the refugees' view of themselves: many endured long-term overcrowding and conflict with other families, even where a solution through personal initiative was possible, while the disappointed hopes for compensation became a stubborn focus for their sense of political and social identity.

Recent Changes

The sense of injustice perpetrated against them continued even when finally in 1972 long-awaited government attention again turned to the issue of refugee housing. The Ministry of Social Welfare instituted formal tribunal sessions to adjudicate contested claims in the Piraeus area and in Yerania much excitement arose at the prospect of better housing. Gradually, cases were called up, many requiring lengthy investigation. But interruptions occurred with the political changes in Greece following the fall of the junta in 1974, and the proceedings dragged out over years. When I returned in 1983 I was told by Ministry officials that the housing problems in Yerania had been settled and that nothing more was due to these refugees. All cases needing arbitration had been investigated and rulings had been made. Further enquiry revealed that only 55 cases had been arbitrated, far fewer than the number of subdivided houses, because a primary criterion for arbitration was that co-resident families be unrelated to one another. Consequently the

majority of subdivided houses, those resulting from dowry provision, were declared ineligible.

In the early phase of arbitration, families who could not prove
a prior claim were given other accommodation, usually a two-
or three-roomed flat in new blocks elsewhere in Piraeus. However, as time passed it became clear that insufficient new
housing existed and at that point government policy apparently
changed. Now it became necessary for the households themselves to reach an agreement about which family would move
out and which would retain the Yerania property. Where no
agreement occurred, the tribunal issued all parties with joint
titles to the property. This happened in 38 cases, i.e. 70 per cent
of those investigated. Similarly, all co-resident families which
were related to one another, as the vast majority were, gained
joint titles to the house and plot.

Consequently a bizarre situation has arisen in Yerania where
a number of separate households, each with titular rights, continue to live on many of the small plots, usually in a state of
extreme conflict with one another. (Even if it did not predate
the intervention, antagonism certainly arose from the so-called
'arbitration'.) In practical terms the granting of joint titles is no
solution since all the plots are too small to be subdivided. Only
the construction of several storeys, one floor per family,
improves the standard of housing provided by these plots.
Rebuilding remains an acute problem, therefore, since it
requires that all co-resident families have roughly equivalent
financial assets or access to credit, a difficult condition to fulfil.
By 1982 only 217 of the original 552 prefabricated units had
been replaced, 130 of these between 1972 and 1982. Overall, in
1982 60 per cent of the original prefabricated units still existed,
most of these along the side-streets, away from the square and
main commercial roads. Their presence is a poignant reminder
of the intractable problems associated with housing provision
and the tenurial rights of sections of the urban refugee population. Sadly for many in Yerania, the poor state of housing
remains in a situation of permanent stalemate. But on the other
hand the 'solution'—the granting of titles to all co-resident
families—has ameliorated the situation in one respect: mobility
is at last possible, for a family can now leave Yerania without
losing its rights to its part of the house.

Although there has never been a period in the past fifty to sixty years when the situation was not in a process of change and development, the period from the mid-1960s saw certain constants in the life of Yerania becoming modified or even disappearing: the rate of mobility out of the area was one of these. Despite the generally depressed level of economic life, possibilities for economic success have always existed for some individuals and the population of Yerania has not been static.

Indications exist that residents who gained wealth in the early days moved to better parts of the city where they could consolidate their success; their places were taken by refugees from provincial towns such as Volos and Kavalla or even Salonika as well as from rural settlements. In the 1972 survey of 62 Yerania households, over four-fifths (82 per cent) of persons over 26 considered themselves to be 'refugees' or of refugee origin, but further examination revealed that only half of them were of the original family. The others had taken over the dwelling from a previous refugee occupant. Since mobility out of the area depended upon some wealth, it was only with the generally greater affluence of the 1960s that more of the concessions were paid. Wealthier families could now choose between leaving or staying in the locality where family ties, neighbourhood networks and friendships had been built up through the years. Some remained; some left, selling their prefabricated homes to newcomers, often now to families from villages who were seeking to create a life in the city. With the granting of titles to plots and houses in the 1970s, Yerania families could now rent out quarters to newcomers. As in other parts of Kokkinia, its population increasingly included people of non-refugee origin.

Migrants who have settled in and around Kokkinia have ended the physical and social isolation which marked its first two or three decades. In the last few years close residential contact has revived that sense of difference between these two sections of the population (see pp. 31–3). This revival is likely to be brief, however, because the underlying conditions upon which the sense of difference was founded and flourished are in themselves changing. Younger people, who no longer live in crowded prefabs with two or three other households, who have attended the brand-new high school, and who have the opportunity to continue schooling, to be trained in skilled trades and find jobs no longer share the experience of marginality and deprivation which marked the lives of their parents, grandparents, and even great-grandparents in some families, nor do they hear the stories told of life in the homeland, as the original refugees pass away. But when I lived in Yerania in 1972, much of the past was still evident in the way of life which had developed just as it was in the physical fabric of the locality.

The following chapters focus on social patterns and cultural values—on employment and economic activity, the house and the family, the neighbourhood, and on the religious dimension of life. This examination reveals a wealth of meaning based on clearly articulated cultural precepts which had been woven into the way of life of these people, deprived though it was of so many material necessities. Yerania acts as the focal point for the analysis, though the whole locality of Kokkinia is the wider context. The discussion explores the main features of a life-style which should be recognizable, not only in Yerania and Kokkinia, but also in many other urban refugee quarters of Greece established at that time, which have shared their historical experience.

5

EARNING A LIVING

Although Yerania was still a disadvantaged district and its image was that of a 'poor neighbourhood' (φτωχογειτονιά, λαϊκή γειτονιά), signs of growing affluence appeared in 1972 as the generally buoyant state of the Greek economy began to affect conditions in all strata of society. The economic climate of the country had reached a new level of expansion and confidence and this had various effects at the local level. First, there was a noticeable alleviation of extreme hardship; secondly, a greater range of choice in economic activity was available; and thirdly, individual enterprise became more of a possibility.

In the past, the social and political isolation of Kokkinia—and Yerania as part of it—had been reinforced by constant economic marginality. These conditions had acted as a framework of constraints within which the problems of survival had to be solved. The desire for security of earnings probably had been foremost. But now, in a situation of expansion, a freer range of preferences in economic activity could be expressed. Choices made in this period revealed the ways in which economic needs were met in accordance with cultural values. This chapter includes case histories of some Yerania men, which illustrate their past economic experience, the effects of chronic poverty, and the way in which personal economic strategies responded to changing conditions. From these, the main themes and preoccupations which characterized economic behaviour for this section of society can be elicited.

The Working Population

Yerania's deceptively attractive appearance initially masked the fact that, even in 1972, economic resources were extremely limited for most families. This became clear in a sample survey of 62 households (see Appendices II and III). These were located in 42 dwellings so that about one-third of them shared the

house with others. The household size in the sample ranged
from a maximum of 7 persons to the single-person households
of a widowed person on a pension. The average size of household in the sample was 3.4 persons (slightly larger than that of
the census figure of 3.2 persons (1971) for the Athens area which
may be due to the larger proportion of younger families in my
sample than in the overall population).

The declared occupations of members of the households provided an indication of income levels: for Yerania households an
average monthly figure of 1,800 drs. per person was estimated
with a range from 1,000 drs. to a maximum of about 2,500 drs.
per head. These approximate figures are significantly lower
than the Greek national average of 2,720 drs. per month (OECD
1972). Total monthly household incomes varied widely, from
about 1,000 drs. for pensioners to around 12,000 drs. in a few
households with two or three working members and dependants.

These figures do not, however, indicate the amount of dis-
posable income. Households with the highest incomes were in
the expansion phase of the family development cycle and
included young adult unmarried children. In these a large proportion of earning tends to be set aside as savings, usually to
provide dowries for daughters. On the other hand, pensioner
households with a low average income per head usually
enjoyed a supplementary source of support in the form of food
prepared and brought daily by a daughter or daughter-in-law
residing nearby: this supplement would represent an additional 300 to 400 drs. per month in cash terms, a 30 per cent
increase. These sample figures provide therefore, only a rough
indication of the economic status of the families surveyed; they
do, however, reveal clearly that the average income per household and per head was considerably less than the national
average.

A further indication of Yerania's economic status was to be
found in analysing the working population of the sample: in
the Yerania households surveyed, the working population
comprised 40 per cent of the total, somewhat higher than the
35 per cent of the Athens area as a whole (calculated from the
1971 census). Many households had more than one earning
member—an average of 1.8 persons employed per household

was calculated (excluding pensioner households). Significantly, a high proportion of the working population was young: 33 per cent of the employed in the sample were under 21 years old while the corresponding figure for the whole of Athens was only 11 per cent. Young people were important in the work-force and played an active economic role in Yerania, though this reflected the low educational standard in the district. A further point of considerable interest was the part played by women in the work-force. In the 1972 household survey, women comprised 23 per cent of the working population. This situation, however, represented a clear contradiction between the explicit ideals of female domesticity and the fact that Yerania women did enter employment, and had done so since early days of settlement.

Categories of occupation in Yerania in 1972, based on the survey, indicated a greater diversity of employment than in 1930 (see Chapter 4, and Appendix III). One obvious improvement was the absence of unemployment and of non-earning heads of households. But again the largest category was the unskilled and semi-skilled (εργάτες) who comprised 42 per cent of the working population. About one-third of the working population were labourers in enterprises other than the construction industry. Skilled trades such as metalworking, carpentry, and shoemaking involved nearly 20 per cent of the work-force, and about 13 per cent were engaged in transport services, both private and public (taxis, buses, and haulage). Among these were a number of men who owned vehicles for business purposes, an enterprise which required some capital and was favoured for its higher earnings as well as for the independence of the self-employed. Similarly engaged in entrepreneurial activity were the 12 per cent recorded as private traders (έμποροι), including neighbourhood storekeepers and itinerant vendors who operated without licences, as well as guild members of the street market. Seven per cent of the working population were classified as 'employees' mainly in low-grade municipal services (rubbish collectors, park attendants), under 4 per cent were seamen, and the single professional person, a retired teacher, reflected the exceptional nature of this occupation in Yerania.

The variety of occupations and the different stages in life cycle were reflected in differences in income levels between households but economic differentiation in Yerania did not appear to provide a clear basis for class stratification. Strong countervailing precepts based on neighbourhood membership existed and were explicitly egalitarian (see Chapter 8). Within Kokkinia as a whole, too, the relative ranking of residential districts tended more to reflect social distinctions based on regional origin, 'character', and 'moral tone' than income levels. Reflecting the situation in Asia Minor, where economic levels were less sharply perceived than the cultural bonds between the Ortho- dox (especially the Greeks), the emphasis in social life in Kokki- nia at this time lay on the urban refugees' common historical experience as distinct from the non-refugee sections of Greek society.[1]

Conditions in Greek Economic Life: The Wider Context

1972 was a particularly interesting time from an economic standpoint. In this year the country's expansion which had started in the 1960s reached the proportions of a boom. The growth of the Greek economy was favourably reported abroad and was given wide publicity by the junta government. The increase in the real GNP was estimated officially at 8.5 per cent (OECD 1972: 47), the inflation rate was only 4.3 per cent in 1972, and the economy was experiencing increasing domestic demand through growing private consumption. Tourism was being courted on a large scale and there was a boom in the con- struction industry. These conditions were a direct result of the permissive monetary and fiscal policies of the government, and the extension of credit (Pesmazoglu 1972; Karayeorgas 1974; OECD 1975: 27–8). Another important feature of the period was the high rate of emigration, especially to Germany, with a con- sequent minimal rate of unemployment and sharp local demand for labour.

The fact that the reckless application of expansionist policies was soon to result in rampant inflation, bottlenecks, and a large deficit in the balance of payments did not concern the majority of people, while those in the disadvantaged areas of the city began to experience a degree of relative affluence for the first time. The alleviation of extreme hardship had begun in the 1960s so that by 1972 even the poorest districts, such as Yerania, showed the first signs of this new wealth in television sets, refrigerators, and other consumer goods. A climate of confidence had developed in which a greater choice of action seemed to be possible for many families. Although the period of buoyancy ultimately proved to be brief, the culturally perceived choices and constraints were thrown into relief, and Yerania as a district was itself altered by the conditions of this period.

One of the most important features of the country's economy in 1972, affecting many related economic pursuits and leaving no part of the city unaffected, was the expansion of the construction industry. Widespread building activity especially of residential structures was encouraged by government policy and construction work began to dominate every part of the city. Throughout Kokkinia the sound of bulldozers, pneumatic drills, and concrete mixers evidenced the effects of these wider economic influences. The high rate of investment in private housing is a constant feature in Greek economic behaviour, a response to a number of different factors, economic and cultural as well as political. It is probably true to say that Greek economic life reflects a chronic lack of confidence in paper assets and that this is partly due to the notorious instability of the drachma through a series of devastating devaluations in the period from the 1920s to the 1960s. The fact that the dowry, an institution of continuing significance in the city, takes the specific form of a 'house' or separate dwelling for the married couple places an even greater premium on real estate than would exist anyway in a rapidly growing urban centre. In the early 1970s official policy further intensified investment in real estate and housing through the extension of credit, special loans for landowners, as well as tax relief for foreign capital imported for these purposes. Thus, investment in building increased from 15 billion drs. in 1967 to 33 billion drs. in 1972, an increase of 115 per cent. In the five year period before the dictatorship, 1961–6, the increase had been 60 per cent (Karayeorgas 1974: 43). Similarly, investment in private housing between 1961 and 1972 went up from 40 per cent of private gross fixed investment to 70 per cent (Campbell and Sherrard 1968; Economist Intelligence Unit 1975: 6).

Another noted and long-established feature of Greek economic life, also reflected in the economic activities of people in

Kokkinia, was the generally small scale of local industrial activity. Even in the main industrial zones of Athens and Piraeus few factories employed more than 300 workers. Only 886 enterprises had more than 30 workers but there were some 30,000 'industrial' enterprises which employed under 5 persons (1971 census). A characteristic feature of Greek industry, this preponderance of small-scale manufacturing (usually under-capitalized family firms with few employees) should be noted as an important indication of the undeveloped state of Greece's economic structure on one hand (cf. Mouzelis 1978) and on the other of the specific approaches likely to be taken by individuals in their economic pursuits.

Economic Activity in Kokkinia

The availability of a plentiful and cheap labour force in the urban refugee settlements has often been noted as an important factor in the growth of the Greek economy. Certainly particular Asia Minor skills provided an inducement to the establishment of many new industries in the 1920s. Indeed a number of the wealthier, more fortunate expatriates with business expertise who had managed to bring or raise capital established new factories in or near refugee quarters. One textile factory started in this way in Nea Ionia illustrates the profitable nature of such initiative. Between 1922 and 1926 it had expanded from a small workshop employing 30 women into a joint stock company with capital of over £250,000 employing 2,400 workers (League of Nations 1926: 188).

In the case of Kokkinia the refugees' labour was absorbed in already established factories on the outskirts of Piraeus, notably the cigarette factories of Papastratos and Kerania. Refugees who sheltered in the factory warehouses were also employed as workers, and after their settlements in Kokkinia and in other Piraeus quarters, many have continued to work there up to the present day. Only in the post-war period were sizeable new factories established in the environs of Kokkinia, in a ribbon development along the main road from the cargo port of Kerat-sini to Athens. An important industrial zone today, this area of the Kifissos river has a number of large factories which service the textile industry (spinning and dyeing mills), the light metal industries, and others which process food. Together with the old and newer industrial establishments of Piraeus and its harbour activities, these factories, some fifteen minutes by bus from the centre of Kokkinia, offered employment of a more impersonal kind, contrasting with the workshop industries located in Kokkinia itself.

In 1972, small workshops in back rooms, basements, and illegally built courtyard rooms were scattered throughout the locality. Typically these employed local girls in making shirts, knitted goods, and other clothing, using hand-operated machines. There were also shoe-makers, metal-welders' yards, and carpenters' workshops where young local boys worked as apprentices, and a few precision workshops such as jewellers and electrical repairers. These concerns were owned by local men and run on their own premises, by hiring workers from the neighbourhood and through personal contacts. Wages were slightly lower than those paid in the larger establishments outside the area, but a local worker saved the cost of bus tickets. An additional advantage from the point of view of parents of young girls was that they were less exposed to the hazards of the city. Growth and increasing trade did come to some of the local workshops and family enterprises during the period, particularly those ancillary to the construction industry; carpenters, plumbers, house-painters, and metalwork shops were all fully engaged while food processing was also profitable.

Some of these local enterprises operated as combined workshops and retail outlets, a situation which was very common in the older parts of the city, but these were gradually forced out of existence by the increasing scale and specialization of commercial and manufacturing activity, and the greater need for capital. These neighbourhood enterprises—a rented shop where the artisan makes, displays, and sells his own goods, sometimes with a helper or apprentice, or a sales assistant—had been viable businesses based on local custom. By the early 1970s, however, television advertising and greater affluence began to affect people's attitudes in Kokkinia. Housewives were no longer content to buy most household goods and clothing locally from the small shops on the commercial streets and squares of Kokkinia, for the large, city shops, whose names were becoming known through advertising campaigns, increasingly attracted their custom. By shopping in the centre of Piraeus, women could compare styles and prices of goods and impress their neighbours with the brand names of their purchases. Since local shops stocked goods which were equally fashionable and somewhat cheaper, clearly the motivation was added prestige and not economic advantage. Television advertising carried a mystique and authority which was having a marked effect on spending patterns. Thus, in a year when customer demand was high, local shopkeepers and artisans noted that customers were being attracted by the window displays of the large stores in the centre and their trade was falling off. In the quieter districts, local producers were forced to close their own retail shops and concentrate only on supplying large retail outlets elsewhere.

Self-employment or Security?

The buoyancy of conditions in 1972, which capped a period of increasing affluence, produced a climate of optimism in all strata of society. It apparently also led to changing responses among the working population in Yerania. Given the concern of men (normally the bread-winners) to maximize their families' incomes in socially acceptable ways, several common trends and tendencies were revealed. In the first place a marked preference for self-employment existed. For men this cultural value is deeply rooted in the notion of independence and ties in with the sense of masculine integrity. It can be seen as the expression of the 'honour' code, well described for rural Greece (e.g. Campbell 1964; Herzfeld 1980, 1985). In an urban economic context the aggressive, self-regarding conduct which among Sarakatsani shepherds, for example, borders on violence is tempered here into a desire for independence and autonomy. It was commonly expressed in the desire 'to have no one over your head' (να μην έχεις κανένα στο κεφάλι σου). It had not been possible to realize this independence under past conditions and so it had coexisted with the desire for security of some kind (either through regular if low earnings, or a pension after years of service). The coexistence of these two responses was reflected in the versatility and flexibility of past approaches to the problems of livelihood. In short, the economic strategy of men in this disadvantaged section of the population can be seen as rooted in adaptability, in taking opportunities as they are offered, in supplementing income through a variety of jobs, and through cooperation with relatives and neighbours. But it was clear, too, that given the opportunity the preferred situation was to be independently employed, one's own boss, with a tolerance of the risks involved.

The main sources of employment were in commerce and vending, construction trades, transport, as factory workers, sellers in the street market (λαϊκή αγορά), in unskilled municipal jobs. Contrasts existed with respect to older and younger generations of adult men (and also women), the former being primarily in occupations which demand few specific skills. Most men under forty, however, tended to have some skilled training, either through an apprenticeship or through attending a technical school. The fact that the majority subsequently become involved in other pursuits reveals, on the one hand, the inability of the economic structure to absorb those with specific training, and on the other, the precarious position of people in this socio-economic class. These observations can best be illustrated in the working histories of local men of different ages.

Shopkeepers

CASE 1: YANNIS

Yannis's career reveals some of these points clearly: born in 1940, he trained as a mechanic at a technical school after completing two years of high school. The prospects were not good at the time. Since he had a younger sister who required help with her dowry, he had entered the Merchant Navy as a mechanic, and spent ten years in this lucrative but difficult existence. For the previous three years he had been running his father's small shop, one of the oldest in Yerania, simply a tiny room added to the original prefabricated refugee house. Profits were small for its stock was limited to cigarettes, stationery, some haberdashery items, but its main service was providing a telephone for the vicinity (instead of the standard charge of 1 dr. per call, the charge was 1.5 drs.). Now that he was married, Yannis preferred this small business to travelling at sea. He supplemented his income by driving a bus for one of the private nursery schools in a nearby residential district, a job arranged through his sister's wedding sponsor, who knew the

headmaster. His rounds took a couple of hours in the morning and afternoon, when his wife or his sister's husband would take over the shop.

Opposite Yannis's kiosk was a popular coffee shop run by Lefteris,
who was six years older than Yannis. He had been trained as a metalworker (σιδεράς). Lefteris found the sociable ambience of the coffee
shop and its easier profits preferable to his own trade, which had only
recently started to offer steady prospects and an assured income with
demand in the building trade.

The Building Boom

In 1972 the construction industry was the key to many changes
and choices made by Kokkinia men providing as it did an
opportunity for self-employment. By convention men involved
in the building trades frequented specific coffee shops which
acted as meeting-places and employment centres for the clients.
In Kokkinia those involved in the construction trade would
gather at three coffee shops just off the square of Ai Nikola.
Here building workers (οικοδόμοι) gathered every morning to
find work and the contractors (εργολάβοι) came to hire a team for
a new contract, or extra workers for a specific job.

In 1972 the changed conditions of the industry were
remarked upon by many with experience in the field. Only a
few years earlier workers would wait for days to be hired under
unfavourable conditions: wages were low and travel costs to the
site, no matter how distant, were met by the worker. Now the
building workers were in demand and could set their terms—
they could refuse a job and wait for a better offer, and demand
travel expenses—while their wages were well above those of
factory workers (an unskilled site labourer was earning 250 drs.
a day while the factory-hand was earning 150 drs. per day).
Construction methods require the use of reinforced concrete;
the preparation of steel rods, concrete mixing, and the throwing
of slabs are skilled and strenuous jobs so that men with these
special skills (μπετατζήδες) were being paid 500 drs. a day. Since
such jobs cannot be undertaken for two to three months during
the winter, the higher pay covers a period of unemployment as
well as the physically taxing nature of the work. The uncertainty

of employment is one of the hazards of the building trade for workers and contractors alike and much depended upon a wide range of contacts. Workers tried, therefore, to get into a team with a well-known contractor which might ensure a longer period of employment in a number of jobs.

The amount of building work going on in Kokkinia itself reflected the government's policy of extension of credit, permitting families to raise loans and rebuild their old refugee houses (provided the legal issues had been resolved). Consequently men with experience in the building trade were encouraged by this local demand to set up contracting firms of their own. With only a small amount of capital it was possible to buy or hire equipment, engage labourers, and undertake demolition and construction of residential buildings.

CASE 3: TASSOS, MILTIADES, AND LAKIS

Tassos and Miltiades were two local men in their late thirties who had both laboured for years at all kinds of construction jobs. Related by marriage to two sisters as *badzanákides* and confident enough of their range of contacts, they decided to pool their savings in 1971 and set up as independent contractors. Their optimism was challenged one day in a long discussion with Lakis, an old friend, who had once worked with them on building sites. Under current conditions he would have been well remunerated since he had been a skilled cement-worker (μπετατζής). But in the late 1960s he had decided that commerce provided the best solution since he could retain his independence and also earn a living in a less arduous way. He started off as an itinerant merchant, buying clothes at wholesale prices and hawking them cheaply on rounds in the poorer residential districts. There were few overheads so he gradually built up the scale of his operations and after only three years he could afford a car (an extremely expensive item in Greece where 100 per cent import tax is paid as well as high monthly circulation taxes). He claimed that his standard takings were 700 drs. a day, and even more when he ran a special offer (such as a line of sports jackets in early autumn) or at the festive seasons (Easter or Christmas). The scepticism he expressed about the building trade's future proved to be well founded a few years later when credit and building licences were restricted, but at the time Miltiades and Tassos thought the risks were worth taking. They argued that a major attraction was taking on the whole responsibility for a job, of being one's own boss; they were prepared to stake their savings on an independent and possibly lucrative enterprise.

CASE 4: DIMITRIS

Similar responses were evident in Dimitris's desire for a new livelihood. He was in his thirties and had been a bus-driver for the previous
seven years, a secure job with a monthly salary and the prospect of a
pension, but one which he said offered no challenges. Following an
apprenticeship after school he had become a carpenter but at that time
there had been little scope for the artisan. He had felt fortunate to get
the job as a bus-driver. With the changing circumstances caused by the
building trade's expansion in 1972, he was encouraged to take the
initiative. He resigned from the bus company job, used his savings to
buy tools, and set up a carpentry workshop in the basement of his Yerania home. Soon he, like others in similar trades, was fully occupied
with orders for work.

Traders

Small-scale trading has always featured as a primary source of
livelihood for families in Yerania and other like districts since it
required little capital, no specific training, and could be geared
to a wide range of needs. The daily calls of street hawkers, as
they moved through the side-streets on foot, in creaking donkey carts, or in small, noisy, three-wheeled vehicles, were
characteristic of life in older urban quarters. When the junta
took power in 1967, however, licensing laws were more strictly
enforced and donkey carts were forbidden. Consequently many
of the older men who had supported their families by hawking
fruit and vegetables in the neighbourhoods were forced to limit
their activities. Their position became even more precarious
since they could not claim pensions. In 1972 many of these
itinerant sellers still operated without licences, having neither the
inclination nor the funds to pay for an official permit (4,000 drs.
in 1972 was a considerable sum). In their sixties or older, these
men would usually be ignored by the police if they acted with
discretion, avoiding a direct confrontation by ducking into a
coffee shop. Their standard stock would be a basket of various
small items—combs, cigarette lighters, matches, plastic mirrors,
'worry beads', sweets, nuts, and religious objects such as
incense, tiny icons, and amulets. Some unlicensed pedlars
would change their goods depending on the time of year. My
neighbour Tollis, a man of 68, used to peddle packets of red dye
and racks to hold eggs just before Easter, and would appear

later in the spring with strings of moth-balls and large plastic bags, catering for the custom that winter clothes are packed away on 21 May, the day of Saints Constantine and Helen.

CASE 5: NIKOS

Other itinerants traded in only one standard commodity for which they knew the variation in demand. Nikos, a friend of Tollis, for instance, hawked only whitewash, sold by weight from the back of a donkey cart at 4 drs. a kilo. This represented a considerable profit since the slaking kiln only a kilometre away sold it for 4 drs. per cwt. sackful, but most housewives were prepared to pay for the convenience of the delivery to their yard.

A way of life based on prudent frugality is common to many families, particularly the older generation. Avraam's life-style stands as a significant reminder of formerly widespread conditions when itinerant hawking was the chief means of survival for a large number of families.

CASE 6: AVRAAM

Avraam was a 70-year-old hawker who had to limit his activities because of stricter controls on commercial activity. He had been a greengrocer with his own donkey cart for many years before 1967. Subsequently he was forced to concentrate his efforts on earning a livelihood illegally by selling garlic on foot in the poorer districts of the city. Surprisingly, from this single source he managed to support three adults: himself, his wife, and a disabled son who received no security benefit. Since the garlic season lasts only eight or nine months there were about four months during which the family effectively had no income and they coped only through efficient budgeting throughout the year.

The year's activities were carefully organized to cover lean periods. The new season of garlic starts in spring. Avraam would begin his trading sometime in March by rising every morning at 2 a.m. to go to the central market of the city five kilometres away. He would start out on foot but would usually get a lift from a truck or three-wheeled vehicle (τρίκυκλο, Plate 14) going in that direction. The market is a convergence point in the early hours of the morning for many Piraeus inhabitants who engage in retailing fresh food, either independently or as members of the daily street markets.

At the market, Avraam would make contact with the wholesale merchants of garlic, help unload their trucks, guard the garlic, and supervise its storage. For this he earned about 100 drs. between 3 a.m. and

7 a.m. daily. After about two weeks of saving he would buy a small amount of garlic after his loading job and start out on his rounds. By noon he would be back at home for a meal and siesta. For several weeks at the beginning of the season he loaded trucks at the market to supplement his day-to-day takings. Once he had collected enough money he would buy a substantial stock of garlic (which he called 'capital' (σερμαγιά), and store it in the yard of his house. In the following months the early-morning visits to the market could be eliminated and he would go only when he needed to restock. By early June the normal routine was established—Avraam would rise at 4.30 a.m. to catch the first bus passing through Kokkinia at 5 a.m., carrying on his back a cloth bag full of plaited strings of garlic. His rounds took him to various parts of the city, usually to the original refugee quarters, such as Kaisariani, Nea Smyrna, as well as to districts of Piraeus. His profit margin was adjusted to the wholesale price, and he could afford to sell for less than the greengrocers. Returning home by 1 p.m. for food and siesta he would give his wife Eliso a daily sum for housekeeping.

Eliso was responsible for the household expenditure, which she planned on a long-term basis, taking into account the winter months when they had no regular income. Avraam would try to earn something when, as they said, he was 'sitting' (κάθεται), by collecting scrap items from neighbours and selling what he could to Piraeus dealers. At the first street market after the earnings started coming in, Eliso always bought a large money-box, and would save coins, ten- or twenty-drachma pieces, until the autumn when she would buy her winter stocks—tins of heating fuel, olive-oil, kilos of macaroni, sugar, and rice. Much foresight went into her everyday housekeeping, which was supplemented if Avraam went past the city market and found cheap fresh meat or fish.

Other characteristic figures in the locality were the sellers of lottery tickets and the pastry vendors, offering cheese pies (τυρόπιτες), raisin buns (σταφιδόψωα), and crisp rings sprinkled with sesame seed (κουλούρια).

CASE 7: CHRISTOS

Old Christos circulated through the streets of Kokkinia every morning, pushing a hand-cart and calling out his wares, his white apron and straw hat proclaiming the legality of his enterprise, for he had paid for the licence to operate openly. His buns and pies were bought early each morning from a large bakery near Yerania, at wholesale prices, to which he added 30-50 per cent profit. Since his rounds included a densely populated district as well as two primary schools which he would attend during the break, he was undoubtedly making a good living with earnings well above the average 3,000 drs. per month.

Entrepreneurs on Wheels

Younger men who hawked goods in the neighbourhoods usually had their own vehicles, small, three-wheeled cycles or vans, which they loaded with special offers on seasonal fruit—oranges, lemons, melons, figs, grapes—obtained from the island boats at the harbour or at the central market. Other itinerant salesmen owned station-wagons from which they hawked household goods, kitchen equipment, bedspreads and curtains, or clothing as Lakis did (Case 3). Their prices were cheaper than those in the shops, since their overheads were lower. Housewives were tempted, too, by the credit offered for they could pay off in small amounts of 20 to 50 drs. at the salesman's weekly visits.

In this locality private vehicles were rare, for they represented considerable capital outlay and running costs. Consequently they were acquired only as a means of livelihood. There were a few privately owned taxis (usually shared by two owner-drivers) and station-wagons used for business. By far the most common were various sizes and types of three-wheeled transport vehicles (τρίκυκλα). The smallest (μηχανάκια), are mere cycles with small, open loading-trays and 250 cc engines which emit an ear-splitting noise as they accelerate up any incline; others are substantial vehicles with two-seater driver's cabs and large covered vans (Plate 14).

The attractions of owning a vehicle were related to the desire for independence and the possibility of self-employment, characteristic and widely expressed preferences amongst the men. One newcomer to the haulage trade, Spiros, had given up a well-paid factory job as a skilled leather tanner, in which he had managed to save the full 85,000 drs. required to buy a transport vehicle. He was enthusiastic about the advantages of his new occupation, expressing it in the telling phrase 'I have no one over my head' (Δεν έχω κανένα στο κεφάλι μου).

The transport trade was thus understandably a popular choice for the entrepreneurial scope it offered, but capital was required. Even in 1972 when credit was easily obtained, the

down payment of 40,000 drs. to purchase a vehicle was a considerable sum, yet increasing numbers of men were managing
to set themselves up in business. Once the necessary licence
was obtained, the transport vehicle could take its place at one of
the particular spots (πιάτσες) designated in various parts of the
city, usually on squares or side-streets, where clients would
haggle with the drivers over the cost of the journey.

CASE 8: PHOTIS

With the increasing number of vehicles, the transport business was
becoming more competitive. One Yerania driver, Photis, noted how
the square in Piraeus where he had worked for ten years had had only
one other vehicle in 1968, but four years later there were seven. Business was inherently risky and earnings could not be assured since
daily takings might vary from nearly 1,000 drs. to a mere 50 drs. or
nothing. This uncertainty could be offset through a wide range of contacts, a steady clientele, and knowledge of local transportation needs.
Photis was undoubtedly successful and experienced: 'I have my own
customers', he explained (έχω την πελατεία μου). In order to qualify for
a pension, he had joined the guild (σωματείο), for which monthly payments were 270 drs., while the other costs—insurance, circulation tax,
normal running—totalled over 2,000 drs. per month. Photis's way of
life, however, reflected the profitability of his occupation. Although
the family lived in a crowded Yerania prefab shared with his wife's sister's family, they owned a spacious summer-house on the island of
Salamina. His home was equipped with many electrical appliances,
including a washing-machine, one of the first in a Yerania home.

The popularity of transport trades was clear—in Yerania they
accounted for about 13 per cent of the total working population,
mainly younger men—and showed the importance of independence to the male earner and of the self-sufficiency of the
family. Those confident of their ability to take on the challenge
of responsibility, which was the main ingredient in success,
accepted the inherent risks of the trade.

Regularity and Risk

There was, however, another response discernable in the choice
of employment, undoubtedly rooted in past experience of
chronic economic instability, and this was the desire for security, with a minimum of risk-taking. For a known, assured wage,

even if it were lower than others available, monotony would be tolerated. This response existed, for instance, among those men who chose to remain in factory jobs in 1972, even when more remunerative employment was available in other pursuits.

Factories have always provided employment for men and women from the majority of families in Yerania and continued to do so in 1972, even though the daily wage was comparatively low. Labour demand peaked at this time of high emigration and expanding industrial requirements, so that factories near Kokkinia were ferrying workers daily in coaches from places as far away as Corinth.

Despite this demand, though, factory wages were lower than those offered in other unskilled activities. Another strategy was practised, therefore, among the men who at this time had only their labour to sell: during the summer they dropped the factory jobs and moved to outdoor labouring work. Such jobs were at the shipbuilding yards of Perama and Skaramanga, for example, as well as in areas such as Liossa beyond the limits of town-plans (εκτός σχεδίου) where small houses were being constructed without planning permission. These jobs paid higher rates, 300 to 400 drs. per day, against the usual equivalent of 250 drs. a day, and of only 150 drs. in a factory. During the winter, however, such jobs were unreliable sources of income, being paid on a daily basis and subject to weather conditions. Thus in winter the men would return to shift-work in factories where steady if lower remuneration was offered.

This attempt to combine higher irregular earnings with a poor but regular source of income inhibits the acquisition of skills and produces a fluctuating labour force. Workers I questioned argued that changing their jobs on a seasonal basis was necessary simply because the rewards for remaining in their factory jobs were insignificant. Even after five years in the same factory, they said earnings would not approach those offered in the illegal construction trade. Thus the seasonally higher rates offset any advantage gained by continuous employment. In order to encourage regular attendance, most factories offered a monthly bonus payment, as well as one for high productivity. One day some factory workers from Kokkinia employed at the spinning mills were discussing the attitude of a group of immigrant Greeks from the Black Sea area of Russia who were known to work hard for a productivity bonus. The local men felt that any extra effort for only 100 drs. a week more (less than the daily wage) was not worth it. Regular attendance, however, was paid on a monthly basis, giving an extra 500 drs. per month, almost a week's pay, and this was more acceptable: it involved no extra effort and was given in a monthly amount. One man who had inadvertently missed a shift because it had been changed was most upset, since the household budget depended upon this essential addition to his earnings.

Wherever people have long been subject to precarious economic conditions, where at times even the question of survival itself has been critical, regular earnings obviously become a major concern. Jobs paid on a monthly basis imply this kind of security and were well regarded particularly by the women who saw them as the most acceptable occupations for a prospective son-in-law or husband. 'Employees' (υπάλληλοι), as they were called, earn monthly incomes either in private concerns, as clerks or salespeople, or in municipal jobs. This latter category, the municipal employee (δημόσιος υπάλληλος), covers a range of activities, however, from white-collar office worker to those of park attendant, street sweeper, or rubbish collector. The fact that no verbal distinction was made between different grades of 'employee' is significant. It suggests that in local eyes the regular monthly income was more significant than type of occupation. Rubbish collectors were no less regarded than others earning monthly wages. This indicated therefore, that social ranking based on occupation was not a marked feature of Yerania people's assessments. Prestige rested on the ability of a family to support itself adequately and not on occupational category, and to this end, as we have seen, a number of strategies were used.

The Street Market

An extremely important commercial activity in the metropolis is the street market (λαϊκή αγορά), which provides an interesting illustration of the two predominant tendencies in economic behaviour already noted. In the organization of the street market the desire for security together with the opportunity for individual enterprise are both allowed expression. Although the street market appears, at first sight, to be a haphazard free-for-all, it is actually an organized guild whose members have a pension scheme and social security benefits. Throughout the metropolitan area in 1972 there were seven separate street market guilds (σωματεία), three operating in Piraeus and four in the Athens area. Each guild had up to 250 sellers (but this did not entitle each member to a stall) and each was run by a committee whose president (πρόεδρος) was normally elected by popular vote (during the junta period he was appointed by the Ministry of Trade for a three-year period). Each market was overseen by an officer of the market control division of the police whose main duty, as one person expressed it, was to 'protect the buyers and sellers from one another'. He in turn had his judgement protected by an extra 2,000 drs. per month above his regular salary. Appeals regarding fair practice and any conflicts could be arbitrated by him as he patrolled the street while the market was open.

Each street market moved to a set locality in rotation six days a week, and since the groups split up to form two smaller markets on certain days, most residential districts of the city were served by at least one. In Piraeus, for example, one group split up three times a week into smaller markets in adjacent residential areas. The whole of Kokkinia was well served by street markets and Yerania was particularly favoured: the Wednesday market took up the length of the main road at the southern border of the district while on Saturdays there was a market to the north about ten minutes' walk from Yerania, and on Mondays another took place near Ai Nikola.

Employment in the street market was highly regarded and it required some influence to obtain a place to open a stall. Positions along the street (closed to all traffic for that morning) were allotted by the committee. Since the market often extended for over 400 metres, the sheer distance between its ends reduced the density of the stalls, and hence the number of customers. Consequently there was considerable rivalry over the positions of the stalls. As a matter of course newcomers were given the least advantageous places at the furthest ends of the lines of the stalls and were mockingly called 'goalkeepers' (τερματοφύλακες) since 'they see least of the action'. The street market rests on a basis of co-operation, however, through its constitution as a guild, and through the agreement of members on various matters, including the position of stalls within it. A sense of permanence and security exists in the organization, therefore, as well as in the pension benefits which accompany membership.

Another equally important aspect of the street market is its basis in 'controlled competition' where those involved may express their individuality and independence. Each stall-keeper was in charge of his own stall and acted on his own initiative, within the official regulations regarding prices and quality of goods. The spirit of individuality was evident in the intense competition and rivalry between sellers, particularly those in the same vicinity stocking the same wares, who engaged vigorously in price-cutting and special bargain offers to increase trade. Not everyone can be successful under these conditions of sharp and unremitting daily competition. Sellers tried to develop techniques to increase the number of customers and their own takings, simply by the variety and volume of calls, some relying on sheer volume, others making original or humorous appeals to the shoppers, or by resorting to less honest means.

Cheating is a feature of the market recognized by sellers and buyers alike so that, although the housewife had the opportunity to purchase high-quality goods at low prices, shopping was not without its hazards. In general, the men took the view that the women were easily fooled and sellers employed various standard techniques of cheating, based on this notion. Some husbands therefore restricted the amounts that their wives could spend at the market, saying that they were only likely to be made fools of and cheated. One seller enlightened me on some of the commoner techniques. The easiest methods of cheating included adding spoilt fruit to items the housewife had chosen to make up the weight, or keeping some items of poor quality out of sight in the weighing-pan before the housewife added those of her choice. Besides outright cheating (which was done imperceptibly and adeptly) another technique was to create a good impression by false means. The seller would tip the weighing-pan slightly with one hand, so that the desired weight had apparently been reached, and then would magnanimously add two or three extra items 'for free' (τσάμπα).

The customer, impressed by this generosity, would return to find him the following week. This effort to build up a regular clientele in different localities indicated the acute and constant competition between sellers, reflected too in the price-cutting of adjacent stalls selling similar produce.

Not surprisingly in this competitive atmosphere disputes between sellers frequently occurred. The arrangements of stalls, a crucial factor in turnover, was not permanent and added another point of tension to the internal organization of the market. For a number of reasons, therefore, it was necessary to ensure the favourable predisposition of persons in authority: good relations with the president, the committee, and the policeman were important considerations.

CASE 9: VASILIS

One dispute illustrates these points: Vasilis, a man in his thirties, had joined the market only a year or two earlier, and had a job selling cigarettes to the sellers in the early hours of the morning before normal trading hours, after which he swept around the stalls during the course of the morning to keep the rubbish out of the way of customers. He received no set wage for this, but at the end of the morning collected a tip of one or two drachmas from each stall-keeper. On three consecutive mornings, one of the stall-keepers chose to ignore his greeting and refused to give him a tip. The following day a row developed between them; Vasilis pushed the stall-keeper into a pile of crates and baskets, and other people had to intervene. The dispute was settled through consultation with the members of the committee and the policeman. Vasilis's complaints were upheld, and the stall-keeper was ordered to give him his daily tip. Regardless of the objective rights and wrongs of the dispute, the fact that Vasilis had been on good terms with the president and members of the committee had been to his advantage. He had established this by performing small services for those people, fully aware of their potential power. He had no guarantee of permanence in his job (which, though one of low status, was financially very rewarding), but he felt assured of his position, for only someone with 'very strong influence' (με πολύ μέσο) could have replaced him. Such influence would mean knowing the president and Vasilis had already established good relations with the committee members from whom any future president might be elected.

This small incident also illustrates a structural feature. Even in the street market, where individuality was given free expression, none the less an informal hierachy of power existed. A man's sense of self-sufficiency could not be regarded as absolute, for as he struggled to support his family he had to enter relationships of dependence with those in more power-ful positions, paradoxically, in order to preserve this independence. By astute management of social contacts, then, and by the recognition of mutual bonds of obligation (υποχρέωση: a key element in the neighbourhood exchanges, see Chapter 8), a man's prestige could be furthered and his sense of integrity preserved, no matter how lowly his position in absolute terms.

Women's Economic Roles

In the 1972 sample survey of Yerania, women comprised 23 per cent of the working population, a figure slightly lower than the 27 per cent recorded for Athens as a whole (census 1971). How-ever, this statistic requires interpretation since it directly contradicts the explicit dictates regarding a woman's role. A well-defined complementarity of roles allocated to men the economic burden of supporting the family and to women the care of the home and family as a primary, even exclusive, obli-gation. For a married woman there was no readily acceptable role in the economic sphere outside the home. An examination of the age of the female working population in Yerania, sheds light on this contradiction. The majority of the employed women—about 60 per cent—were under 21 years old, and therefore most were unmarried. The importance of the dowry is evident here; indeed, young girls who earned money to provide dowry for their future marriages were employed in a culturally justifiable way (cf. Lambiri 1968 on factory employment in Megara).

Just as the priorities for a married woman centred on the family, for the unmarried the goal of marriage was paramount. A dowry, considered the essential precondition for marriage, usually consisted of a dwelling of some kind as well as most of its furnishings (Chapter 6). This considerable outlay could not be met by male members of the family alone, especially if there was more than one daughter. Consistent with long-standing traditional practice, then, a girl's capacity to contribute towards her dowry through her earnings was acceptable. The contingent nature of a woman's earning capacity was clear. Once married, a woman was expected to take her place as 'mistress of the house', *noikokyrá*, (*νοικοκυρά*) as a full-time all-encompassing commitment.[2] Since marriage was the aim and female chastity was a primary concern for most families, employment outside the home with the dangers of a girl's exposure to the outside world posed problems for parents. It was not unusual for a father to check on an 18-year-old daughter's movements to and from work. Parents also tended to treat their daughter's work companions with caution if not hostility. Many parents preferred to arrange a job somewhere in the locality where surveillance was easier. Small-scale family businesses also benefited from this supply of labour.

CASE 10: THE PYLIDES FAMILY BUSINESS

The salami factory of the Pylides family was situated in Korydalo about ten minutes' walk from Yerania. It had been started in the 1960s by the father and in 1972 supported two of his married sons as well. Run typically as a family business, it employed eight women workers, all unmarried. The wife of one of the Pylides sons, herself from Yerania, had recommended five of the workers, young girls whose families were known to hers, and whose parents were glad that their daughters were employed in a more amenable family environment.

In the early 1970s many girls in the locality were leaving the high school at 15 or 16 to take up apprenticeships. A skilled trade was seen as particularly suitable: before marriage the girl could contribute towards her dowry, and after it, should the need arise, she could practise her skills from home. Thus, the most popular trades were hairdressing and dressmaking, as well as shirtmaking and tailoring (*φραγκοραφφτική*), all of which offered employment in the locality.

Whatever employment a girl took up, however, it was always seen as entirely secondary to her ultimate destiny (*προορισμός*) in marriage, childbearing, and housekeeping. It is interesting that attitudes regarding a woman's employment after marriage remained so clearly defined and modelled along a rigid division of labour by gender, despite the decades of need which had forced contradictions in practice. Only under conditions of particular hardship was a wife's employment acceptable, justified in the context of self-sacrifice which places the family's survival above all other considerations.

Although negative attitudes generally attached to married women undertaking employment, in most Yerania homes women were actually in charge of all running costs and had considerable autonomy regarding the allocation of household expenditure; they were said to 'be in command' (κάνουν κουμάντο). Their ability as housekeepers was a joint source of pride for both spouses. In a poor locality such as Yerania, it is no exaggeration to say that a household's survival would depend on the housewife's prudence and ingenuity in handling resources. Not surprisingly, therefore, great emphasis was placed on the thrifty management of household income and on general housekeeping ability. A woman's economic role lay *within* the home and was of considerable importance. Men and women alike subscribed to the notion that their roles were separate and complementary. Indeed some older people, asserting this division, even said that money earned by a woman 'brings no success' (τα λεφτά της γυναίκας δεν έχουν προκοπή). In this view money did not have a neutral cash value, it was qualitatively related to gender and was seen as an integral aspect of masculine competence. A woman's earning capacity was seen as somehow superfluous and it could even threaten her husband's social reputation and self-respect, but her management ability was highly valued.

It is significant that these values were so resilient and persisted even against the extreme pressures of material needs. Possibly the tenacity of the concepts regarding the division of labour was a defensive response to the stresses of chronic poverty and threats to family integrity over the years. Since key values designated to a woman a chaste image and the attainment of virtue within her family, these precepts were used as the foundation of family stability. In the past, however, sheer necessity had forced women into paid employment, either as sole supporter of a family or as an additional working member. No woman over her mid-fifties had escaped paid employment for the financial support of her family. Even if they had not worked in the first years after the settlement, the period of the depression followed by war and the German Occupation, when even greater hardship struck the urban refugee quarters, made everyone's contribution essential. There was little food available in the city and the refugees were the most vulnerable, for, unlike many local Greeks, they seldom had connections or relatives in nearby villages where food could be obtained by barter. At this time it was the fortunate women who managed to find jobs—whether for money or for food—in domestic service, or in the military hospital and army barracks situated near Kokkinia.

In 1972 married women who worked did so, in the main, in order to cover the family's basic living costs. Since the single wage of a male factory worker or municipal cleaner covered little more than subsistence needs, it was necessary for their wives to take employment outside the home. A few of these women, unskilled and mostly over 35 years old, could earn cash at home doing simple piece-work (packaging moth-balls, carding hair-grips) but the majority could get jobs only in factories or as cleaners. The contemporary emphasis on practical training for girls reflected the awareness of the exigencies of economic life, while the favoured trades were ones which offered the chance of home-based earnings.

Views on the relative merits of different jobs for women further indicated central cultural values. Given the emphasis on women's domestic roles, one might have expected a preference for housework, the more so because at that period wages for domestic work were considerably higher than those in other unskilled pursuits: in 1972 a cleaner or cook could earn 180–200 drs. per day with coffee breaks as well as a midday meal, while a female factory worker earned only 97 drs. a day. But wealthier households in Athens could not easily get domestic help—the level of wages reflected the demand. Apparently, women from poor localities like Yerania preferred to take factory jobs despite the lower daily wage. One obvious advantage of factory employment, not to be ignored, was that social insurance and pension benefits (IKA) were automatically available.

This was not the total explanation, however, since such benefits could also be negotiated through domestic employment. The preference existed in a wider set of values. In accepting a domestic job a woman takes a subordinate position under another woman, her employer, who could criticize her performance in keeping house. For the women of Kokkinia, housework was not an impersonal activity; it was not seen as a necessary evil at the margins of one's real concerns. House-keeping, in all its aspects, from the most tedious routine tasks to the intricacies of pastry-making, was a crucial expression, the essential manifestation of a woman's character and worth. Both her self-esteem and her social prestige were inextricably bound up with her performance as a housewife. Housework was not easily detached from a woman's sense of self, therefore, nor could it easily be given a commodity value. Thus a woman who, like most, prided herself on being a 'good housewife' (καλή νοικοκυρά), a primary female aspiration, could jeopardize a central dimension of her personality if placed in the position of employee caring for another's home.

Koula, a woman of 40 married to a labourer, explained emphatically that her factory job where she earned only 97 drs. per day was preferable to house-cleaning at twice the wage. 'I couldn't stand another woman telling me how to sweep or dust. Far better to hand over my machine at the end of the shift and go home with a quiet mind (. . . με ήσυχο το κεφάλι).' Her remarks were revealing: like other women she described domestic employment as 'degrading' (υποτιμητικό). The term is suggestive for it contains the notion of honour or price, τιμή, indicating that social worth and honour is involved. Thus, monotonous shift-work in a factory with low wages and some long-term security was preferred to a better-paid, more varied, and familiar domestic job without security where, however, one's self-esteem, something beyond monetary value, would be subject to another's judgements. The reluctance of Yerania women to take on these well-paid jobs makes sense in the light of these values.

Among the unskilled jobs available to women, one considered most desirable was, significantly, that of early-morning cleaner in an office building or bank. Such jobs offered lower wages than domestic service but did carry social security benefits (IKA) while the short working hours (5–8 a.m.) allowed the woman to run her home the rest of the day. The work itself was familiar, and in this impersonal setting the woman as cleaner was not subject to another woman's judgements about the state of her home. For these reasons, such jobs were in great demand but, people said, without an influential sponsor (μέσο) applications were simply ignored.

Among Yerania residents I discerned a clear division in public attitudes to married women taking employment. On the one
hand, sympathy was extended to those women of poor families,
like Koula, who worked from sheer necessity. Public opinion
tolerated their absence from home because it was seen as a sacrifice made to enable the family to survive. However, when
family circumstances improved, public approval would be
withdrawn if they did not give up their employment and
devote themselves more to the home.

Open criticism was directed at married women whose employment was seen to provide funds for superfluous spending.
In a sense, they were breaking the rules of the game in which
families were engaged: the rivalry for prestige in the narrow
confines of neighbourhood life. Their family's material success,
displayed in modern appliances, renovations, or the purchase
of a plot on Salamina island, would provoke envy together with
a sense of outrage. About such a woman people would typically
comment, 'What is her complaint? Her husband earns enough.
It's all for extravagance, she's insatiable' (Τί παράπονο έχει; Ο
άντρας της φέρνει αρκετά. Για λούσα είναι αυτά είναι αχόρταγη).
Through contravening the norms of complementarity which
designate women's and men's different contributions to the
household, these women laid themselves open not only to the
criticism of neglecting the home but also to the charge of
greed (πλεονεξία), a term carrying strong moral implications,
for it was among the causes which, in the religious world-
view, condemned man to a fallen existence. Greed is linked
with sensuality (cf. Staniforth 1968: 150 n. 3) and both are seen
as primarily feminine weaknesses. It is the domestic priorities
of women which should counteract these inherent flaws of
character.

Although some of these women did work at home as uphol-
sterers, dressmakers, or hairdressers, they were frequently criticized for neglecting their duties. Regardless of the actual state of
the house, public opinion stigmatized its disorder and inadequate care and the woman's reputation suffered. These women
were aware of the disapproval and, characteristically, were critical of the unpleasant aspects of neighbourhood life. Since their
husbands must have approved their activity, these married
couples were jointly acting in the spirit of *symphéron*, the

pursuit of material success, translated as 'self-' or 'family-interest'.³ The notion of *symphéron* is one which men apply continually in their economic activities; it is an essentially competitive drive, grounded in gaining advantages, often at the expense of others, and its effect may often be to limit possibilities for co-operative effort. Together with the desire for independence, *symphéron* was a guide-line for masculine achievement and its locus was in the market-place. *Symphéron* seeks the increase of family wealth, another goal for men. In contrast, women were not expected to increase the family's material wealth (their dowry portion was an initial endowment, a foundation upon which the husband based his future efforts) but to conserve it. The guiding economic values for a woman thus stressed prudent management and the conservation of resources in the home. The married woman's concerns should primarily be for raising children, complementing the husband's efforts to support the family, and with promoting a harmonious, well-ordered environment in the home and the neighbourhood. The clearly defined division of labour upon which the family rests reflected values of an economic nature which were gender-specific, applying differently to men and women (cf. du Boulay 1974: 135). Those married women who were criticized for earning money had embraced one of the values associated with competitive, masculine activity, and were acting in a manner inappropriate to their designated role. A woman's labour was not to be detached from her role as 'mistress of the house', and her earning power, whether before or after marriage, was seen as secondary and subordinate to this goal.

The division of labour according to gender was clearly articulated and explicit. Less obvious perhaps, but equally interesting, was a separation of generations in terms of values and aspirations. Older people, usually those over sixty, had a definite philosophy, articulated in various stock phrases and sayings, which could be characterized as 'other-wordly'. By contrast, the struggle for achievement and material success characteristically occupied the energies of younger adults with growing families. Their life-style involved competition, rivalry, the pursuit of *symphéron* and material gains, all appropriate at this stage of life, but not in old age when transcendent values emphasizing non-acquisition and spiritual realities would come to the fore.

This chapter has shown how material conditions set up the constraints within which key cultural values lie dormant or continue to operate despite countervailing pressure. Thus, long periods of economic hardship have meant that security of earnings became a goal, but with buoyant conditions offering a greater range of opportunities, the preference for self-employment surfaced again. The desire 'to have no one over your head', as Yerania men put it, widespread in Greek society, is reflected in the proliferation of small family businesses and industrial concerns employing under five workers. This can be seen as the expression of honour values translated into an urban, industrial, market economy. The family's integrity is expressed in the autonomy of its male head. Linked as it is with the notion of *symphéron*, seeking one's own interest, the effect was to set men in adversarial positions; but they did not challenge one another as individuals, since the framework of social life centred on the family. The family was the keystone in the pattern of social life which had developed in this locality, and it is to this base, from which adult and child alike identified self and others, that attention now turns.

6

THE HOUSE, THE DOWRY, AND MARRIAGE
Continuity and Adaptation

Those people who finally received houses in Yerania had been living in various makeshift shelters for anything up to six years. When they were handed the keys to their dwellings a few days before the Christmas of 1927, their joy and optimism were overwhelming. The provision of a house meant protection; it conferred security and stability and, for most, it represented the only item of substantial property. These houses can be examined, therefore, from a number of different angles: the failure of successive governments to redress the housing problems in the poorer urban quarters turned the house into a political issue, tied up with the refugee identity. It became the material sign, even the proof of dispossessed status. In the early phase of settlement, however, the house provided the first opportunity of normal family life for the refugees, it became the focus of their adjustment to their new environment, and the centre of their social and symbolic world.

The Marriage Imperative

Flight and expulsion had meant to the Asia Minor Greeks the complete disruption of hundreds of thousands of families as well as entire communities. In the upheaval following the military campaign, kinsfolk disappeared, men were detained, and social connections were lost. For a large section of the population 1922 is a sharp dividing line when genealogical depth and the extension of kinship ties were irrecoverably extinguished. Survivors were often reluctant to recall the period of their flight but it was clear from their stories that it was difficult to keep even the elementary family together. Right into the 1980s appeals were broadcast daily to trace people dispersed during the 1920s.

A marked feature of life in Yerania was the emphasis on social continuity, expressed in the concern with preserving family stability, on maintaining harmonious neighbourhood relationships, and, at the symbolic level, on the value of life, generation, and sociability. The emphasis on life and continuity is certainly not unique to this section of the Greek population, but it is probable that their experiences endowed it with fresh significance and immediacy. An intense and pressing problem was the welfare of the younger generation, and the need to reconstitute family life put marriage at the forefront of people's concerns. Parental obligations, entailing a life-long commitment, self-denial, and responsibilities which culminated in the successful marriages of their offspring, were not relinquished but were maintained as cultural dictates. Thus, parents were held responsible for children's marriages and, in the case of daughters, for providing the dowry portion which was considered an essential prerequisite for it. Marriage was seen by all as a turning-point in the life cycle, conferring on the young the status of recognized adulthood and on their parents the recognition of successfully discharged obligations.

As everywhere in Greece, marriage was considered imperative for all men and women (excepting only the physically and mentally handicapped and those who entered celibate monastic communities). It was not considered to be an optional matter, nor one of choice, but rather a matter of 'destiny' (προορισμός). The appropriate path for both sons and daughters was to move straight from their families of origin to new roles as spouses and later as parents in the family of marriage. In the urban setting of Kokkinia in 1972 there was no accepted stage of independent unmarried adulthood such as exists in western cities where young people live alone or together, supporting themselves before settling down in marriage. From the point of view of young people in Kokkinia, therefore, marriage was the only accepted means of establishing full adulthood and maturity.

The importance of marriage was particularly impressed on young girls who, from an early age, were inculcated with the notion that no other fulfilment was possible for them. A woman's destiny was to bear children and raise her family as mistress in her own household and no acceptable alternative existed. The Greek language abounds in conventional phrases and wishes: ritual sayings used for various occasions. Among those directed incessantly at young girls were: 'To your joys!' (*Στις χαρές σου!*), 'Here's to a bridegroom!' (*Μ' ένα γαμπρό!*), and 'Married next year!' (*Του χρόνου παντρεμένη!*). The most significant of these was the exhortation, 'Get married and open your house!' (*Παντρέψου ν' ανοίξεις το σπίτι σου!*), a metaphor associated with the pervasive symbolism of 'open' and 'closed' categories of orientation.

The vulnerability of women outside the house was a theme in their upbringing. In all contexts marriage was presented as an auspicious state, as the only safe and appropriate condition for adulthood. In essence a girl passed from the protection of her father to that of her husband. In the ideals of this society the less she was exposed to the outside world, the better. 'She's straight from her mother's arms' (*Απ' την αγκαλιά της μάνας της*) or 'She never goes beyond the front door' (*Δεν βγαίνει απ' την πόρτα της*) were two common ways of expressing approval of such girls. Significantly, it was her husband who would 'take her out into society' (*θα την βγάλει έξω στην κοινωνία*), and only through her conjunction with him could a woman play a full and acceptable role in adult social life.

The importance of a husband's presence is also thrown into negative relief. In this area of the city the position of a widow if she was under fifty was almost untenable. Her every action would be observed by the surrounding neighbourhood and her behaviour had to be extremely circumspect. A recently widowed woman of forty was advised by her elderly neighbour, 'Get married again. You will never be at peace until you do' (*Παντρέψου ξανά αλλιώς δεν θα ησυχάσεις ποτές*). An older woman who had been widowed during the Occupation but remarried five years later corroborated this view: 'Don't I know it? People keep asking, "Where are you going?" "What are you wearing?" "When did you return?" Not even a tom-cat came into my yard for five years. It was only when I remarried that they quietened down' (. . . *ούτε σερνικός γάτος στην αυλή μου. Μόνο όταν ξαναπαντρεύτηκα ησυχάσανε*).

For men marriage was also seen as a necessary state though the emphasis was slightly different. The informal age limitations for men were less rigid and they could enjoy a longer period of unmarried adulthood. As a man approached thirty,

1. One type of refugee housing provided by the Refugee Settlement
Commission in Kokkinia

2. Yerania. View of a main street leading to the square and parish
church of Evangelismos

3. The primary school on the edge of Yerania serves two residential areas. Prefabricated houses set on plinths above ground permitted the addition of basement rooms

4. One half of this prefabricated dwelling has been replaced by a modern structure, only possible when full titles have been paid for by the family

5. This corner-house facing on to the main square has no courtyard since the addition of the adjacent two-roomed house for the daughter's dowry. The small boy is playing at the entrance to his grandparents' excavated basement quarters

6. The need for additional living space accounts for extensions of various kinds on to—and under—pavement areas

7. Despite overcrowding and inadequate public facilities, Yerania presented a neat and attractive appearance

8. Whitewash was frequently renewed. Other typical features include the basement quarters, indicated by the ground-level window, and the chair on the pavement

however, public pressure encouraging his marriage intensified, for every man is expected to undertake the duties and responsibilities of family life. An unduly prolonged bachelorhood indicated avoidance of the full status of adulthood, suggesting certain deficiencies in character: weakness, frivolity, and, ultimately, lack of masculinity. For men the emphasis was on becoming the head of a household as well as on the creation of a family. Unmarried men were urged to 'Get married so that you can have a family' (*Παντρέψου να κάνεις οικογένεια*). The principal concern was to produce sons who would continue the family name.

Arranged Marriage: The Proxenió

Among the findings of this study was the fact that continuity was maintained in all aspects of culture and social life in the urban refugee quarters, despite the tremendous psychological trauma and social disruption which these people had suffered. Given the stresses and difficulties which faced them for many years after settlement, conditions which might have prompted totally different reactions and even caused a severe breakdown of the social order, the degree of social adjustment was remarkable. Alternative attitudes to social and biological reproduction do exist and anthropological studies document their rich variety. Given the extent of community disruption, the Asia Minor Greeks might have abandoned the conventions regarding family organization or the provision of dowry. But they did not. Their cultural precepts, reinforced by the notion of the intrinsic value of tradition itself, were reiterated in the new context.

Historically, the basis of their culture, founded in Orthodox Christianity, presents marriage as a sacramental tie, ideally permanent and indissoluble (though up to three marriages are permitted by ecclesiastical ruling). The permanence of the marriage bond and the importance of family stability were frequently and explicitly emphasized values. Young people often heard the warning 'Choose well, [marriage] is until you close your eyes, there is no other' (*Διάλεξε καλά—είναι μέχρι να κλείσεις τα μάτια σου. Δεν υπάρχει άλλο*). I often heard admonitions such as, 'Marriage requires great caution, you must consider it very carefully' (*Ο γάμος θέλει πολύ προσοχή, Πρέπει να το μελετήσεις πολύ καλά*).

Possibly some of the anxieties generated by the past and present stresses of Yerania life were reflected in this constant barrage of advice offered to young people. Television was a recent innovation (in 1972 about one-third of the houses had a set). *Peyton Place,* an American soap-opera, was a popular serial at the time, and Western-style romance was being widely projected. But threats to family stability were not new in Yerania. Excessively crowded conditions and economic pressures had obviously contributed to the conflicts, some extremely bitter, within the local group. Marriages were not always harmonious, divorce was not unknown, and in part the district's poor reputation was attributed by outsiders to the prevalence of conflict. In the emphatic expression of ideal values, however, there was no indication that divorce or separation was condoned. On the contrary, cases which had occurred were deplored and used as negative examples in pejorative contexts.

It was quite clear that the preferred form of marriage was one which followed a set and formal procedure, called the *proxenió,* roughly equivalent to 'arranged marriage'. In the Greek case of 'arranged marriage' varying degrees of pressure may be applied, but there is no question of compulsion. In essence the *proxenió* is a formalization of marriage proceedings which involves both younger and older generations of the families. It includes a third party, *proxenitís (προξενητής),* to act as go-between, to arrange an introduction, and to aid negotiations between the two families. These negotiations concern the material basis of the marriage and involve ascertaining the assets, both dowry and income, which each partner would provide. The continuing preference for the *proxenió* at that time reflected a pragmatic approach to marriage, essentially a deep concern with the economic viability of the new household and the personal suitability of the spouses, crucial factors in ensuring the stability of the marriage. It should not be regarded as an odd, outdated, and anomalous 'survival' of 'traditional' ways among three to four generations of urban dwellers, since some of the functional advantages of marriage by *proxenió* are evident.

First, the pool of possible candidates is enlarged when others besides the immediate family are included in the selection of suitable spouses. The *proxenitís* or go-between, who is not necessarily related to either family (though he or she may be), enlarges the social network of prospective candidates. In this way people living in a locality of limited opportunity and mobility are in effect tapping the social resources of the city more efficiently. In addition, reliable information about unknown families is of crucial importance in the city whereas first-hand information may be easier to obtain in smaller settlements in the countryside. Thus the go-between plays an important, responsible role verifying claims made by either side regarding the qualities of the prospective spouses. Although this is an unpaid, non-specialist role, the go-between has a highly valued social function. Another important advantage of the arranged match is that, through the mediation of the third party in the crucial negotiation stage, a face-saving institution exists. Pretexts and excuses can be more acceptably presented by the go-between and thus the public face or honour of both parties can be preserved should the proposed match fail.

The *proxenió* can be seen as a means whereby attributes of individuals and their families are matched, since the suitability of the prospective spouses is a central issue. Various criteria were involved in the notion of suitability, one being the imprecise notion of *seirá* (lit. 'series, row') or rank. A common expression was 'You will marry someone of your own *seirá*' (θα πάρεις κάποιον της σειράς σου). The idea of *seirá* lay behind the choice of suitable partners, so that marriage in this locality was not, normatively, a means of social mobility. This contrasts with the explicit goals of marriage in some Greek rural communities (cf. Friedl 1962, 1976; Allen 1976).

Among the criteria of suitability, the economic and educational levels of the two families were very important, while an additional consideration was place of origin. Even in 1972 it was clear that marriages were preferably contracted from within the 'refugee' population. People in Kokkinia often used the common Greek proverb, 'Shoes from your homeland, even if they are mended' (Παπούτσι απ' τον τόπο σου κι ας είναι μπαλωμένο). Other important considerations for which the go-between should check were personal qualities such as health, diligence, and virtue (or rather, the reputation for it). Once the suitability of the match has been established, a formal introduction takes place in the presence of the couple's parents and other close kin, together with the go-between, usually at the home of the girl (where her dowry may be covertly assessed). If the young people agree, a stage of negotiations follows in which the interested parties discuss the material contributions to the marriage, seen as essential for the viability, existence, and well-being of any newly established family in the city. In the parleying over material issues parental concern may generate antagonisms which can, and often do, affect their later relationships and those between affines are notably fraught with tension.

It is clear that in both moral and practical respects parents were considered responsible for securing a proper match for a child; until their marriage children of both sexes remained in the parental home and were not considered fully adult, regardless of age. The parents' active interest and guidance was considered essential at least by the older generation, because without it, the son or daughter might fall victim to passion or to unscrupulous persons. Since the world is seen to be inherently flawed and human beings imperfect, driven by the desire to advance their own interests, so marriage may be manipulated to the advantage of some and the detriment of others. Parental involvement ensured the proper attention to social, economic, and practical factors without which the foundation of the marriage would be shaky; by their involvement parents protected the interests of their children. Furthermore, parents were considered responsible for initiating this process at the right time, and those who neglected to do so or who made only half-hearted attempts were criticized by others.

The *proxenió* procedure itself follows a set pattern but it is flexible and may be initiated in many ways (cf. Bernard 1976: 297), a factor which has undoubtedly contributed to its continued use in city life. In some cases, neither the candidates nor their parents know one another, and in this 'blind' *proxenió* the go-between is the only link, conveys all the information, and has a great deal of responsibility for the outcome. The introduction could be made by a sibling or close relative who would then play the part of the go-between. Sometimes the parents of the young people meet and themselves judge that a suitable match could be made, and a mutual acquaintance is approached to play the part of go-between. In all these cases, the final decision depends on the personal feelings of the young people. Parents seldom desire to impose their will—forced marriage is agreed to be unacceptable—so that even if all other factors appear ideal, the match will not proceed in the absence of the candidates' consent.

The way the *proxenió* works is illustrated by the case of Nikos.

THE RELUCTANT BRIDEGROOM

Unmarried and in his early thirties, Nikos was causing his parents considerable concern. In a period of five months he had been introduced to over twenty suitable women in various residential areas of Piraeus, but without success. Each introduction entailed a lengthy visit to the home of the prospective bride accompanied by a parent and the 'go-between', usually a married couple, friends of Nikos's parents, who had a wide range of acquaintances.

I was invited on one such *proxenió* visit to Amphiyali, a new suburb several kilometres from Kokkinia, together with Nikos, his hopeful mother, and the elderly couple who had arranged the meeting. The newly built, two-storey house was in a quiet street, with a small, well-kept garden. The two families were introduced and we visitors were ushered into the best room for the customary *kérasma* (chocolates and liqueurs offered to guests) followed by home-made sweets, a cake, and ice-cream. Conversation was general and drifted over impersonal topics in the main, besides some comments indicating how domesticated the prospective bride was. Both young people were tense and exchanged only a few words with one another. After nearly two hours of pleasantries the visit ended. Returning home, the go-between informed Nikos that the dowry home offered was the whole upper floor of the house, furnished in the same style as the parents' home on the ground floor. While Nikos's mother had enjoyed the family's warmth and been impressed by the young woman's modesty and lack of ostentation, Nikos was downcast. Although she was obviously very suitable, he said, she just did not attract him; he did not wish to pursue it further. His parents' disappointment only intensified when they later received a message through the go-between that her family were keen to continue, but Nikos could not be persuaded to change his mind. Excuses were conveyed to the girl's family; Nikos's parents and go-between began again seeking other possible candidates. In these cases people say that one's luck has not 'opened' (Δεν άνοιξε η τύχη), that the correct time has not occurred, and the only remedy, therefore, is simply to continue with the search. Several months later, however, through a different go-between, a workmate of Nikos's, a successful introduction did occur, and marriage arrangements proceeded smoothly, much to the delight of his parents.

In the urban setting where young people, both male and female, are involved in wage-earning and have some freedom of movement, it is increasingly common for the proceedings to be initiated by a young person, usually the boy, after seeing or meeting a girl who appeals to him. Once the suggestion is made and approved by the parents, however, it is the parents who organize the usual *proxenió* procedure. Many couples who say that they married 'for love' indicate that the initial suggestion was theirs, based on attraction, but in fact the formal *proxenió* then took place. Clearly the chances of a match being concluded are higher when a degree of personal interest has already been established and the initiative comes from a young person while the 'blind' *proxenió* is less likely to lead to marriage. Regardless of the way in which it is initiated, however, the *proxenió* follows the same stages, and, as noted, its very formality serves several useful purposes.

The widespread preference for marriage by *proxenió* was linked with disapproval of romantic love as a basis for marriage. 'Love', in a stock phrase used by old and young people alike, 'is a bad thing; it brings catastrophe' (*Η αγάπη είναι κακό πράγμα. Φέρνει καταστροφή*). Love, a force which by nature is not controlled or regulated, produces disorder. Love disregards the correct order of priorities: the factors of suitable background, health, and economic viability, essential to the process of matchmaking and to the success of the marriage, are ignored. Since emotional factors override practical considerations a match based on love provides a totally unsuitable basis for marriage. In addition, even if a *proxenió*-type of procedure is followed, the open declaration of sentiment by one of the young people destroys the negotiating position of the parents when the material transactions are discussed. Parents would not be able to protect the interests of their child in this situation and the marriage would therefore be seen as starting out under a handicap.

One particularly interesting case, that of Michalis and Toula,

illustrates several of these themes and shows the kind of freedom young people have both within and outside the preferred
approach to marriage.

THE FAITHFUL SUITOR

Michalis was an eligible young man of 26 when he fell in love with
Toula, a pretty non-refugee girl who had recently moved to a rented
flat in Yerania with her parents who were from a village in the Pelo-
ponnese. Michalis's mother, a widow of long standing, had always
held high expectations for his marriage as he was the youngest of her
three children. She had worked hard to raise and educate him, and he
was industrious and responsible. He earned a good wage as a skilled
metalworker and had managed to save the considerable sum of 200,000
drs. His mother objected strongly to his interest in Toula and forbade
him to see her; she also intensified her attempts to marry him off by
arranging a number of *proxenió* visits to the houses of girls of refugee
origin who were suitably endowed with dowry homes. Although
Michalis was co-operative he declined all other possibilities. After
three years had passed, he again broached the subject to his mother.
Her adamant demand and characteristic complaint centred around the
issue of a dowry house: 'Why should he not get a house?' (*Μα γιατί να
μην πάρει σπίτι;*). But finally she capitulated unwillingly and sent a go-
between to Toula's parents and stipulated that a house or flat be provided for the new household. But they did not even respond—they
were sure of Michalis's feelings and knew that his mother had no basis
for negotiating. To avoid further deadlock, Michalis suggested an
unusual solution—*he* would buy a flat with his savings. Toula's
parents immediately agreed to the match and offered to provide the
furniture. The formal engagement took place and people in the district
commented on Toula's extraordinary luck. Congratulatory remarks
addressed to Michalis, however, were those required by convention
alone. Neighbours were ambivalent and the general consensus was
that he had made an unfortunate match: he had been a victim of love.

Michalis had lessened his own public estimation by not holding out for a dowry which was seen to be the due of any respectable groom. There were also implications of imprudence. The
economic pressures which have taxed every Yerania family
place a premium on cautious assessment of the future. The prospective husband and father should calculate the level at which
he can maintain his family and weigh this against personal and
emotional factors. A man whose prudence and forethought
is overruled by passion is likely to be considered a 'fool'

(*χορόιδο*) (cf. Friedl 1962: 70). Similarly, a girl who marries without providing a dowry house was not admired nor could her parents pride themselves on this; it is taken by many as evidence of failure and expressed to the girl's demerit in a sexual idiom: she is said to be 'without pants' (*ξεβράκωτη*), a far from respectable image. Typical comments were: 'Have you heard— Michalis is getting married?' 'Oh! Did he get a dowry?' 'No— the fool. She hasn't even got pants' (*"Εμαθες; ο Μιχάλης παντρεύεται.' "Ετσι, έ; Πήρε προίκα;' "Οχι, ο βλάκας, ξεβράκωτη είναι'*).

Marriages based on romantic love without regard to the other considerations were not approved. Inevitably such marriages have occurred but confidence in their success was limited. Couples who married for love in the face of parents' and relatives' objections contended with general scepticism about their choice. Stella and Prokopis well remembered the objections they had to overcome. After seven years of clandestine courtship they had finally married. In their late thirties with two children, they were still conscious of their relatives' criticism and were always careful to present a picture of total domestic harmony to them. Although love is not considered a necessary precondition for marriage this does not mean that emotional bonds have no place in the relationship of the spouses. The order of priority, however, and the type of emotion is different. In general, erotic love or passion, allied with sensuality, was seen above all as a force for disruption and disorder, which should be contained and controlled.

Since the *proxenió* is treated as a formal but flexible approach to marriage, it accommodates the great variety of situations which urban life presents. In summary, the *proxenió* contains the recognition of calculated material advantage together with that of individual attraction. In any particular match material gain and emotional attraction are weighed up and balanced. Although parents may try to influence a child, the *proxenió* does not entail the forced choice of spouse and final acceptance always rests with the young person. Similarly, the *proxenió* can be stretched to include instances of strong personal attraction with the formal procedures still observed so that economic considerations are included. My conclusion is that arranged marriage, the *proxenió*, has proved adaptable and eminently suitable for contemporary urban conditions, given the values associated with family life. Far from being an incongruous, fossilized institution, the *proxenió* expresses an essentially pragmatic approach to marriage, where provisions for the new family and its stability are primary considerations.

The Dowry

Marriage is the point at which property is transferred between groups of kin in many societies, including Greece (Hirschon 1984: 10 ff.). The provision of wealth at the time of marriage, particularly but not solely by the parents of the bride, has always been an important custom in the Hellenic world, from classical through medieval and modern times. Despite considerable variation in the amount and type of wealth, its social consequences, changes in various periods, and regional differences, the dowry's continuing importance in contemporary Greece is shown in continuing debates surrounding recent legislation regarding dowry provision.[1]

Recollections of the older people showed that the provision of dowry had always been a matter of considerable parental, indeed corporate familial concern. They recalled that marriage proceedings in their home communities, in regions as diverse as Broussa, Ankara, Smyrna, and Pontus, a girl was expected to provide a certain amount of wealth on marriage. In some regions this was a house but in others it took the form of movable goods such as cash, gold coins, or household linen and equipment, items regarded as endowment for the new family and returnable to the girl if the marriage failed. Here, too, marriage was contracted through the formal arrangement procedure, the *proxenió*. Since in these communities people usually knew the resources of other families, either at first hand or through others, lengthy negotiations and haggling could be avoided in contrast to what my elderly informants noted as a distasteful feature of contemporary marriage proceedings.

The situation in Yerania reveals various contrasts as well as continuities: dowry continued to be provided by the girl's family, some of which came from the bride's own labour (in many Asia Minor and other Greek communities her own hand-woven and embroidered goods; in Yerania household

equipment purchased with cash earned and saved before marriage). In some Asia Minor communities, however, the bride left
home accompanied by her dowry; in Yerania the standard dowry
provision was separate living quarters in the bride's family
home. Although in 1972 the dowry could take a variety of forms,
the most essential element was the provision of a house. Indeed I
was often reminded pointedly that 'Without a house a woman
does not marry' (Χωρίς σπίτι η γυναίκα δεν παντρεύεται). An
attractive girl who could not provide a dwelling however minimal could hardly expect marriage, people said, while one who
had a house but very little personal charm had better prospects.
The worried parent of an unmarried 20-year-old girl concluded
that, 'Furnishing, everything else can be found when you have
a house, but without it, everything else is difficult' ('Έπιπλα, όλα
γίνονται όταν υπάρχει σπίτι αλλά χωρίς σπίτι όλα είναι δύσκολα).

As a consequence of the form of dowry, the groom in Yerania
moved out of his parents' home and usually lived with or close
to the bride's kinsfolk. The provision of dowry in the form of
living quarters, therefore, determined the composition of the
local group: those who lived in close proximity were usually
related through women not men (see pp. 158–9). In part, the
adaptability of the type of house in Yerania accounts for this
but other factors too played a part in producing the predominant pattern. Some of these pertain to more general conditions
in Greek society for Yerania is by no means unique in having
residential concentrations of families related through female
kin. In fact the house as dowry is a common feature throughout
the city.

The Dowry House

A complex set of factors can be seen to bear upon the provision
of a 'house' in Yerania. Economic resources were clearly
extremely limited throughout the history of this district, and
the means of livelihood precarious. The house represented a
resource of practical utilitarian value as well as embodying central cultural notions regarding family integrity and independence. Its particular significance can only be appreciated,
however, in the light of the wider historical and social setting.

In the major urban centres of Greece—Athens and Salonika—

housing shortages were endemic, predating even the tremendous, sudden influx of population caused by the Asia Minor
débâcle. Athens in 1920, for example, had an estimated ratio of
ten persons per dwelling; Salonika suffered a catastrophic fire
in 1917 which destroyed entire areas of the city leaving thousands homeless. The arrival of the refugees from 1922 onwards
simply exacerbated, to an extreme degree, a problem already
present in both cities. The provision of housing never caught
up entirely with real needs as large-scale migration from the
countryside, provoked initially by the Civil War, continued at
an increasing pace through the 1950s and 1960s. Thus, demand
for shelter in the cities has been a constant factor and has
enhanced the intrinsic utility value of home ownership.

The country's economic vicissitudes over the past fifty years
have affected attitudes to real-estate ownership and to various
kinds of property. High land values already characteristic of
densely populated urban areas further reinforce the economic
evaluation of home ownership. In the absence of adequate state
welfare provisions for the poor, the insecurity of a tenant's position in rented accommodation was sharply felt. As one Yerania
man put it, 'You can economize on food but not on rent. If you
can't meet your rent payments your family will be out on the
streets at the mercy of God.'

Combined with this endemic sense of economic insecurity,
other forces, derived from cultural precepts regarding the
values of family life and of home territory, reinforced the
perception of the centrality of the house. The abhorrence for
paying rent was related to the marked emphasis on the independence of each family-based household in Yerania. The position of a tenant, paying rent to the owner of a dwelling, was
seen as one of dependence and rank inferiority. The head of the
family (νοικοκύρης, lit. 'lord in/of the house') should be master
of the house—but the tenant cannot be. It is interesting that
even where a house purchase may not have represented the
best use of resources in economic terms (and rents in Yerania
were low in comparison with earnings: about 1,000 drs. would
get a three-roomed house with courtyard, or a new two-roomed
flat), it was none the less given unquestioned priority.

Another factor directly connected with a house as dowry was
the division of labour. In this urban district married women

were not expected to play any part in the economic support of the family. In the provision of the family's shelter by the wife at the time of marriage, however, the complementarity of male and female roles was expressed. The *past* efforts of the wife's family are represented in this substantial economic contribution while the husband's responsibility is directed to the *future* support of the newly-established household. The differentiation between initial provision and subsequent maintenance, with the wife laying a secure economic foundation and the husband being allocated a continuing role, reflects also the equivalence of their contributions. In this as in other aspects of social life, the marital relationship is founded in complementarity. The emphasis on home ownership must be understood in the wider context of values involving gender roles, the independence of the nuclear family, and considerations of relative rank, and not simply as the response to urban living conditions and the economic pressures which prevailed over several decades.

In the case of the urban refugees, however, another factor also influenced the nature of dowry provision. In so far as records exist, they show the early demographic imbalance in the refugee population. In four urban refugee quarters of Athens and Piraeus, including Kokkinia, a marked shortage of men in the adult age groups existed in 1926 due to the conditions of the flight and of war-time experiences (Table 1, p. 38). The high proportion of widows (25 per cent) in the adult refugee population was an additional feature. Since these women with children would have qualified for housing, a competitive situation may have arisen in the urban quarters related to the remarriage of widows, a shortage of adult men, and the need to provide dowry for daughters. At the very earliest stage of settlement young widows may possibly have had an advantage since they were able to offer a home to a man on remarriage. Parents with limited resources and marriageable daughters may possibly have employed a similar strategy in order to attract a groom, by offering part of the family dwelling. Some parents who had salvaged or accumulated wealth were able to marry off their daughters more easily. But for most families during the early period of settlement when thousands awaited some form of housing, even ten years after arrival, the offer of separate living quarters however inadequate by present standards could well have been the most appropriate and attractive dowry. The state of destitution of many families and the minimal level of earnings under sharply competitive conditions enhanced the value of a house, for it simultaneously met basic physical requirements and certain cultural prescriptions. One possible alternative (although culturally unacceptable) would have been to abandon the provision of dowry as an impossible expectation under the conditions of the period. This could have entirely prejudiced the girl's chances of marriage, however, and resulted in unmarried female dependants, or else have incurred a ruined social reputation (since female chastity was a major criterion of family honour).

Taken together, the force of historical circumstances, economic constraints, cultural prescriptions, and the particular demographic characteristics of this group all add up to an almost predictable result: after settlement, dowry continued to be provided—probably even more of a priority, given the lack of available men—and it took the form of the most highly valued asset in the circumstances, namely separate living quarters in the home of the bride's family.

Patterns in Dowry Provision

The distinctive character of Yerania which evolved through five decades was to a great extent the product of the interaction of durable cultural values with a particular type of housing adaptable to the changing needs of the inhabitants through time. Extensive modification of housing also reflected weak administrative controls since additional building was usually carried out illegally and few houses remained in an unmodified form by 1972. In Yerania the solution to the problem of dowry provision was developed with some ingenuity: the prefabricated houses proved eminently suitable for the creation of additional living quarters (see pp. 63–7). Thus, to provide dowries, several households could be accommodated on a single plot with little outlay or effort.

Although variations exist in each case, depending on the number of daughters, size of plot, historical events, and individual chance, common features in the provision of dowry can be summarized. Indeed, the process followed a characteristic pattern. The first and second daughters would be given the original prefab rooms on marriage, and their parents would take up residence in the basement rooms excavated to accommodate this expansion. Extra kitchens for the younger housewives would also be provided, usually as alcoves in the basement area. A younger daughter would be provided with a dowry house in the courtyard of the dwelling and, in time, even the next generation would be provided with dowry in a similar fashion. This procedure for the long-term provision of dowry is clearly illustrated by the history of the dwelling inhabited by the Yannides family (see Fig. 4).

THE YANNIDES FAMILY HISTORY

In 1928, just after the allocation of houses in Yerania, the Yannides family—parents, a daughter (Vasso) and two sons—solely occupied a dwelling with a large courtyard situated on the centre of a block (Fig. 4A). Over the next few years another son and two daughters, Anthi and Soula, were born. By 1938 eight people made up this single household (Fig. 4B). In 1940 the first subdivision took place when Vasso got married. Her dowry consisted of the front room of the house and when her husband, a Yerania man, moved in, they excavated a basement room under their own as a kitchen/living-room. The rest of the Yannides family occupied the two back rooms of the house. In 1940 two households and nine persons were resident on the plot (Fig. 4C).

During the war years the picture changed considerably. The three sons left home, joined the Resistance, and later married (into dowry houses provided by their wives). Vasso had a daughter, and Anthi got married. As her dowry, Anthi took over the two back rooms of the prefab house. The Yannides parents moved down into a second basement room excavated at the back of the house and occupied it with their youngest daughter, Soula. In 1950, when Anthi had a child, the dwelling contained three separate households and nine persons (Fig. 4D).

Five years later Soula was ready for marriage. Two rooms were constructed in the courtyard as her dowry home, one as a bedroom/living-room, the other as a kitchen. In 1955 eleven person lived on the plot, since Anthi had had another child. There were four separate households—the Yannides parents in their basement, and the three married sisters in their respective dowry quarters (Fig. 4E).

By 1960 Vasso's only child, a daughter, had reached marriageable age. As her parents had done before her, Vasso gave the front room of the house to her daughter and she moved her quarters down into the front basement. Two small kitchen alcoves were excavated partly under the pavement, one for Vasso and one for her newly married daughter. Now at its most crowded, the house in 1960 contained five households and twelve persons. Characteristically the older couples lived in the basement rooms and the younger married couples occupied the original dwelling and courtyard rooms (Fig. 4F).

By 1970 the number of occupants and households was declining: the Yannides parents had died, as had Vasso's husband. Vasso's daughter with two children was finding conditions too crowded in her portion of the house (one room and a kitchen alcove). As her husband's income was increasing they were keen to move out. Anthi's eldest daughter had married and left Yerania for Athens where she and her husband rented a small flat. Anthi, her husband, and younger child were still resident in their own quarters. Soula remained childless and lived in the courtyard house with her husband. At this time four separate households and ten residents occupied the plot. The use of the back basement, vacant since the parents' death, was being disputed (Fig. 4G).

In 1972, when I first got to know the family, only six people were resident in three households. Vasso lived alone in the front basement; her daughter and family had moved out, but their living quarters remained empty. Anthi had taken over the basement formerly occupied by her parents: her youngest daughter of 23 was preparing for marriage and would be given the two upper rooms of the dwelling, once Anthi's own dowry portion. Soula and her husband were still living in the courtyard house (Fig. 4H).

This example illustrates how dowry provision affected the composition and density of the domestic group at different points in the family's life cycle, as, in the course of time, the Yerania house came to contain a number of separate households.

Contemporary Dowry Strategies

Even in the early 1970s the dowry for many Yerania families consisted of separate living quarters in the bride's family house, so that the groom moved in to live with his in-laws while sons moved out to homes provided by their wives' families. But by 1972 a wider range of options had become available to Yerania families through the generally increasing affluence in the locality, with the granting of credit for the purchase of flats (previously unavailable) and, in the years of the junta

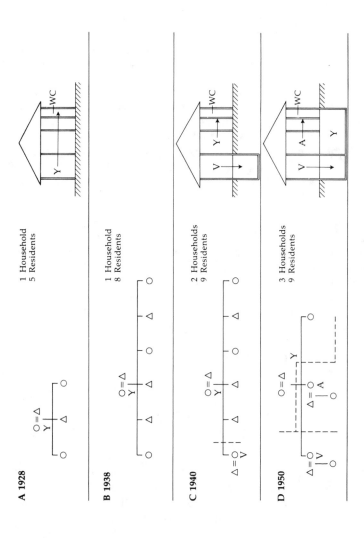

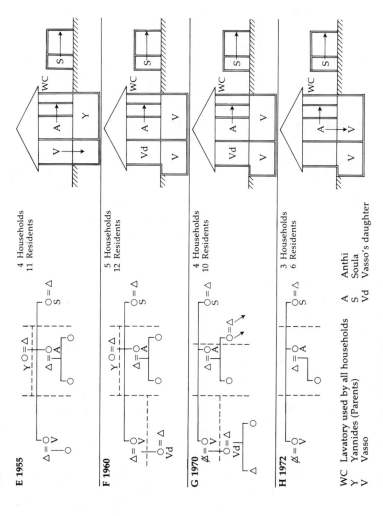

WC Lavatory used by all households   A   Anthi
Y   Yannides (Parents)   S   Soula
V   Vasso   Vd Vasso's daughter

FIG. 4. Yannides Family History, 1928–1972

government, of credit for landowners who wished to build on their own property. In a period of economic expansion the variety, type, and value of the dowry reflected these wider opportunities, and the family's initiative as well as its means.

It became possible, for example, to buy small plots of land on the outskirts of the city in places like Liossa, or Loutsa, or on the nearby island of Salamina where a small summer cottage could be built. Another possibility was to purchase a flat in nearby residential areas since, with the building boom, many new apartment blocks were being constructed here as in all parts of the city. Alternatively, a family could demolish the original pre-fabricated house and build a new family dwelling. This option, however, was only available for families who had bought the title rights to their plots and was usually ruled out in Yerania wherever subdivision of the house had occurred since co-resident families seldom agreed on contributing to this payment.

The newly-available alternatives required considerable cash sums: rebuilding the family home was the most costly, above the means of all but a few families (e.g., the family who inherited a million drachmas from an American relative, and the family who won a similar amount in the Christmas lottery). In 1972 construction of a two-storey building, 6 m. × 15 m., cost about 500,000 drs. and would have provided only one dowry residence in addition to the parental home (see Plate 4). Purchase of a new flat became possible at this time through the availability of credit but half the sum had to be given as an initial deposit. A two-roomed flat in the locality cost between 250,000 and 270,000 drs., again beyond the means of most families since furnishing, essential as part of the dowry, would have raised the dowry cost to over 300,000 drs.

Clearly, therefore, the family home itself remained the most important asset for purposes of the dowry, especially as urban land values continued to rise. But simple subdivision of the original residence was no longer an adequate offering for the next generation in a situation of 'dowry inflation'. Modern expectations dictated extensive renovation of the Yerania prefab dwelling at the very least as well as the addition of a bathroom, still an innovation in 1972. Alterations required about 30,000 drs. while a new set of furnishings cost another

60,000 to 80,000 drs.: the minimum expenditure, therefore, would still have amounted to over 100,000 drs.

The purchase of a small plot of land outside the city had also become a possibility for some Kokkinia families during the mid-1960s, particularly at Loutsa and Salamina where land values were low. Although this may not have been the original intention, it was clear that by 1972 some families with young daughters were planning to supplement dowry living-quarters in Yerania with a small, seaside cottage. At that time an average plot in Salamina (under 250 sq. m.) cost between 40,000 and 60,000 drs.; larger and better-situated ones ranged from about 80,000 drs. to 100,000 drs. A small deposit of 5,000 drs. with monthly payments over two years would secure a purchase and made it feasible even for poor families. Since these plots lay outside approved settlement zones, permanent structures could not be erected. The prefabricated houses which were put up, however, were in many cases substantial and solid buildings, very attractive additions to the intended dowry of a daughter. A simple summer cottage of prefabricated materials could be erected for 60,000 drs. and furnished at a reasonable cost, less than the furnishings required for the town home, and together the combination of urban living-quarters and seaside cottage, however modest, was considered sufficient to equip a daughter for an appropriate match.

The evidence shows that Yerania parents at all periods have desired to see their daughters and sons settled in marriage and have maintained their responsibility for this. They have approached the need to provide dowry with a degree of calculation and flexibility in order to obtain the most successful result under whatever current economic conditions. I maintain that the central concerns have been constant, but that the strategies and kinds of dowry have varied in response to opportunities and circumstances.

Indications exist, for example, that shortly after the Civil War (around 1950) some Yerania parents were keen to marry their sons to the daughters of villagers (preferably from families of Asia Minor origin). Following the war, the village girls' dowries consisting of gold coins represented a most attractive resource for townspeople. During the worst period of the Occupation and after, many urban families had been forced to barter all their possessions, coins, jewellery, and other valuables, to obtain food from villages as supplies ran out in the city. Thus, when peace returned, the most highly valued asset was realizable cash, especially needed to establish young men, now released from military service, in their own businesses.

Two examples illustrate this. Maria came from an olive-growing district near Lamia and in 1952 was married by arrangement to Tassos, the eldest of four brothers in a Yerania home. The family used her fifty gold coins to open a leather workshop for the sons; later the other boys married local girls with dowry dwellings. Olga was born in an Epirot village of refugee parents. They had connections in Kokkinia and she was married there in the early 1950s, bringing a dowry of gold coins which was used by her husband to purchase a vehicle for the haulage business.

Yerania family histories indicate how the priority of settling offspring in marriage led to a flexible attitude to dowries; their strategies have reflected current economic concerns, the particular needs of families, and their means. In the present period the continuing demand for dowry, the anxiety generated around the marriages of girls, and the increasing amount of wealth required, all suggest that a market situation with a shortage of men, acute in the early years of refugee settlement, has recurred in the post-war period when emigration abroad took place at an ever-increasing rate, especially from 1950 until the mid-1970s. Since younger unmarried men are more likely to emigrate than women, a resulting imbalance in the critical age group would produce an inflationary situation where fewer available young men make increasingly high demands for dowry.[2] Many parents and girls alike saw that provision as an essential precondition for marriage, and the indication of awareness that the girl's family were at a disadvantage was succinctly expressed by those who said, 'Nowadays it's the men who make the stipulations' (Σήμερα οι άντρες έχουν τις απαιτήσεις).

A House is Not Enough

Dowry demands are not necessarily stated explicitly but the expectations are recognized on all sides. For the girl's family it was not enough to provide only separate living quarters; the dowry had to include furniture too. Among the essential items provided by the bride's family was a formal dining-room suite consisting of a large rectangular table (1.3 m. × 1.5 m.), six matching chairs and a buffet-display cabinet, glossily varnished, and costing about 20,000 drs. in 1972. Even in the crowded conditions of Yerania homes the dining-suite was deemed essential and all families with more than one room at their disposal had the large ceremonial table, used for special occasions. Modern electrical appliances were provided wherever possible, often through the girl's own earnings, saved and supplemented by the family. The employment of young unmarried daughters undoubtedly reflected the considerable cost of even a modest dowry but, since 'She's working for her own things' (Γ*ια τα δικά της πράγματα δουλεύει*), and the goal was marriage, this activity was acceptable. Brothers were expected to contribute part of their earnings to a sister's dowry, and sisters would also help one another add to the large sums needed for expensive household appliances. The groom was expected to provide only the bedroom furniture at the time of marriage.

The joint contribution of a girl's family was reflected in the preparation of other items in her dowry, often for many years, even before the girl reached puberty. One elderly woman from Pergamos, crocheting yards of fine lace-edging for pillowcases for her 9-year-old granddaughter, quoted to me the homeland maxim, 'The baby in the cradle and the dowry in the trunk' (*Στην κούνια το μωρό και η προίκα στο μπαούλο*). Sheets, towels, table-cloths, and blankets were collected or made and stored by the mother years in advance, thus spreading the expense over a longer period. A series of popular Tupperware parties held in Yerania in the spring of 1972 revealed the characteristic forethought associated with dowry provision. Several mothers with young teenage girls were buying items to put away with other dowry objects, using their savings out of the weekly housekeeping money. After a Tupperware gathering one mother invited me home to see the items which had been accumulated for her eldest daughter. The impressive range, taking over an hour to unpack, included a large trunk full of matching sets of bed linen and towels, numerous table-cloths, blankets, a full set of Tupperware kitchen goods, and three imitation Persian rugs. A new washing-machine wrapped in polythene stood in the basement: several years of storage lay ahead for the aspiring bride was only 13 years old and in the final year of primary school! Her father spent every weekend on the island of Salamina supervising the construction of a summer cottage also intended as the girl's dowry.

The provision of dowry can be seen to have wide ramifications, from being a response to the shortage of housing and the need for shelter to being a focus of the corporate efforts of all family members; furthermore, since it became the determinant of residential proximity, the dowry affected all aspects of kinship relations.

Property without Ownership

'Ownership' is not an entirely appropriate term in this refugee locality since in 1972 the vast majority of Yerania houses were occupied by right only, not through full entitlement by concession. For the inhabitants themselves, however, ownership in the sense of exclusive rights to use was informally recognized. I was struck by their conduct which suggested that living quarters provided as dowries for daughters, informally and without contract, were treated as inalienable property by the rest of the family and others. Notwithstanding the absence of legal transactions, the dowry provision was considered as exclusive to the family created by that marriage. Even when vacated, these quarters were not used by other residents, regardless of the pressure on living space. In the shared dwellings where a daughter's family had left to live somewhere else this was particularly clear, as the following examples show:

Mr and Mrs Nikolaou lived in a dwelling shared with an unrelated family. They had given their only daughter their portion of the house, two back rooms, and had themselves moved into a basement room under it with a kitchen above. After twenty years during which three families lived on the plot sharing the toilet and courtyard (the Nikolaou couple, their daughter's family, the unrelated family) the daughter and family emigrated to Australia, leaving the oldest son, aged 18, in the care of grandparents. The old couple Nikolaou continued to live in their basement room despite the damp and its steep entrance steps. The grandson slept in the smallest room of his parents' quarters, which remained vacant but were regularly aired and cleaned by Mrs Nikolaou. Although she was not in good health and Mr Nikolaou, aged 70, had a heart condition, neither complained nor even contemplated using their daughter's ground-floor rooms for themselves.

Mr and Mrs Makris were another elderly couple living in a basement having given the whole of the dwelling to their only daughter on her marriage. Their unmarried son aged 40 still lived with them as part of the parental household. The married daughter's family had been living in Athens for the previous five years and only sometimes returned to Yerania for weekend visits. The ground-floor rooms were, therefore, unoccupied. Mrs Makris took regular care of them and again, the elderly couple did not consider reorganizing the living quarters although they both suffered the infirmities of old age and their basement rooms were poorly ventilated.

In these and other similar instances parents stated simply 'It is our daughter's' (*Της κόρης μας είναι*). Parents clearly felt that once a dowry had been given they had no right to claim it back or even to make use of the living space, despite the discomforts which they might be suffering. Even in the absence of full legal entitlement the marital home was regarded as exclusive to the family which occupied it. Furthermore, it appeared that inherited rights to a portion of the dwelling were recognized. For example, in one very crowded Yerania house shared by separate but related households, an elderly widow died leaving vacant the single room which had been her home. The other occupants went to great lengths to trace her heirs. Her only son had long ago left Yerania and no relatives had visited her for years. None the less members of co-resident households in need of extra space scrupulously traced them before the room was taken over by other occupants.

The refugees' legal status regarding compensation undoubtedly played a part in regarding a family's living quarters as separate and inalienable. Since the government would not recognize claims for compensation by refugees who had voluntarily moved out of their houses, the preservation of a family's quarters helped retain refugee status on behalf of an absent family. Thus the informal recognition of 'ownership' acted to preserve refugee rights *vis-à-vis* the authorities, given their continuing claims for compensation, especially for adequate housing.

But another aspect also exists, the symbolic association of the house or living quarters with the family, where it represented the independent existence of the family. When vacated it remained unoccupied despite pressure on space and the needs of the aged. The empty house stood as a spatial reminder of the absent family. Were these living quarters to be reallocated or used, the autonomy of the absent family would be violated. In some sense, the house is the spatial, material expression of the life and existence of the family (cf. du Boulay 1974: 17 ff.).

A revealing case shows how the integrity of the family was bound up with the recognition of its exclusive space. A married woman abandoned her husband and child and went to live in another part of Piraeus with a lover. Her husband, a Yerania man, returned to his parents' home with their child. The woman's widowed mother and her married sister, co-occupants in the house, then took over the quarters she had received as dowry, threw out the furnishings, and decorated and completely renovated it. These measures, expunging the woman's disgrace and the shame of a broken marriage, suggested an act of catharsis.

In this chapter various aspects of the house in Yerania have been discussed. The house was the key to understanding patterns of residence: it became the major economic asset for these dispossessed people and provided living quarters for the dowry of daughters. These factors can only be comprehended in the context of values regarding marriage. The preference for arranged marriage by the formal procedure of *proxenió*, I have argued, reflected concern with family stability and the permanence of the marriage bond. Marriages should be set up on a sound practical basis, it was believed; thus, the guidance of the older generation and their active involvement were required in negotiations regarding the material assets upon which the match would be based. Personal qualities were not disregarded, however, nor were the feelings of the potential spouses. Romantic love, a disruptive force from which young people needed to be protected, was considered dangerous, and an unsuitable basis for marriage.

The house stood also for the autonomy and integrity of the

family. The abhorrence of paying rent and the preference for being 'master of the house' reflected the desire for autonomy already noted in economic spheres of activity. When living quarters in the parental home were given as dowry, the preservation of an absent family's living space as inviolate property, even under extreme pressure of space, reflected both respect for the symbolic connection of the house and the family (an ancient etymological link exists in the terms for house (οἶκος) and family (οικογένεια)), and the staking out of claims for compensation and better housing. The significance of the Yerania house in physical and material terms can be more fully understood by examining further its social and symbolic dimensions.

7

THE HOUSE
Symbolic and Social Worlds

Previous chapters have indicated the political importance of the house in the refugee experience, its flexibility in providing shelter, and hence its negotiability in strategies surrounding marriage as well as its symbolic association with the autonomy of the family. In Yerania the house became the locus of an integrated social and symbolic world. It provided the central point of orientation for individual identity and emotional attachments. Family and kinship relations centred here, their organization resting on the complementarity of gender and age categories. In examining Yerania homes further, the principles which define the social personality and roles of men and women, the autonomy of the household, patterns of relationships between kin and affines, and the salience of symbolic categories also become clear.

Symbolic Furniture

As already noted, the original single dwelling and plot in Yerania usually came to contain a number of independent households. This expansion of accommodation came about through extensive modification and reallocation of living space, the excavation of basement rooms and alcoves, and the addition of extra rooms in courtyards. There was a tremendous increase in living area (total floor area increased by an estimated 117 per cent), but even so, most rooms in Yerania houses had to serve various functions. The original kitchen of the prefab house, often enlarged, was usually converted into a bed-living room in many cases, while the two main rooms, provided originally as a reception and bedroom respectively, were used in various combinations for sleeping, reception, eating, and for food and household storage.

The jumble of different uses in these rooms led to an odd mixture of furnishings. Entering, one was immediately impressed by the scrupulously neat and clean appearance, by the congestion and lack of free space, but most of all by the orderly arrangement of incongruous furnishings. The main room where visitors were received, for example, was inevitably crowded. Typically it contained a central dining-table, six matching chairs, a buffet-display cabinet glittering with rows of decorative china and glass, one or two sofa-divans (beds for children) and a clothes alcove in a corner. Another typical arrangement would include the central dining-table with six chairs, a single bed, a wardrobe, a refrigerator, and some occasional chairs. In a household with even less space, the main room might contain the dining-table and chairs, the double bed of the couple, as well as a wardrobe or fridge, and might have only 10 per cent of the floor area free for circulation.

The use of items in these rooms was also interesting. In terms of frequency or duration of use the main room would qualify as a bedroom or storage area. Its actual significance, however, lay in its use as a formal reception room since the most important item was the dining-table where the formal gestures of hospitality were performed. The glossy dining-table was an essential item of furnishing in a Yerania home. Thus, the main room was presented and preserved as a reception area, regardless of the other uses to which it was more frequently put. If a choice had been possible the Yeraniots would undoubtedly have allocated separate rooms for reception, sleeping, eating, and food preparation but extreme pressure on space had dictated that different uses be accommodated in the same room. Consequently, at first sight, the functional confusion in Yerania rooms suggested an unconsidered approach to spatial arrangements.

This attitude to interior space was also characterized by the impractical, solid items of furniture considered essential, without which the home would have been incomplete. Here, conventional expectations obviously played a part. One housewife, for example, whom I complimented on her spacious reception room with its low coffee-table instead of the central dining-table, responded apologetically that this was a source of embarrassment—they were saving to buy a full dining suite, for, 'How can you receive people into your house without one?'

Oddly in Yerania homes easily stored items (convertible or foldable beds, folding chairs) were not adopted even under the long-term conditions of crowding. In Yerania, space-saving furnishings were far from common although they were available on the market, a contrast, for example, with the minimal furnishings used in compact, crowded Japanese homes.

It took me a while to interpret this apparently irrational and impractical attitude to household interiors. The key lay in the house's symbolic attributes, where practical or rational considerations are subordinated to metaphysical issues. In non-Western societies the house is recognized as a 'cosmic building', a 'transcendent space' (cf. Eliade 1959; Raglan 1964). Yerania homes too cannot be understood simply as secular structures; the use of space and furnishings was patterned on the symbolic world and expressed a sacred dimension in everyday contexts. Thus, two different levels of reality coexisted in the multi-purpose rooms with their unwieldy furnishings; on the one hand the room served an everyday, practical function and on the other, its furnishing had an expressive function, a symbolic significance superseding mundane considerations. In the face of apparent functional confusion there was another level, of distinct symbolic clarity.

Tables, Beds, Chairs, and Icons

Among the items considered essential in the home were the dining suite, the bedroom suite, numerous chairs, and the *iconostási*, the icon-shelf, and each represented the metaphysical dimension present in everyday life.

The dining suite ($\tau\rho\alpha\pi\varepsilon\zeta\alpha\rho\acute{\iota}\alpha$) is suggestive. An item of considerable expense, it was an integral part of the bride's dowry and without it the house was not properly equipped. Over two-thirds of the houses had a large dining-table (1.3m. × 1.5m. × 0.8m. on average), and usually an entire suite of six matching chairs and a buffet-display cabinet. This large table potentially offered a useful working surface (food preparation, ironing), but in fact Yerania housewives seldom used it for anything other than offering formal but infrequent hospitality. This was partly because kitchens, located in basement alcoves or attached to courtyard rooms, were too far away since the large table was accommodated in one of the main rooms. In most homes therefore, a smaller table usually foldable, was used for most purposes. Situated in the kitchen or the room nearest to it, this work-table was always covered by a brightly coloured plastic cloth printed with designs of fruit, fish on platters, or other motifs representing food. In contrast, the formal dining-table was always covered with a textile cloth of velvet or hand-embroidered cotton and usually carried a vase of bright, plastic flowers as the centre-piece. This difference served to underline the separate purposes of these two items of furniture, the one predominantly utilitarian, the other an object for ceremonial or ritual use.

The significance of the meal, of commensality, in Greek culture sheds further light on the importance of the large dining-table. In Yerania houses an icon of the Last Supper hung on the wall over or near the table. Sometimes a comment would make explicit the parallel between Christ feeding his disciples, the Communion service, and the food shared at a meal. Before eating, the sign of the Cross was customarily made. Bread was always served with every meal and it was treated as a special substance. Pieces which remained were never thrown away and if bread was dropped on the floor it would be kissed. Every meal, daily as well as festive, was clearly patterned on a sacramental basis, that of the Eucharist or Communion service (cf. Campbell 1964: 341; du Boulay 1974: 54–5). This major sacrament in Orthodox Christian practice provides the charter for the common participation in food and drink, which sanctifies and raises it to another level of experience.

Taken in this light, the dining suite provided by the bride indicated specific values attached to her new role in the home: the provision of sustenance for the family and the offering of hospitality to outsiders. (Normally, a man did not offer refreshments to visitors but was served along with them by his wife.) People spoke of the formal meal which marked special occasions—weddings, baptisms, funerals, name-days, and other celebrations—as 'making a table' (κάνοντας τραπέζι). Thus: 'I'm making a table for Dimitris's name-day' (κάνω τραπέζι για την γιορτή του Δημήτρη), as if the ritual offering of hospitality contributed towards the construction of the table. This verbal idiom suggests that the physical object is in some way incomplete in itself, and that it requires ritual involvement to take on its complete form.

While the dining suite was associated with the bride's nurturing role, the groom was expected to provide for the marital home. The symbolism of the marital bed and its association with the groom, I suggest, underlines his role in creating a new line of descendants, maintaining the family's identity through its name, and giving it continuity through time. In Yerania homes the marital bed was a space-consuming item, sometimes taking up about a third of the room's floor area and never less than one-fifth of it. This bed was not, however, used for seating. People were always offered chairs or ushered onto sofa beds; I was told that it was not done to sit on the marital bed. Treated as a special object, set apart, its particular form and use suggested again a dimension beyond that of practical necessity.

Indeed, the marital bed was itself celebrated in a special ritual a few days before the wedding (usually the Thursday preceding the Sunday ceremony). Young people of both sexes, friends and relatives of the couple, were invited to the new home to a party 'for the bed' (για το κρεββάτι). The bed would be made up by young unmarried girls as everyone gathered round to watch. Sometimes one of the men present would try to undo their work so that a struggle over the sheets would take place. Then a little boy would be thrown onto the prepared bed amid cheers. Everyone present would throw money onto the bed and then refreshments were served. On such occasions, young people have time to chat, new acquaintances can be made and possible matches be initiated.

The ritual practices associated with the bed were indicative of its significance: the farewell to virginity (the unmarried girls, the struggle for the sheets), the wish for prosperity (money gifts) and for offspring (the little boy). The marital bed contains the sexual union of man and wife, a union which is seen as a religious bond, with a sacramental significance. The bed is part of this ritual dimension of the conjugal bond. It also comes to represent the unity of the marriage: to vacate the bed after a row and to sleep separately was taken as a serious rift. The treatment and use of the marital bed, therefore, reflected values of a sacramental character related to marriage, procreation, and to conjugal unity.

Chairs were another item of furnishing demanding interpretation. The kind of chair referred to here—wooden,
straight-backed, rush-seated, and uncomfortable—is familiar
to all who know Greece. It does not stack or fold, and yet these
chairs predominated in all Yerania houses. They are sturdy,
small, and lightweight, which may account for their popularity, which is undoubtedly reinforced by customary seating
habits and convention (Thakurdesai 1974). Once again the
presence of these chairs strikes one's attention, not because of
their size this time, but because of numbers. Households were
well endowed with chairs—an average of three chairs per head
was calculated. One household with three persons, however,
had sixteen chairs, another of four persons had thirteen. These
figures can only be interpreted in the context of values emphasizing neighbourhood exchange and sociability: chairs are
essential for daily contacts with neighbours and other visitors.
Every afternoon during the warmer seasons (about eight
months of the year) they are brought out onto the pavements
where they are offered to those passers-by whose company is
desired. Despite the crowded rooms, far more chairs existed
than were required for the family's needs alone. Thus, the
chair represents the need for communication with the wider
world, with others outside the home, and it expresses the
value placed on communal life and participation. Further, its
significance derived from its ability to bridge the divide
between 'house' and 'road', between family and outside
world. The chair offered for company on the pavement
mediated the opposition, symbolic as well as social, between
these two contexts, by extending the house's boundaries into
the road.

Yet another indication of the symbolic richness of Yerania
houses was evident in the *iconostási*, a small shelf or alcove
adorned with lace curtains, usually in one of the main rooms
and properly located in an eastern corner. Despite Kokkinia's
reputation as a left-wing locality, and although the degree of
overt religious observance varied widely, no household was
without a niche for icons and other holy substances. Even in the
least devout homes, attention was paid to the *iconostási* twice a
year at the major festivals. The oil lamp (*kandíli*) suspended in
front of it would be lit at that time; in the homes of devout

women, it was lit every evening or at least every Saturday evening. Other sacred substances kept on the icon shelf included a phial of holy water (αγιασμός), usually renewed once a month, sprigs of dried flowers which have adorned special icons, the twig given as a palm on Palm Sunday, and other items from shrines throughout the country. The housewife was responsible for maintaining the stock of holy substances, the spiritual resources of the household used in protecting members of the family.

The icons on the *iconostási* provided further insights. They varied in number from two or three to over a dozen, some of which were heirlooms preserved in the flight from Asia Minor, others cheap paper versions sold locally by itinerant vendors or at country shrines. Essential among these were icons of Christ and of his mother, the *Panayía*, the 'All Holy One', as she is most usually called by Greeks. The figure of the *Panayía* had a special significance for the women of the locality, and provided the archetype of redeemed womanhood. The total world represented by the house, as microcosm, is borne out too, by the correspondence between the house and cosmos, the woman and the *Panayía*. One articulate woman expressed it well: 'The *Panayía* is for the house. Can there be a house without a mother? So the *Panayía* is the mother of all the world (*Η Παναγία είναι για το σπίτι. Υπάρχει σπίτι χωρίς μάνα; Η Παναγία είναι μάνα για όλον τον κόσμο*).

These sacred points of reference in the Yerania house reminded its inhabitants constantly of the presence of another dimension, the metaphysical realm, an area of experience beyond that of the tangible world. But in it, the spiritual dimension was not separated from the everyday concerns of life. Indeed, it is a fundamental precept of Orthodox thought that the material and spiritual worlds interact and are unified. In holding out against the pressures for rational and practical solutions to the use of space, Yerania homes preserved the precepts of their religious tradition. The sacramental nature of commensality and of the conjugal union, the symbolic importance of sociability and exchange, were represented in material form by the dining-table, the marital bed, and the numerous chairs, while the presence of the *iconostási* endowed the house with its sacred character.

9. Before the roads were tarred and traffic increased, the unpaved side-streets were used for recreation

10. Afternoon gathering on a side-street before roadworks started

11. Men spend time at coffee shops

12. Women enjoy sociable contact outside their homes. Clothes and
fabric are appropriate to the stage in the life cycle

13. Afternoons are for leisurely social contact. This woman will not be alone for long

14. Three-wheeled vehicles used in the haulage and transport business favoured by entrepreneurs

15. Neighbours chat and pass the time

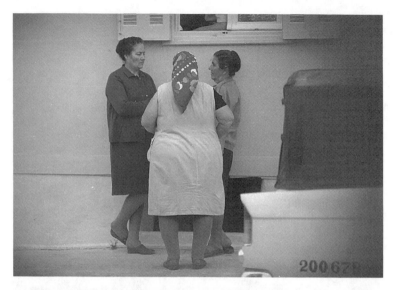

16. Gossip is inevitable—and essential—for women are active in the dissemination of news through the locality, and in the assessment of the reputations of other families

Men and Women: Complementarity and Asymmetry

In Yerania, as in Kokkinia and indeed all over Greece, the separation of men and women in activity and in conceptual terms pervaded all aspects of life in the 1970s. The gender dichotomy is a fundamental ordering principle in Greek life, its rationale derived from a number of sources; possibly its foundation in the cultural interpretation of biological differences felt to be immutable and part of the natural order, gives this a particular intractability. In this way of thinking, men and women are endowed with entirely different natures. With different bodies and physiological capacities, their physical natures are entirely distinct, a difference which extends to all aspects of their being. Following this, their emotional constitutions are construed as essentially different, and their symbolic attributes are correspondingly distinguished (cf. Hirschon 1978). Since men and women are endowed by nature with different capacities and capabilities, they are not interchangeable entities; they do not and cannot replace one another. They are created as unique and distinct; their relationship is defined as one of complementarity, of fundamental interdependence. Each is essential to the other and at the time of adulthood this complementarity must be met. The single adult is incomplete, whether male or female. It is as a married couple that a man and woman form a totality. This helps explain the emphasis on marriage as an imperative and it follows from this, too, that there is no complete state achieved by the single individual. Each person is always part of a family unit.[1] Indeed, I would argue that the notion of the single individual as it is understood in the West may still be inappropriate for understanding contemporary Greek society, even with the rapid changes which have occurred in the 1980s.

According to these ideas, men and women as adult married persons have separate spheres of competence, of authority, and of fulfilment. The complementarity of the sexes is matched by the separation of their lives into distinct and essentially different sets of experience. In Kokkinia, these principles demarcated appropriate areas of activity for men and women both within and outside the home. Although there was a division between the home/family unit and the road/neighbourhood which applied in certain situations depending on time and context, a division which corresponds to a spatial dichotomy between 'public' and 'private' areas, it was not absolute and did not correlate with gender (cf. Chapter 10, n. 3). Thus women were not associated solely with the home, nor were they confined to the domestic, private realm. Rather, in my view, they acted in both private and public arenas, just as men did, but for different purposes. The attitudes to women's employment, considered inappropriate after marriage (see Chapter 5), might suggest that women's activities were to be solely domestic, located in the home. However, a most important dimension of married women's lives, particularly in later life, was their involvement in many ritual and religious observances which took them away from the home and, I suggest, gave them an accepted role in the public world, removed geographically and socially from home and neighbourhood.

My interpretation of roles in Kokkinia, therefore, does not rest on a correlation of gender with public/private but, rather, on the complementarity of men and women in all aspects of life, extending from the domestic to the public. This had a spatial expression, for men and women used different meeting-places in the neighbourhood (coffee shops and barbers' shops for men, grocers and hairdressers for women). Admittedly, the emphasis was not equal. Men were chiefly involved in matters outside the home, in economic activities (and, had circumstances in that period been different, in political action), while women were primarily concerned with affairs in the home and neighbourhood, their involvement in the public arena having a specifically religious purpose. Stating this in more abstract terms, women's public activities were related to the *spiritual* needs of the family while men's were directed to *material* and worldly concerns. A further general distinction should also be made since the emphasis varied according to stage in the life cycle. Economic pursuits were undertaken most vigorously by the *younger* married men whose families were in the expansion phase of the developmental cycle, while religious duties were undertaken chiefly by *older* women with married children, who were less involved in the struggle to improve their social and economic standing.

Complementarity implies functional interdependence. This was most evident in the activities surrounding the home and family. The relationship of men and women in the home entailed the provision of different services, related to cultural notions regarding their different capacities. Men were the providers of income, they were said to 'bring things into the home' (ο άντρας φέρνει πράματα στο σπίτι) and a husband's success was measured by his capacity to fill the home with things, or the money to buy them. The woman's role was to convert these items from the outside world into sustenance and comfort, to create an ordered environment in which the family could flourish. To explain the mutual dependence of men and women in the home, the house would be likened to a bird's nest: 'The male bird brings things to the nest, the female builds it. The male brings grass and twigs and the female makes the nest.'[2] Both spouses were essential for the home to function properly. As one woman put it, 'There can be no home without a woman. The woman warms the house, she is its golden quilt, covering and warming it and she is essential. But the man is also essential. He is the pillar of the house, he is its base.'[3]

Marriage was seen as a co-operative effort, essentially a working partnership founded on the separate qualities of men and women. The notion of incompetence further reinforced the separation of their activities. Since gender roles were defined in terms of 'natural' capacities rooted in biological difference, the tasks allocated to each were held to be the only possible ones. Men and women alike asserted that men were unable to deal with household chores, and that women were incompetent in dealing with the business world or political matters. The belief in incompetence is a powerful force for maintaining the status quo. In 1972, these views went largely unquestioned by the married adults I knew although some of the younger people queried them. They undoubtedly provided the guide-lines for an approach in which marriage was to be preserved as the stable foundation of social life.

This was further reflected in the pragmatic approach guiding the formalized arrangement of marriage, the *proxenió*, and in the explicit denouncement of romantic love, *érotas*, as an unsuitable and dangerous passion. Indeed erotic love and sexual interest were not considered an entirely appropriate bond between the spouses (see pp. 114–16). Love was said to develop through the common commitment to the family and its welfare, and in time the husband and wife would achieve a sense of understanding (συνεννόηση), the ability to arrive at mutual agreement. In old age the spouse as companion or comrade (σύντροφος) would provide company against the state of loneliness which falls to the widowed or single person. Though it is used in a positive and affectionate sense, the term 'companion' does not, however, convey individual compatibility or personal communication. It refers primarily to the state of harmony achieved after a shared life and long-term co-operative effort (see Frontispiece).

The roles of husband and wife in the home were defined clearly as separate and as complementary. Their status relationship, however, was not one of formal equality. At the formal level, the husband had ultimate authority over his wife and she was subordinate to his will and decisions, features which reflected the precepts of the previous Greek Family Law (changed by the socialist government elected in 1981) and which endowed the man, as head of the family, with considerable power over other family members. The subordinate position of women is also reflected in the fact that a woman's surname in Greek is always given in the genitive (possessive) case; she is either her father's or her husband's: thus, (ο Κύριος Μαύρος, η Κυρία Μαύρου, η Δεσποινίς Μαύρου) translate as Mr Black, Black's Mrs, and Black's Miss. In common speech, one often heard that women were 'inferior' (κατώτερες), and they were held to be the 'weaker sex', the 'weak link' (αδύνατο φύλο, αδύνατο μέρος). Women were expected to defer to men in final decisions, most evident in the district of Yerania where housing conditions forced clear articulation of principles and where each man had unchallenged authority over his household. There the autonomy of each marital household was maintained through the recognition of the husband's ultimate powers (see pp. 155–8).

The structurally subordinate position of women was reflected also in an interesting verbal idiom. In references to housework or accounting for the way they spend their time, women would say 'I have my obligations' (Έχω τις υποχρεώσεις μου). Men, however, did not use this phrase when speaking of family life. The significance of the idiom lies in the notion of the 'debt', since the word for obligation (υποχρέωση), contains the word for debt (χρέος). This highlights the asymmetry of male and female statuses. A woman's position in society, her attainment of full adulthood as mistress of the house (νοικοκυρά) depended upon marriage, and thus upon her husband. She was indebted to the family for her social existence, therefore, and also for the possibility of redeeming those inherent flaws in her nature which devotion to her roles as wife and mother could overcome. For the woman then this debt was one which could never be totally discharged.

Of course, another side to the picture exists since women do exercise considerable influence over men. Their more subtle power has both recognized and unacknowledged aspects. Thus both women and men would say, 'Women are in command— they decide' (H γυναίκα κάνει κουμάντο, εκείνη ορίζει). It was clear that within the home women had autonomy in certain matters, those relating to household management and to the spiritual welfare of the family. The household budget, for example, was almost without exception under the control of the wife. In some families she was allocated a sum by her husband (who kept the rest of his earnings), in others all family earnings were turned over to her and she set aside the sums needed for various purposes. In all homes, expenditure for food, household maintenance, and clothing requirements were decided upon by the housewife, except if she had proved herself an untrustworthy spendthrift (only one case was known to me). Even though husbands were said to have the final word in matters of major expense, wives would be involved in the preceding discussions where their influence would be considerable. Each woman prided herself on her skills in this: 'I have my way' she would say cryptically (Έχω τον τρόπο μου). With its innuendoes of sexual cajolery, the 'way' was never openly discussed in my presence.

In a poor locality where every penny counted, the control of household resources conferred a position of considerable power. Women had autonomy in allocating sums from the budget for expenditure as well as for savings (for excursions of their own or for adding to a daughter's dowry). They took pride in their ability to budget thriftily, an essential quality complementing the husband's earning efforts. If the wife were profligate, his endeavours would come to nothing. Thus women and men readily concurred with the common saying, 'Everything depends upon the woman: she can make her husband or she can ruin him' (*Όλα εξαρτώνται απ' την γυναίκα. Εκείνη φτιάχνει τον άντρα ή τον χαλάει*).

Again, as with a woman's 'way', nuances were attached to the belief in a woman's ability to make or ruin a man. These attached to the general belief in the destructive potential of her sexual nature (see p. 149). These notions present a paradox in the light of her status of inferiority in formal terms and ideas about women's weakness and vulnerability.

Gender and Symbolic States

The cultural definition of gender, built upon perceived differences in biological attributes, was part of a wider set of notions of a metaphorical and symbolic order. These notions were expressed figuratively in two contrasting spatial metaphors, the 'open' and the 'closed'. Corresponding with this was what I have called two modes of orientation, ways in which social relations were ordered. The metaphors are commonly used and apply to a number of different contexts, they constitute indigenous categories; the modes of orientation are an analytical construct, based on observations and interpretations of patterns of social behaviour in different contexts (discussed more fully in Chapters 8, 9, and 10).

The notion of open and closed states as related to gender reflected the asymmetry of men and women's lives. Openness, a metaphor with positive connotations—associated linguistically with the divine realm, with new life, light, luck, sociability (see pp. 235–7)—was used idiomatically to express the state of marriage for women. On marriage a woman was said to 'open a house' (*ανοίγει σπίτι*) and it was the highest aspiration for her, for within marriage she was mistress of her own household. The Greek term *noikokyrá*, inadequately translated as 'housewife', is a position to which women aspired. Through marriage and in conjunction with one man, her husband, a woman achieved this state and, with it, the potential for procreation and for redemption of her nature. The sense of unending obligations, the debt which cannot be fully discharged, was also contained in these sets of notions.

Men, on the other hand, were not urged to 'marry and open a house'. For them the equivalent wish was to 'have a family' (*να κάνεις οικογένεια*) indicating the primacy of their role in perpetuating the family's line, particularly through the name. The absence of men is expressed idiomatically with the negative state of closure. Thus when the Greek Army was mobilized in 1974 with the Turkish army's invasion of Cyprus, I heard women weeping at the docks and railway stations saying 'Now we close our houses' (*Τώρα θα κλείσουμε τα σπίτια μας*). This phrase was also used to signify the end of a family's line with the death of an only son. Alexander Onassis's accidental death, for example, was said to have 'closed the house' of the wealthy shipowner (*Έκλεισε το σπίτι του*).

The state of openness conveyed by marriage has two connotations. One is a purely social aspect, the fact that marriage is the creation of a new social unit, an autonomous household, which enlarges the social field and implies the continuity of society itself. For the woman marriage held the promise that she would 'go out into society' (*θα βγει στην κοινωνία*). Her husband was the one who would 'take her out' (*θα την βγάλει έξω*). The status of a married woman conferred a kind of freedom, with the autonomy gained as mistress of her house. Furthermore, once married, neighbourhood life with its explicit injunctions to sociability occupied the major part of a woman's time (see Chapters 8 and 10).

The second set of notions associated with marriage and openness refer to the procreative aspect of marriage. Marriage has procreation as a primary aim; it means opening a new line, and confers continuity through time. For years young people have been told 'You get married to have children' (*Παντρεύεσαι για να κάνεις παιδιά*). Then from the first moments after the wedding ceremony they are repeatedly wished 'With children!' (*Με τέκνα!*). Childless couples, seen as incomplete units, were generally pitied, and considered extremely unfortunate. Young couples felt the continual social pressure; fear of sterility could only be allayed by the birth of a child and some young parents told me that they had decided to have the first child soon after marriage, before they felt quite ready, 'to stop people talking', or 'to keep the in-laws happy'.

This concern with childbearing and family continuity may

somewhat reflect the refugee experience, though it is also a general feature in Greek culture, for the emphasis on procreation is bound up with religious notions regarding the purpose of the sexual act and the definition of female sexuality. In Orthodox tradition the sexual act is considered polluting, requiring abstinence from Communion. It is somehow ambiguous, and was sometimes referred to as the 'evil act' (κακή πράξη). Again, however, translation misrepresents the word, for κακός is not 'evil' in the absolute sense conveyed by the English. (A parallel ambiguity exists in the English 'naughty'.)

The procreative purpose of female sexuality is also emphasized. It is a woman's destiny (προορισμός) to bear children, her path to fulfilment, since in motherhood a woman approaches the ideals represented by the archetypal figure of Mary, the Mother of God. Pregnancy is an admired state, a cause for pride (not shame as, for example, among Gypsies, see Okely 1975). Pregnant women and mothers of young children are treated with consideration and, especially in pregnancy, with a deference which contrasts with attitudes to them at other times.

Indeed, the positive connotations of the open state were used explicitly to denote the changes which marriage brings to a woman. A fusion of metaphorical and folk-physiological notions occurred so that the effects of marriage on a woman's body were characterized in terms of 'opening': with marriage, 'her body opens' (ανοίγει το σώμα της). Through childbearing a woman's body does actually open to allow for the growth and birth of the infant. Since Greek women tended to become plump, even matronly, in the first years of marriage, these notions were validated. Plumpness was also held to indicate well-being and good fortune. I have heard these ideas conflated and summarized: 'After marriage you become serene and so you get fatter. The body opens, that's why' (Όταν παντρεύεσαι ησυχάζεις και παχαίνεις. Ανοίγει το σώμα, γι' αυτό).

The vulnerability of women at certain times was held to be acute and was reflected in the rituals of seclusion after childbirth. The newly delivered mother (λεχώνα) was expected to remain at home with the infant for forty days following birth, a period terminated by a short service in church when the mother and child were blessed by the priest. In the old days in the homeland, a new bride was secluded at home for eight days after the

wedding. Recounting these customs older people would con-
nect these two states (cf. Hirschon 1978: 81). Both the bride and
the newly delivered mother were 'open' and therefore vulnerable, particularly to the dangers associated with social life and
the outside world.

The differences between men and women's sexuality were
seen as extensive and fundamental to their separate natures. In
the cultural interpretation of biological difference female and
male sexuality were held to be fundamentally different drives.
A man's sexual drive was held to be physiologically imperative,
uncontrollable, and diverted only with dire consequences (both
masturbation and homosexuality were said to lead to serious
mental and physical disorders). However, a woman's sexual
drive was believed to be subject to her conscious control.
Although recognized as a real force, provoking the parents of
adolescent girls into thoughts of early marriage, for 'the blood is
hot' (βράζει το αίμα), it was seen to be physiologically control-
lable. Typically it was said that 'a woman can last a hundred
years but a man cannot control himself' (Η γυναίκα εκατό χρόνια
να πάει, μπορεί να κρατηθεί, αλλά ο άντρας δεν κρατιέται). These
views make women responsible for maintaining the moral
code: since women have the power to control their sexual urges,
they are at fault when transgressions occur. For example, when
a wife learned of her husband's infidelity with a woman in the
locality, she said nothing to him but sought out the other
woman and attacked her physically, since she was the responsible party.

But women can only be the seducers if men are susceptible.
The recognition of a woman's sexual power reveals an area of
male vulnerability. The imperative nature of a man's sexual
drive casts the woman as a constant potential threat. Her
sexuality, if not properly controlled, might undermine her own
honour, that of her family, and destroy a man's integrity, sedu-
cing him away from his commitment to his own family. In various images woman was portrayed as a catastrophic force: 'Fear
only three things,' goes the proverb, 'fire, water and woman'
(Τρία πράματα να φοβάσai μόνο—φωτιά, νερό και γυναίκα). An
elderly woman, explaining these aspects of a woman's power,
put it graphically, 'She wags her tail and the whole world turns
upside down' (Κουνάει την ουρά της και ο κόσμος πάει πάνω κάτω).

Women in this view present a potential threat to the whole social order, they are powerful and dangerous.

Clear ideas associated women with restraint and control, with the creation and maintenance of harmony both within the home and in relations with others. Positive evaluations of a woman focused on her modesty and prudent comportment. A particular vice was 'to have a tongue' (ἔχει γλώσσα), or 'mouth' (στόμα), even to the extent of spoiling a girl's chance of marriage. It was said of Pitsa that her bad tongue had ruined her reputation and she would have difficulty finding a husband even though she was a 'good girl' and tidy in the house. Likewise, though an energetic and efficient housewife, Tasia was criticized by relatives and neighbours alike for her sharp tongue: 'With that tongue of hers she loses everything' (. . . τα χάνει όλα). The tongue causes havoc through gossip and quarrels: a woman's ability to keep silent even under provocation was considered an admirable virtue.

A woman's activities were very clearly specified and concentrated her daily efforts in maintaining the household. Her ability as a housewife within the domestic realm was a major criterion of her self-esteem and prestige. Although the house was an area of limited access, people could assess a housewife's competence from other things—the state of the courtyard, the pavement and street outside her home, the state of the family graves in the local cemetery, the appearance of her children's and husband's clothing, and her ability as a cook. The latter was judged through the frequent exchanges of small plates of food, samples of special dishes prepared for the family and given in return for favours to neighbours (see Chapter 8). One interesting insight was provided by my landlady who was from the Ankara region and had lived in Constantinople as a young married woman. Real culinary skill, she said, lay in making dishes such as *moussakás*, stuffed vegetables and vine leaves, very fine strudel-type pastry dishes (φύλλο), as well as the great variety of fruit and vegetable preserves, all of which involve many steps and hours of preparation. In the homeland, she said, grills and quickly prepared meals (της ώρας) were called 'prostitute's food' (της πουτάνας το φαΐ). The implication was clear: a woman's virtue can be demonstrated when her time is fully occupied in domestic tasks. Cooking and food preparation conventions can thus be seen as a mode of social control over women.

A woman's role in the home should be one of wise management regarding conservation of resources. She should be guided by the virtue of self-sacrifice, serving the needs of husband and children before her own, and be able to control her appetites and needs. Together with uncontrolled sensuality, greed was considered a serious flaw of character. It is involved with the banishment of Adam and Eve from Paradise, and, like sexual desire, it is a consuming appetite, one which can become an end in itself. Indulgence of that kind is not acceptable, though in Orthodox thought there should not be a denial of the flesh but its transformation. Neither the material world nor the body need be rejected as evil but they must be transformed and imbued with spiritual values (Ware 1979: 63–4, 79–80). Thus, sexuality has a procreative end, eating and drinking become a ritual of communion. In Orthodoxy the aim is to transform the weaker, fallen aspect of human nature and this is achieved partly by attention to the roles ordained for men and women.

For women, in symbolic terms two archetypal figures present images of womanhood, that of Eve in the Old Testament, and that of Mary in the New Testament. The figure of Eve represents the unregenerate female, submitting to temptation, weak, and given to sensuality. Eve embodies the dangerous element in woman's nature, its potential for chaos and destruction. Mary, on the other hand, represents the redeeming power of female qualities, the submission to divine will, the image of purity, of human perfectibility. Her willing acceptance of God's incarnation places her, to quote the most frequently used hymn in her praise, 'more honourable than the Cherubim, incomparably more glorious than the Seraphim'. Her subordination through active complicity in the divine plan has glorified all humankind. In Orthodox thought, Mary was fully human and had free will. She could, therefore, have refused but did not, and thus she made possible the redemption of the human condition. This active and simultaneously passive participation of Mary in the incarnation is of great importance in understanding the position of women in Greek thought. She appears subordinate and yet stands out among all human figures; for her

co-operation she is granted pre-eminence in the spiritual hierarchy, and yet this glory is deceptively silent.

The qualities of Mary conveyed in Orthodox iconography
emphasize her motherhood. By far the most common representations are those of Mary holding Christ as a child in various
poses and this icon was present in every home. Women
appealed to the *Panayía*, the All Holy One, for compassion, for
aid and intercession in everyday problems, and in crises of illness and sorrow since they felt able to identify with her. Significantly, she was seldom referred to as the 'Virgin' (*Παρθένα*).
Indeed, it is a noteworthy distinction between Eastern and
Western forms of Christianity that in the Eastern tradition Mary
is more often thought of and addressed as *Παναγία θεοτόκος*, All
Holy Mother of God (lit. God-bearer). In contrast with the Catholic tendency to portray her as a young girl and to dwell upon
her virginal quality, the Orthodox leans towards her maternal
aspects. I would argue that this difference in emphasis, both in
theology and in lay perceptions, results in subtle yet significant
differences in the position and experience of women in these
societies. For Orthodox women, some of the tension in the irre-
concilable contradiction between virginity and motherhood is
reduced. The Orthodox definition of the female role, giving pre-
eminence to the woman's childbearing capacity, alleviates the
ambiguous demands of these two contradictory female states.
Certainly women I knew did not appear to feel a burden of guilt
requiring a lifetime to expiate their inherited sin, nor were they
preoccupied with repentance, in contrast with attitudes
expressed in parts of the Catholic world (cf. Christian 1972;
Warner 1976: 224 ff.). Confession, a voluntary practice, was not
often undertaken. Religious duties were seen as part of the
expectations of a woman's role, tasks with a transcendent purpose, undertaken in a matter-of-fact way without self-conscious
piety.

The emphasis on control and restraint is a theme among the
ideals prescribing conduct for women and it can be read in
several ways. First, it constitutes an acknowledgement of
power, since the woman can maintain or destroy order through
her own volition. Secondly, it can be seen as a means of social
control over women since actions are circumscribed by a variety
of restrictions. Thirdly, this emphasis is part of a cosmology

offering women two opposing archetypes, Eve and Mary, with the possibility of aligning themselves more or less with either the negative or positive qualities associated with female nature. The particular character of Orthodox Christianity, in contrast with Western forms, provided for these women the possibility of overcoming the negative aspects of their nature as these were culturally defined. Associated with the archetypal seductress Eve, a woman's potential for destruction and disorder could be counteracted by continual reference to the life-giving and caring qualities associated with the archetypal mother, Mary.

Family Relationships: Co-residence and Autonomy

The house contained the joint effort of husband and wife for the creation, sustenance, and furtherance of the family. An ancient etymological link suggests the connection between house (οἶκος) and family (οἰκογένεια). What is interesting in Yerania is the subdivision of the physical structure into a number of different 'houses' strictly corresponding to the number of families/households on the plot. Given the closeness of living conditions, the exigencies of survival and the primary bonds of kinship which bound many of the co-resident households, co-operation within an extended family group might have been a feasible arrangement. But, strikingly, the co-residence of kin in Yerania homes did not result in joint households. On the contrary, the independent and autonomous existence of each elementary family was socially reinforced. After marriage the young couple constituted an entirely separate household, sharing only toilet facilities, with living quarters set aside for their sole use. Each constituted a separate unit of consumption with a separate budget based on the husband's earnings. The household included those who regularly ate together, and its existence was marked physically by the kitchen, however small, exclusive to each housewife.

The autonomy of each household was probably a response to economic forces and pressure on housing within a specific cultural setting. It could be that the dictates of economic conditions prevented any other form of family organization. Wage-earning in a restricted labour market and limitations on co-operative enterprise where capital and credit were lacking may help to explain the marked emphasis on family autarky in this locality. As a self-sufficient unit, the household revealed the importance of a husband's authority at its head as well as the clear division of labour of the sexes. With the stresses caused by housing, economic, and political difficulties in Yerania, concern with the permanence of marriage led to a clear definition of household boundaries and of the precepts which define residential group organization. The following analysis indicates how family stability was based on the minute demarcation of social and spatial boundaries.

Parents explicitly acknowledged the immediate separation of the new household once their child married. As several of the older parents put it, 'When you give your child away in marriage, he/she becomes independent' (Όταν δίνεις το παιδί σου στην παντρειά, νοικοκύρης/νοικοκυρά γίνεται). The term used, noikokýris/noikokyrá conveys autonomy and independence— etymologically, 'master/mistress of the house'. Ideally, parents would not interfere in the domestic life of the married child; if conflict between spouses occurred, they were expected to retain an impartial stance. Interference of any kind provoked criticism by family, affines, and neighbours alike. Thus, even in the close confines of co-resident related households, parents' neutrality was to be maintained, regardless of the objective justice of the situation. In these prefabricated houses, conversations were audible from one room to another, so that disagreements could not be hidden, but parents had to refrain from any kind of involvement. One mother, explaining how distressed she had been by the frequent quarrels of her daughter and son-in-law said, 'I'm a mother—but even so I never interfered' (Μάνα είμαι αλλά ποτές δεν ανακατέφτηκα). Ideally a mother would maintain impartiality and respond with exhortations to greater patience and fortitude (υπομονή, κουράγιο). When a married child confided problems, parents were to emphasize the positive aspects of the marriage, the spouse's good qualities, the children, or whatever might promote reconciliation, for the primary concern was to preserve stable family life.

THE ROW

These precepts are clearly illustrated in the case of one married couple, Tassos and Dimitra, who had formerly enjoyed a harmonious marriage. They began to face problems when Tassos's business fell off sharply and he was forced to close his shop. One day a row about money developed between him and his mother-in-law, a tactless woman who lived in the same house. Dimitra's indifference to the row irritated him and he left the house threatening not to return. By late evening he was still absent, so, in some consternation, Dimitra went to call on Tassos's mother who lived near by. She complained of Tassos's recent moods and depression, but although the older woman was aware of the reasons for her son's frustration, she listened quietly but barely commented. The next day Tassos appeared at his mother's door, having been away all night. She welcomed him and gave him a plate of food but far from showing him sympathy, she praised Dimitra's virtues, reminded him of their happy marriage, and advised him only to ignore his mother-in-law. Then she suggested that he return home at once. Later she explained to me that, as his mother, she naturally felt sympathy and recognized that some of his grievances were justified, but it was the spouses' own problem which they alone could resolve. In her view a parent's duty was to support the marriage bond itself, not the individuals; the objective justice of the situation was of secondary importance. A parent should avoid taking sides since this would only aggravate the division between the spouses.

The Groom's Position

It follows from these notions that parents were expected to accept the authority of their son-in-law as a household head. In Yerania a groom had the right to define his wife's activities, to limit her contacts, and to restrict her movements when he thought that his authority should be exercised. Provided that his own conduct was socially acceptable—and here the emphasis was on his responsibility for supporting the family—his authority was undisputed, regardless of his wife's parents' and siblings' presence in the same dwelling or on the same plot. Parental intervention would only be acceptable if the foundations of marriage were violated through abandonment, inadequate provisions, or violence, and then every effort would be made to effect a reconciliation. In the late 1960s and early 1970s divorce was resorted to only under the most extreme circumstances.

The fact that conflicts between co-resident families were common—many cases could be cited and tales of conflict were a major part of the repertoire of daily conversation in Yerania—

must reflect the tensions which were bound to arise in crowded flimsy houses with inadequate space and cramped facilities. Remarkably, marriage stability had been preserved in the face of these adverse living conditions, and it is probable that the emphatic definition of household autonomy was a response to the pressures on family life. The recognition of the husband's authority as head of the household provided a basis whereby the boundaries of obligation could be sharply delimited. Co-resident women who spent most of the day on the same plot did have many opportunities to co-operate, especially as they were often related as sisters, or as mother and daughters, but these contacts could be forbidden by the groom. The justification was that a woman's primary obligation was to her own family of marriage, in which all her energies should be concentrated. The situation of conflict which developed in a house in my neighbourhood clearly illustrates these patterns.

MARO'S ISOLATION

This corner house was shared by four separate households. Here eight adults lived under very crowded conditions since the plot was small and had been entirely built over (see Fig. 5). One toilet and washbasin was shared by all and, not surprisingly, relationships were under some strain. The longer-established households were those of two widowed sisters, Theodora (70) who kept house alone since her sons had left the dwelling on marriage, and Chara (63) who kept house with her unmarried son of 30. Chara's only daughter, Rosa (40), lived with her husband and an unmarried daughter in the basement. Their older daughter Maro (23) lived in the front room of the house given to her dowry on her marriage (previously Rosa's own dowry home).

Maro's husband Kostas was a metal-welder earning a good wage. They lived well, but the marriage of some five years was incomplete for they still had no children. One hot summer afternoon a disagreement between Kostas and his mother-in-law Rosa became increasingly vituperative. When she produced the ultimate insult, 'You are impotent!' (Είσαι ανίκανος), Kostas retaliated with some innuendo, 'Ask your daughter if I'm impotent—she's the one who can't have children' (Ρώτα την κόρη σου αν είμαι ανίκανος—εκείνη είναι που δεν κάνει παιδιά). Thereafter Kostas ignored Rosa entirely, forbade Maro contact with her family, and closed his home, the front room of the dwelling, where the family usually met in the evening to watch television.

Now a regular exodus took place at nightfall, as Chara, Theodora, Rosa, and her young daughter crossed the street to spend the evening

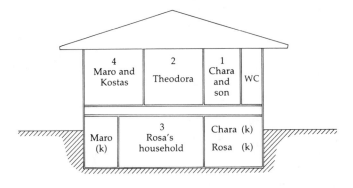

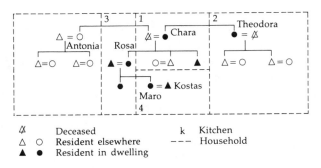

⚠	Deceased	k	Kitchen
△ ○	Resident elsewhere	---	Household
▲ ●	Resident in dwelling		

FIG. 5. Maro's Isolation

at the home of Antonia, sister of Chara's late husband. Since the other two men, Maro's father and her mother's brother, were usually in a coffee shop, Maro was left watching television alone or with her husband.

Two weeks after this incident, Chara's unmarried son (Maro's mother's brother) announced his engagement. Neighbourhood speculation centred on Kostas's reaction, since the families of the engaged couple planned expensive formal celebrations, but he was unyielding—neither he nor Maro would attend. On the evening of the engagement party a month later he returned home, and, ignoring the family, ordered a tearful Maro to get ready and took her out to visit friends of his who lived in another district.

Weeks passed but Kostas showed no signs of relenting. Since Maro was not short of money nor was she being neglected, family intervention was inappropriate. Her husband was within his rights in restricting her associations; indeed his reaction could be justified in the light of his mother-in-law's injudicious insult which might have led to further disruption if she were to continue her relationship with her daughter. Although the women of the family complained about Kostas and made threats over morning coffee to 'throw him out', they could do no such thing. Only Maro's father could have intervened but his daughter was not being ill-treated nor was she short of money so there were no grounds for him to do so.

In spite of the spatial proximity of these families whose close relationships potentially challenged the existence of independent nuclear family households, the recognized authority of the groom allowed him to create social distance by defining the boundaries of his household.

Co-resident Women

While it is true to say that each Yerania household was governed by its male head and that the wife was formally subordinate to him in all ultimate decisions, none the less a prime consequence of dowry provisions was that emotional support could and did continue between mothers, daughters, and sisters by virtue of their physical proximity after marriage. The bride was not isolated from her kin but derived support from the presence of close relatives and yet was granted full autonomy from them in her own living quarters. The close bond between mothers and daughters was reinforced through their common experience as married women; daughters often remained emotionally dependent on their mothers and relied on them for practical help and advice especially through pregnancy and childbirth, and with child-rearing. But the readjustment of obligations which marriage entails inevitably led to a separation of interests between related women. The family of marriage had to take prior claim to an individual's loyalties: relationships with spouses and children were given precedence over those with siblings or even parents. Since the integrity of the family unit was a central value, any criticism of one's spouse by parents or siblings was to be rejected, however well intentioned.

Even the intimacy which normally characterized the relationship of sisters through childhood and adolescence was gradually reduced after marriage. They could continue to co-operate

in household tasks and with child-care but the common identity which they once shared had ended, and, as each woman
became more involved in promoting the welfare of her own
family of marriage, their relationship tended to take on an
increasingly competitive tone. Rivalry between unrelated
women usually centred on housewifely competence while
between sisters it focused on the success of husbands and the
progress of children. Obviously variations existed, but this
general pattern of growing separation resulted from the emphatic boundaries drawn between households.

Co-resident Men

It is interesting to note, therefore, that these internal divisions
between households appear to be maintained more by the
women and not, as might be expected, by unrelated men, the
in-marrying grooms. In fact the relationships between these
men who marry sisters were notable for their general level of
amity and warmth, sharply contrasting with other relationships
created through marriage. In general, relationships between
affines were marked by degrees of mistrust and hostility. The
badzanákides, men who marry sisters, often formed friendships,
however, and attempted various forms of business collaboration. A common expression was 'my *badzanákis* is better than a
brother' (. . . *καλύτερος από αδελφό*). Indeed their desire to
retain close ties with each other was not always reciprocated by
their wives, the sisters. For example, Yiorgos and Christos
attempted to purchase a plot of land in Salamina. Together they
could have afforded a larger plot, but the objections brought by
the sisters indicated a clear reluctance to enter a long-term commitment. Although both families were on good terms, the plan
was finally abandoned. The close relationship of the *badzanákides*
was also sometimes expressed in the face of their wives' hostility.
When Prokopis's wife and her sister quarrelled during the Carnival, the family's joint festive meal was called off. Prokopis
returned from work that afternoon and was so upset that he sent
his son to the home of his *badzanákis* (they lived in different
houses) with a slice of bread on a plate and his greeting, com-
plaining 'How can I not eat with my *badzanákis* tonight?'
    It is not easy to account for the different responses of men and

women in these circumstances. Possibly the need to maintain harmony under conditions of high density, given the whole range of cultural prescriptions regarding family life and reputation, induced in the women the preference for reducing as far as possible the involvements which already existed daily and could not be avoided (cf. Wright 1981). Indeed, the importance women attached to separate kitchens can also be interpreted as a way of minimizing sources of conflict. Men possibly find it easier to adjust to the reorientation that marriage entails because of mobility and their more diffuse ties in the family. Men and boys are freer in their movements and contacts; in addition their employment usually means that they are absent from home for much of the day and they are not, therefore, subject to the continual presence of other persons in the vicinity.

The experience of men and women in Yerania houses was different since their prescribed roles and spheres of activity were so clearly separated. Within the family, as already noted, brothers and sisters were subject to different constraints and expectations. Unlike sisters who retained residential contact even after marriage, brothers were dispersed earlier through employment and army service and, although they remained in the parental home while single, the pressure was usually for an early marriage especially where dowry could only be provided by subdividing the family home. In this case, brothers were little involved in the marriages of sisters. However, the increasing affluence of the early 1970s and alternatives for dowry provision as well as the greater cash outlay required, meant that brothers and even sisters were making some contribution to dowries out of their cash earnings, thus reinforcing their joint involvement and interest in one another. Even so, married brothers had to make special efforts to maintain regular contact with their family of origin and they tended to meet mainly on family name-day celebrations.

Thus, one of the consequences of residential patterns which result from dowry provision is that brothers are seen as allied with their wives' families' interests, which are generally believed to prevail. For example, in cases where brothers could not reach agreement on a family matter such as contributing towards the payment of the 'concession' titles to the family home, people usually attributed this to the wives' influence over their husbands. This reveals an interesting facet of social relationships in Yerania: despite the recognition of overt male authority, many contexts existed in which women exercised considerable power. Here, they appeared to maintain the divisions between households. Men indicated their sense of inefficacy when they said that women 'have the devil in them' (Έχουν τον διάβολο μέσα τους). It is clear, then, from various aspects of life in Yerania, public as well as domestic, that women played a central and powerful role, complementary to that of men, one which was more complex than the simple attribution to them of a subordinate position in social life.

The 'In-law Problem'

Yerania parents were closely involved with their children: again, the power of family bonds and commitment may reflect a reaction against their refugee experience and the centripetal forces of urban existence. Thus a son's departure from the parental home after marriage was deeply regretted by his parents. Since employed men were at work and even the self-employed were occupied elsewhere, parents would usually see a son infrequently after his marriage unless he resided in the vicinity. Inevitably this soon led to complaints of neglect and dissatisfaction stemming from the presumed alienating influence of his wife. Indeed, the bride was in an invidious position, one of divided loyalty and conflicting ties, for she had to balance the expectations of her husband's parents and those of her own. Since women were held to be responsible for promoting harmony in social life, the onus fell upon her. Even if a young woman observed the obligations to her in-laws she would seldom be given credit, or else she would fall foul of criticism from her own parents claiming that too much attention was being paid to them. In some cases she would even have her attempts to reconcile these demands frustrated by her husband's indifference to this social pressure.

Clearly, therefore, the points of greatest structural tension in relationships were the positions of the daughter-in-law, *nýphi*, and mother-in-law, *petherá*. The groom's mother was caught in ambivalent feelings for her son's marriage: she would realize that the daughter-in-law's affections were centred in her own family of origin and she also recognized the influence a wife has over a husband. Thus, it was noticeable that after the wedding the *petherá* characteristically adopted a conciliatory attitude towards her *nýphi*. One elderly woman, somewhat of an expert with four married sons, expressed it succinctly, 'Daughters-in-law must be handled with kid gloves. Everything depends upon them—what they say goes' (*Με τα γάντια να τις έχεις. Όλα εξαρτώνται απ᾽αυτές—ό,τι θα πούνε γίνεται*). In many cases the tensions between *petherá* and *nýphi* had their origins in the period before marriage when dowry offerings were assessed. Many mothers tended to take a great interest in their son's marriage arrangements and they appeared to feel that their sons deserved larger dowries than those offered. Such views expressed before the marriage could have long lasting ill-effects. The girl who had to be diplomatically pleasant before the wedding would feel free to express her resentment after it. Secure in the presence of her own kinsfolk near by, she could show indifference or even hostility, while the groom's parents had to display goodwill, or risk increasing alienation from their son.

At the same time as a marriage creates a new social unit it reorders previously tightly knit relationships and it entails the realignment of personal loyalty and identity. In this process the relationship between the two sets of parents (*συμπέθεροι*) was generally less than harmonious. This is a consequence of two social concerns: the commitment to the furthering of family interests (*symphéron*), and the pragmatic emphasis on a sound economic basis for the marriage. Previously, the contact between co-parents-in-law had been part of the prenuptial negotiations regarding material provisions for the new household when they confronted one another from opposed, even antagonistic positions. Furthermore, parents were predisposed to suspect each other of collusion and secrecy with their respective child in accordance with precepts of family loyalty. For example, when Ritsa got married, an open row developed between the two sets of parents only hours after the wedding ceremony. The groom's mother arrived at the new home of the couple and started counting the wedding gifts which had just been transferred from the bride's home. When challenged by the bride's father she expressed her suspicion that some gifts had been retained by them. Later when Ritsa recounted the incident to her friends she admitted laughingly that her *petherá*'s fears were justified—Ritsa had already given some of the wedding presents to her mother!

The birth of grandchildren could be a point of mutual interest to consolidate the relationship between co-parents-in-law. Given their characteristic antagonism, however, it was more likely to be another source of rivalry and discord. As a consequence of dowry provision and post-marital residence patterns, paternal grandparents tended to see their grandchildren less frequently, while a much closer bond developed with maternal grandparents and other matrilateral kin. Besides accusing the *nýphi* of purposeful neglect, the husband's parents frequently expressed their dissatisfaction through criticism directed at their grandchildren's progress. Lack of manners, poor health, school problems were usually attributed to the incompetence of the *nýphi* or her parents.

Household and Family Boundaries

We have seen how the house was a central focus of each person's social life, loyalty was related to membership in the domestic group, and how kinship and affinal ties were subject to attenuation as residential distance increased. Household membership created exclusive ties, secrets were shared 'within the house', but the awareness of obligation to those related by kinship or marriage, wherever they lived, always persisted. An additional force which affected the conduct of Yerania's residents was their concern with preserving the family's reputation, a source of some anxiety since reputation was chiefly assessed by neighbours who were not necessarily favourably disposed. The characteristic relationships between kin and affines and the tensions associated with maintaining reputation in the immediate community are well illustrated by the truancy of Takis, a 14-year-old boy in the second form of the local high school.

THE CONCEALED TRUANCY

Quite unknown to his parents Orestes and Noula, Takis started playing truant with a class-mate about six weeks before the final exams of the school year. He was a bright student and had become bored in the school with its huge classes of over seventy pupils. His absence from school went unnoticed for two weeks but one day a class-mate mentioned to Tasia, a relative of Noula, that Takis had been away ill for a long time. Tasia lived in Chalkidona, about fifteen minutes walk from Yerania and worked as a upholsterer at home, so three days passed before she found time one morning to visit and enquire about Takis's absence from school. Taken aback by this information, Orestes went at midday to the school gates and waited for his son, but Takis did not appear with the rest of his class though he returned home at the usual time carrying his school bag. Under questioning, Takis admitted that he had not attended school for two weeks: he had forged an excuse claiming ill health using a rubber stamp from his father's shop.

Parental reactions were revealing: Orestes was enraged and beat the boy roughly until Noula intervened. Takis was sent to his room without food, but late that night they relented and took him a meal. His pocket money was to be stopped and he was forbidden to go to the seaside or cinema, the usual recreation at weekends in summer. Orestes warned him that he would be followed to and from school in future since they had lost all confidence in him (χάσαμε την εμπιστοσύνη μας). A few days later, however, the father laughed secretly at his son's daring actions and ingenuity as a forger, but the incident was not related to outsiders. The parents expressed their disappointment and discussed where the fault lay. However, an immediate effort had to be made to protect their reputation. That afternoon Orestes went to a local doctor's surgery and, for 1,000 drs., got a signed medical certificate stating that Takis had been treated for a stomach complaint over the previous fifteen days. It was important that his truancy be concealed because a child's success at the high school, it was believed, depended to a great extent on his good conduct. Once 'bad conduct' was written in his reports, he would be stigmatized and his chance of passing the exams would be prejudiced. The parents could not expose their son to the consequences of his act for that would have affected the good name of the family as well as his own progress. Takis returned to school and was followed to and fro by his father for several weeks. Every evening he was supervised at homework although Orestes, like many men born in Kokkinia in the early 1930s, had not himself finished primary school. Their relationship became even more strained than it normally is at this period in a boy's life.

Besides Noula's mother, who lived in the same house, and me, no one was told of the incident. Significantly, Noula's mother, the resident grandmother, was particularly anxious to conceal the incident from the other grandmother, Orestes's mother, who lived in the next block, for it could be interpreted as her family's inability to control and bring up the children. The ambivalence of affinal relations is clear: Takis was grandchild of both women yet one considered the other an 'outsider'. Takis's parents complained too about Tasia's tardiness in reporting his absence. While indifference was to be expected from unrelated people in the locality it was inexcusable in relatives. 'If I had seen Tasia's daughter roaming around in school hours I would have told her immediately', Noula complained; 'Neighbours [may] mock but relatives care' (*H γειτονιά κοροϊδεύει, οι συγγενείς πονάνε*). Tasia's defence indicated how physical distance can effectively limit inter-action even though, in absolute terms, the distances were not great: 'If I lived one step away would I have delayed? I would have told them the same moment, but I didn't have a chance to leave home', Tasia pro-tested.

Indeed, those relationships which were based on geogra-phical proximity, especially between neighbours, provoked most concern in matters affecting the family's reputation. Although it was unavoidable that some neighbours would have heard about Takis's truancy from their own children, no public admission of error was made. The fact that his family had acted immediately and effectively to protect its position was import-ant. To some extent children's misdeeds were seen as inevi-table—far more serious was the inability of a family to protect its reputation by not covering up an error. In the case of Takis's truancy the defence of the family and their expectations of sup-port were revealed in an exemplary fashion.

As a centre of exclusive loyalty the family took precedence over relationships with outsiders in most contexts of life. There was another important realm of social action, nevertheless— that of the neighbourhood, where explicit obligations and expectations were defined, but where values and precepts stood in sharp contrast with those of the household/family realm. In the next chapter some of the contradictions which arise out of the opposing contexts of family life and of neighbourhood activity are explored.

8

NEIGHBOURHOOD LIFE
Integration and Ambiguity

In Yerania the family and the household were the main focus of individual loyalty and identification. Household autonomy was clearly defined; the house was an area of limited access, the family an exclusive unit. These features can be seen to divide and fragment relationships in the community. The notion of *symphéron*, of self/family interest, tended to generate competition, envy, even hostility between families. However, another key institution existed around which Yerania life was organized, that of the neighbourhood, *yeitoniá*. Neighbourhood relationships were informed by explicit and contrasting values which specified sociability, co-operation, and a high degree of exchange, both tangible and intangible. In terms of these values, neighbourhood life ideally was integrative and egalitarian (since it excluded none and its code applied to all). Because of the contradictory dictates of family membership, however, ambiguity and tension were built into the situation. All the same, the precepts of neighbourhood obligation counterbalanced any possibility of family isolation or of individual alienation. At an abstract level of analysis, neighbourhood principles expressed a mode of orientation which could be characterized as open and communal, since they tended to override divisions and to equalize differences. In contrast, the family being closed and divisive, tended to fragment the community into exclusive units. Throughout the locality, however, linkages existed through various networks of neighbourhood relationships, of friendship and of *koumbariá*, spiritual kinship. These different social institutions tended to overlap in interesting ways, resulting in ambiguities and tensions as well as clear areas of harmony and integration.

The Quality of Neighbourhood Life

The intense vitality of neighbourhood life was one of the most striking features of Kokkinia and other old refugee quarters in the city. This life in *yeitoniés* is recalled by older Athenians with nostalgia for it has disappeared from many areas of the city with the encroachment of high-rise buildings. But in localities like Kokkinia in 1972 neighbourhood life was a predominant part of daily experience, and a major aspect of social organization. With Greece's mild climate, outdoor life continues for most of the year. In Kokkinia, the streets, street corners, pavements, and *plateías* (squares) provided the arena where neighbourhood activity took place. From the early spring, streets and squares became alive as women gathered outside to chat, or to sit in groups on pavements, crocheting or knitting. The unpaved side-streets were used as play areas by children and men would set up tables there to play cards or backgammon (Plates 9–13, 15–16). Noise and activity increased with the warm weather until the peak period in May and June. During this period the streets would not empty until almost midnight, and on the hottest days people would offer their shade or a cool spot to passing company. Then, with the school holidays, many families left the locality to spend the summer in cottages, either their own or those of relatives, at nearby resorts (Salamina, Loutsa). During the hottest months, July and August, the locality was visibly depleted of its population and only in September with the start of the school year did it come to life again. The evenings being shorter and cooler, the streets emptied earlier but right into November people still sat outside for an hour to two on fine afternoons. A common remark at this time was 'Winter is coming and people gather into their houses' (*O χειμώνας έρχεται και ο κόσμος μαζεύεται στα σπίτια του*). For the next few months houses remained shuttered against the sharp winds. The streets were deserted except for a few housewives hurrying from the shelter of the bakery or grocer's shop to the warmth of home. The casual daily meetings between neighbours, so important for social life, took place in these local shops or briefly on street corners in milder weather. The major religious festivals and name-days, however, did provide occasions for sociability when people would be expected to visit one another's homes.

The different kinds of seasonal sociability are suggestive and reflect the two modes of orientation which patterned social life in this locality. 'Gathered into their houses' in winter, people were less accessible and more family-oriented; community life was attenuated. Openness, sociability, and exchange were specifically bound up with religious events such as feasts and name-days when the house would be open to all-comers. In general, this contrasts with the patterns of sociability and exchange which predominated in the warmer months when neighbours spent much time in one another's company but outside their homes, public sociability being a prescribed part of neighbourly conduct. Now the home would be visited only by those whose relationships were defined by ties other than neighbourhood (coffee-drinking, friendship, *koumbariá*, see pp. 183–7). During afternoon gatherings on pavements outside the home, women extended their domestic space and again, selectively, offered company and hospitality to others.

The vital bonds between neighbours demonstrated the elaboration of social relationships within the urban refugee quarters which have developed through the decades. At the time of Kokkinia's settlement residents came from various regions of Asia Minor and from different economic backgrounds; indeed, ties between households seldom existed in this initially heterogeneous population. In a few cases, kin or friends managed to get houses near one another but mostly throughout Kokkinia adjacent houses were allocated to virtual strangers. Gradually bonds developed through residential proximity, reinforced by marriage and *koumbariá*. The result is a tightly knit set of social relationships, of cross-cutting ties which ramify throughout the district (Hirschon and Thakurdesai 1970: 190–1).

Several factors have played a part in this elaborate density of social ties. The fact that some of the urban quarters were geographically separated at the outset combined with the growing mutual prejudice between local Greeks and refugees initially contributed to a sense of isolation. In any case, a conscious preference for marrying compatriots existed, suitability for marriage being thought to depend largely on the place of origin and thus the boundaries between the host and the refugee population were maintained. Political isolation, limited mobility, and consequent lack of contact with influential patrons meant that spiritual kinship ties tended to concentrate within the community, with kinsfolk, workmates, or with neighbours themselves. The highly developed, conscious nature of neighbourhood ties based on recognition of mutual obligation among those residing on adjacent territory, reflected the social, political, and physical isolation of this section of the population from the current of life in the city. But this was undoubtedly also because in the homeland before the expulsion, neighbourhood life had been a well-developed feature: separate ethnic groups had resided in different quarters of a town, each group having its own *mahallá*, or quarter. Older people often recalled the exchanges which took place between neighbours within and between different quarters of the town (see pp. 28–9). These memories undoubtedly played a part in the re-establishment of social patterns of exchange which came to characterize neighbourhood life in the urban refugee quarters, based as they were on the recognition of reciprocity, mutual dependence, and the need for co-operation.

The Neighbourhood Defined

For Yerania families the home and the 'outside world' were separated in interesting ways. Beyond the home the surrounding built-up area which represented this outside world was perceptually arranged into areas of differing physical scales. The residents' bonds with the wider locality were, however, only vaguely defined in daily life, for the major locus of personal identification was the small neighbourhood close to home, where concentrated social life occurred. The same Greek word *yeitoniá* (neighbourhood) had varying spatial referents, so that when people asked 'In which neighbourhood do you live?' (*Σε ποιά γειτονιά μένεις;*) they may have been referring to the larger districts, such as Yerania, Chalkidona, and Ai Nikola, or more frequently and significantly, to the immediate home area. The following analysis represents the way in which people themselves experienced and defined their notion of 'neighbourhood'.[1]

The primary basis of neighbourhood was territorial, so that it included all those who lived in close proximity whether or not actual relationships existed. This was revealed when people said, 'We are neighbours but we are not on speaking terms' (*Είμαστε γειτόνισσες αλλά δεν μιλάμε*) and contrasts with the attitudes described in some Greek villages (e.g., du Boulay

1974: 216). Physical proximity, though necessary, was not a sufficient criterion, for the neighbourhood never encompassed a whole block: families living 'back to back', their plots separated by walls, were not neighbours. The most crucial feature, therefore, was visibility on a daily basis. Consequently, a neighbourhood tended to centre on the street and seldom extended around a corner; it had no standard shape or extent. The actual area of each neighbourhood depended upon contingent factors such as position of house (corner, middle of block, side-street, or main street), the proximity of kinsfolk or spiritual kin; as well as individual factors such as personality, attitudes towards sociability, and age (cf. Davis 1973: 66 ff.) Thus 'neighbourhood' was marginally different for adjacent houses. The neighbourhood was a subjective construct, it was defined in relation to a house or plot, essentially similar for all co-resident there, but its outer limits were ego-based, depending on a number of individual factors. In short, for each house it constituted the visually accessible area where frequent contacts, informed by definite expectations of conduct, occurred. Expressed differently, neighbourhoods were subjectively defined, overlapping groups having an ascribed basis in physical proximity.

It is significant that Yerania neighbourhoods were not ranked or internally differentiated even though there were different levels of income (cf. Brandes 1975: 145; Pina-Cabral 1986: 150–2; but contrast Davis 1973: 69); also, as in other parts of the European Mediterranean, neighbourhood life chiefly concerned women (cf. Cutileiro 1971: 139; Davis 1973: 71–2). Although the men of Yerania were away from home most of the day at their places of employment, they did participate as neighbours in the late afternoons and on Sundays. But some men—the local grocer, baker, greengrocer—were important figures in the neighbourhoods and had detailed knowledge of the lives of many families who resided in the vicinity, for their shops were meeting-places where women spent much time in conversation.

The Neighbourhood's Presence

One could not live in this locality without soon becoming conscious of the lively interest in one's every action. Spatial proximity and high population density probably played a part in this overtly sociable attitude. In fact, to withdraw from social contact required conscious effort and would lead only to isolation; one only had to open a window or to sally beyond one's front door in order to be well informed on many local occurrences. The vigilant eyes and ears of neighbours were felt as a constant presence, and, in order to avoid simply being a passive object of talk and observation, one had to venture out of the home and enter actively into the various exchanges which took place. In my own experience I found that association with neighbours was not really a matter of choice, it was inevitable and imperative. A revealing proverb was 'Don't choose a house, choose a neighbourhood' (*Μην πάρεις σπίτι, πάρε γειτονιά*) (cf. Brandes 1975: 148).

An interesting expression of the strength of the relationships based on residential proximity was the conceptual personification of 'neighbourhood'. Frequently heard phrases were: 'The neighbourhood judges' (*Η γειτονιά κρίνει*), 'Ask the neighbourhood' (*Ρώτα την γειτονιά*), and ultimately 'The neighbourhood is my witness' (*Η γειτονιά είναι μάρτυρας*). Joy and sorrow, failure and success were equally recorded by 'the neighbourhood'. For those whose lives had been difficult yet observant of conventional precepts, a sense of vindication existed: 'The neighbourhood knows what I have suffered' (*Τι τράβηξα εγώ, η γειτονιά ξέρει*). The neighbourhood recognized merit, albeit somewhat less readily than it noted deviations from norms of conduct. Neighbourhoods were not, however, bounded or segmented entities. They were essentially overlapping sets of relationships from which information was relayed throughout the district and where knowledge was pooled about events and personalities in distant localities. In this way the neighbourhood was a system of relationships which promoted and integrated social life through the transmission of information. At the same time neighbourhood relations acted as a force which controlled and sanctioned conduct within the community.

Frequent contacts and their importance in sustaining neighbourhood life placed a high premium on houses which had access to the greatest activity, 'in the midst of the action' (*μεσ' την κίνηση*). Front rooms overlooking the street were more desirable than those in the courtyard, secluded houses in quiet areas were stigmatized by their 'solitude' (μοναξιά) and 'confinement' (κλεισούρα). This was not simply an interesting cultural turn of phrase but expressed a more fundamental set of values related to the pervasive metaphorical opposition of 'open' and 'closed' states (see Chapter 10).

Neighbourhood Exchange: Conflicting Values

Within the neighbourhood co-operation and participation was expected. The appropriate conduct of a good neighbour was made explicitly clear: she should be open and sociable, she should greet others cordially and be willing to pass the time of day in casual conversation, even while involved in her daily tasks. She ought therefore to accept and offer company and she should give aid in times of crisis. Furthermore, she should be willing to give and accept small titbits of food, an important aspect of neighbourhood exchange, and to offer invitations to drink coffee, a step leading to greater intimacy. Although the duties and obligations of neighbours were clearly stipulated, they were not formalized (as among urban Japanese, Dore 1958: 252–63), nor did they involve specific duties among designated categories of neighbours (as in the Basque country, Douglass 1969: Ott 1981).

Neighbourhood life in Yerania emphasized sociability which was generated through non-systematized exchanges of all kinds; it was rooted in the notion of reciprocity and, consequently, the recognition of obligation. Neighbourly relations were egalitarian and universalistic, including all and exempting none. But in this respect an in-built contradiction existed since the actions of giving and receiving entailed an inequality of status. Whoever received any prestation or gift, whether material or intangible, was placed under obligation to the giver (Mauss 1969); the balance had to be reasserted through a counter-prestation, and thus another obligation was set up.

Certain of the tensions observable in Yerania life are hereby explained. Neighbourhood relations depended on reciprocal exchange and the consequent recognition of obligation. Significantly, the Greek word for obligation (υποχρέωση) contains the root χρέος, meaning 'debt'. Indebtedness is, however, an abhorrent state for those who desire autonomy. Neighbourly relations therefore involved conduct which directly contradicted the values of family integrity and the emphasis on the independence of each household. Conversely, concern with family autonomy and the furtherance of its interests stood in direct opposition to the precepts upon which neighbourhood relations were founded.

The neighbourhood then, was an inherently ambiguous area, where these opposing values were expressed. Any individual was both a member of the family and of the neighbourhood and had therefore to balance the conflicting expectations implied by these two social contexts. Co-operation, participation, and willingness to accept the offerings of neighbours were tenets of conduct which had to be observed, for prestige and approval could only be attained through the positive assessments of others. At the same time family interest and integrity required some distancing; this too was a socially defined expectation, for loss of prestige and public censure followed if family members behaved imprudently.

The terms used for neighbours were revealing, pointing to the inherent ambiguity of neighbourhood life in the overall context of social relationships. A good neighbour who readily offered aid and participated was called a καλή συντρέχτρα (lit. 'one who contributes well'). The willingness to accept company and be involved in neighbourhood life was approvingly expressed in the adjective καταδεχτικός, 'one who deigns to accept'. From the verb καταδέχομαι, which also means 'I condescend', the word conveys the bridging of status differences. Two contrasting actions were expressed here: an active offering, which takes the initiative, with a more passive but essential willingness to receive. Those who tried to remain uninvolved were stigmatized as having their 'nose in the air' (ψηλή μύτη, lit. 'high nose'). These verbal designations are suggestive. They imply on the one hand relationships of social distance and on the other those of equality. A good neighbour was one who stooped to exchange sociability, to join other residents on a basis of equality. Thus, neighbourhood involvement brought everyone to the same level and produced integration, while family-centredness created distance. The coexistence of these two social contexts has multifold significance.

The conflicting values which pertain to the different contexts of family life and the neighbourhood were well illustrated at the weekly occasion of the street market. Every Wednesday the street market would take place on Yerania's southern boundary, the road marking the end of the prefabricated houses. Here women from nearby districts would spend the morning shopping for fresh produce, clothing, and household goods, making several trips to and from home if they were within easy distance. On this day women neighbours puzzled me by their mutual indifference, which noticeably contrasted with their usual daily conduct. Whereas normally they would exchange greetings and have a sociable if brief conversation, the same women were barely civil on Wednesday mornings, displaying an attitude which would have caused affront on any other occasion. The street market was no great distance from any part of Yerania so that many shoppers knew one another—yet they acted as strangers. With a curt greeting, if anything at all, each woman concentrated upon her purchases, pushing and shoving to find the best bargains and freshest provisions.

My explanation for this is that the street market was treated as socially and spatially distinct from the area of neighbourly association. Each woman appeared to be totally motivated by family interest, to seek bargains and manage the cost of purchases most effectively. For that time, she would suspend the precepts of neighbourly sociability. However, once the market had closed, women would conduct themselves as neighbours once again, sitting together and cleaning the vegetables purchased, comparing prices and quality. But a noticeable edge of competitive assessment existed in their conversations, for the morning's housewifely activity had clearly been motivated by single-minded emphasis on *symphéron*, the protection of family interest.

The ambiguity which results from this coincidence of two sets of contradictory values in a single social arena can be further illustrated. Borrowing and lending, the most obvious contact between neighbours, is inherently fraught with this tension. Lending items is problematic because, as good neighbours, women are expected to demonstrate generosity but, as efficient housewives, they also ought to conserve the family's resources and household property. A special piece of equipment (e.g., a grater for preserves, a pastry cutter) might be in demand by other housewives but its loss would diminish the household and would also create discord. In order to avoid lending goods and to preserve cordial relations, therefore, housewives tended to make excuses or resort to lying about their possessions. Equally, borrowing items from another housewife was to be avoided: it served as an admission of incompetence since a good housewife ought to be prepared for any contingency. Women known as borrowers were mocked and lost prestige. Consequently, most women tried to run their homes as self-contained units, and avoided as far as possible either borrowing or lending goods.

But to share facilities which others did not have was expected of neighbourly relations. Private telephones were rare in Yerania homes: thus those who had a private telephone were expected to make it available to neighbours. This, however, implied a degree of trust and intimacy since its use entailed entry to the neighbour's home and, once there, conversations could be overheard. It was clear that most people preferred to make their calls from the local kiosks or grocery stores where a sense of anonymity existed, however specious, and where no obligation was incurred.

The sharing of courtyard space in this crowded district was another expectation of neighbourhood life, and one which involved little inconvenience or disruption. Even so, it gave rise to feelings of obligation in those women who needed to hang laundry out in other people's yards, either because they had large families, or because their homes had no open courtyard (through extensive building on the original plot). 'How can I keep going into her yard? Once or twice is all right but not all the time' was a typical expression of unease. Some women would carry their laundry a few blocks away to the house of a relative, *koumbára*, or special friend, where the implications of dependence were less damaging.

In all these situations neighbourly co-operation was expected, yet women attempted to maintain their sense of independence by avoiding, wherever possible, too great an involvement. There were, however, two contexts in which the full expression of neighbourly conduct could scarcely be avoided, in the preparation and exchange of food and in verbal communication.

Competing with Food

Food preparation took up much of a housewife's time. In this locality it was a matter of central importance, associated with the woman's symbolic role as provider of sustenance for the family as well as with the social evaluation of her competence and worth. A woman's skill in preparing food was a major basis for her reputation. The fact that neighbours willingly offered help and accepted it from others when they were busy preparing the ingredients was significant. Time-consuming tasks such as cleaning vegetables or chopping nuts for a sweet pastry were often done in the yard where passing neighbours would call in and offer help. The standard acknowledgement for this help is a small plate of the finished dish, called a 'titbit' or 'morsel' (μυρωδιά, lit. 'smell'), which is taken to the house of the helper and presented with the words 'Just a morsel/titbit' (Μία μυρωδιά μόνο). The plates with their 'morsels' represented one of the most characteristic signs of reciprocal exchange in the neighbourhood. Since the plate had to be returned to its owner, and must never be returned empty, this provided an opportunity for each woman to display her culinary ability. Usually a specially prepared dish was selected for the return offering. In this way not only was the obligation inherent in the acceptance of food cancelled out, but one's own skill could be demonstrated in returning the plate.

Undoubtedly, however, the most vital links between neighbours were verbal and took many forms—through the exchange of information and concern, through criticism and maligning in vicious gossip, through lying and deception. The action of the neighbourhood in this respect was effectively one of social control. Again, the ambiguities of the situation were clearly revealed.

Dangerous Words

Notably in Greek as in English there is only a limited set of terms for various kinds of verbal exchange (conversation, chat, debate, quarrel, gossip). Finer distinctions such as those described by Gilmore in an Andalusian town (1978) do not exist. The Greek word for gossip (κοτσομπολιό) covers all kinds of verbal communication whether malicious or not. It is especially used for women's talk, though, and seldom for men's.

Casual conversations between women formed the basis of neighbourhood life though these can be seen to have several different functions. In a positive way, they served to link families throughout the locality by forming a network of information. This helped promote a sense of integration which counteracted the tendency of fragmentation arising from the emphasis on exclusive ties in the family. In this respect women can be seen as agents for social integration together with their participation in religious observances beyond the home (see Chapters 9 and 10). In both these spheres, that of neighbourhood life and of religious activity, their actions effectively promoted a sense of universality, of community, and of wider solidarity which transcended the particularity and narrow loyalties of family interest. Local people were less aware, however, of the positive and integrative function of verbal communication; for them attention centred on its negative and restrictive aspects.

In this respect, verbal exchange or gossip was not socially approved yet it was seen as an inescapable aspect of neighbourhood life. Inevitably gossip flourishes where families are concerned with social recognition and prestige and closely observe the lives of others. Women tried to avoid being characterized as gossips (κοτσομπόλες), however, though this was not easy since they were all involved in the pursuit and dissemination of news in the neighbourhood, an essential part of the process whereby the relative prestige of each family could be assessed (see Plate 16).

The active involvement of women in daily verbal exchange in the neighbourhood was not directed only at assessing the conduct of others; it was an important check of neighbourhood opinion on one's own family, for this was continually being revised and modified with every bit of new information. The competitive striving for recognition and consequent prestige which took place here meant that the neighbourhood was clearly an arena of social control, one in which there was considerable ambiguity in the contradictory expectations of the conduct of its actors.

From the perspective of the home, therefore, the world

beyond might seem treacherous territory. Since the information gathered by the neighbourhood about one's activities formed part of a continual assessment of prestige and esteem, it posed a threat to the ideal reputation of each family. But simultaneously families were dependent upon one another for the recognition of merit; thus some degree of involvement in neighbourhood life was essential. Each family was also concerned with promoting its own interest; hence relationships were marked by competition, and this generated a level of latent antagonism.

These inherent contradictions explain the widespread view that neighbours were not disposed to favourable comment. The predisposition of others to pass unfavourable judgements was believed to have no limits: anything and anyone came under scrutiny, and some grounds could always be found to denigrate or criticize the activities of others, particularly since the values specific to different contexts of action might be sharply contradictory.

The hazards of contact with neighbours were further increased because *any* information was deemed to be accessible. I was struck by the absence of limitations on the kinds of questions which could be asked; topics which we consider private, or which presuppose some intimacy before being discussed, were freely expressed here. Unrelated people questioned one another in a free-for-all atmosphere on any subject, however personal, and could enquire about others from third parties who knew them better. The responsibility for discretion and for maintaining privacy rested to a great extent with each individual. A woman who proved incapable of defending her family from prying questions, it was said, 'has no sense' (Δεν έχει μυαλό), was considered unworthy of trust by her own relatives, and might herself be excluded from family secrets. Discretion was also needed when asking and answering questions about unrelated families. Too great a freedom would lead to one being characterized as a gossip.

Defensive Techniques

Women had little confidence that their activities would be accurately interpreted or represented. In response to this anxiety and to the tension between neighbourhood and family expectations, various defensive techniques were employed. One of these which effectively dealt with prying questions was the use of rhetorical answers such as 'How should I know?' (Ξέρω 'γώ;) or statements such as 'I neither know nor care' (Δεν μ' ενδιαφέρει ούτε και ξέρω). This kind of curt reply prevented any further questioning on the same topic. No offence was taken since the person answering had an accepted right to parry unrestricted questioning. Another common response to personal questions was an evasive or non-committal answer such as 'Something will turn up' (Κάτι θα βρεθεί) or 'We'll see' (Θα δούμε). Alternatively, some kind of joking or entirely improbable reply might be used if the relationship was sufficiently informal, characteristically among the older generation of women whose talk often had a bawdy tone, full of innuendo.

Deception was another common technique for keeping one's activities, however innocuous, out of the public scrutiny. Since any information might be used to the detriment of the family, concealment was considered an acceptable expedient action. If a piece of furniture was sold, for example, it would be removed at night to avoid the prying eyes of neighbours and inevitable questions about reasons for the sale, or the price. A simple transaction of this kind could be interpreted to indicate the family's declining or improving economic status, or an impending engagement. Similarly, a woman preferring to hide the frequency of her visits to a friend would set out from home in another direction, possibly to buy something from a kiosk, and take an indirect route to her friend's house. Unnecessary speculation by neighbours was to be avoided.

Direct questioning could also be dealt with by lying. Since questioning was unrestricted, lies were commonly employed as a means for gaining privacy (cf. Sciama 1981), especially to conceal domestic matters. Food preparation provided a clear example. Women who met casually on the street would tend to ask standard questions, among them 'What are you cooking today?' This apparently innocuous question was often answered with a lie. If the meal was not fish, meat, or a special dish requiring some skill, a woman would probably tell a lie, or answer vaguely, 'Oh, something will turn up' (Κάτι θα βρεθεί) rather than admit to serving bean soup, lentils, or vegetables yet again.

Deception on so routine a matter occurred because little information was socially neutral. Enquiries about food preparation, for example, might serve two ends: to estimate the other family's relative affluence and to assess the housewife's competence, cooking skills being a primary criterion. Through casual questions regarding the midday meal women tried to gain information indirectly about the economic and social standing of other families. Since all were engaged in the same enquiry and true answers need not be given, this was not a satisfactory method. A more effective, direct way of assessing one another's ability was through the actual exchange of 'titbits' of food between neighbours.

Significantly, lies were more often used to protect one's family privacy or simply to make a fool of someone; they seldom took the form of false malicious stories or slander (contrasting with du Boulay 1974: 193–7; 1976). Since city people are not as dependent upon one another's services in practical and economic aspects of life, the pressures to overlook misconduct because of expediency may appear to be less in an urban locality than in a village. However, in places like Kokkinia people were greatly dependent on others for approval and recognition, and for the assessments upon which reputation was based. Here the prestige of a family depended to a great extent upon the good opinion of others. Malicious stories and slander might rebound and have more harmful effects on the slanderer than on the victim; certainly, slandering others could result in severe social censure, avoidance, and even isolation.

Gossip and Social Control

The expression of critical opinions about others was itself an inevitable aspect of gossip. In the interest of preserving harmonious relationships with neighbours, however, talk of this kind was limited to a few trusted confidantes. It might happen that two women would just finish criticizing a third, when she would appear. They would exchange greetings and engage in warm conversation; thus, what can be called 'acceptable duplicity' was a characteristic feature of neighbourhood association. But since women's relationships tended to follow fluctuating patterns of intimacy and distance (see below), duplicity itself had limits, because continual contact in the neighbourhood could result in greater involvement with the very women one had criticized. Should the bounds of 'acceptable duplicity' be overstepped, therefore, and a woman become known for being 'two-faced', she might be avoided by others as being totally untrustworthy.

The common anxiety underlying these various constraints was phrased most frequently as 'What will people say?' (Tί θα πει ο κόσμος;).[2] The force of public opinion promoted a high level of social conformity in neighbourhood life. What was feared above all was mockery, especially where directed against pretentious behaviour. The charge of conceit (φαντασία) was a severe one. Criticism of pretentious behaviour and conduct appropriate to a more elevated position in life was related to the drive for prestige and the competitive element in family relationships. Fear of mockery induced people to toe the line. Conformity was reinforced by the belief in the harmful power of both envy and admiration which was expressed in the evil eye (το κακό μάτι). Envy was seen as a powerful force which, once provoked, destroys the ideal harmony and sociability of neighbourhood life. Those families who experienced economic success in 1972 became anxious about arousing envy among their neighbours. One woman cautioned her married daughter while their refugee house was being demolished, 'Be sure to greet the neighbours—now that you're building you own house, they'll say that you've become conceited (Έχεις ψηλή μύτη).' But as good luck or success was also cause for pride (as the basis for increased recognition and prestige), again malicious gossip might easily result. In a social environment where each family desired to improve its position in relative and absolute terms, where little remained unknown, and proximity permitted easy comparison, gossip was a natural outcome.

The Preservation of Harmony

It may seem surprising at first that life in an urban neighbourhood entailed such immediate constraints on conduct and that public sanctions should have such direct force. Certainly, conditions of high-density living in which the potential causes of friction were numerous and diverse partly account for this. Privacy was almost impossible. Quite apart from the values which stressed sociability, the physical setting precluded it since the houses were closely built and in some areas were far from being sound-proof. In Yerania prefabs loud conversations, not to mention quarrels, were audible through the partitions which separated households and families; where possible, people would discuss private matters in basement rooms.

Harmony in the neighbourhood was valued, however, and a high priority given to preserving smooth social relationships. A revealing maxim summarized this: 'A bad year passes but a bad neighbour never does' (Η κακή χρονιά περνάει, αλλά ο κακός γείτονας ποτές). Among the ideal qualities of a woman was the ability to maintain order and good relations (see pp. 149–51). It was a damning fault to have a bad tongue (Hirschon 1978: 84–5). Women tried to avoid 'misunderstandings' (παρεξηγήσεις) and severely stigmatized those who became known as trouble-makers (καυγατζήδες). A characteristic technique for avoiding quarrels was to express one's complaints to a third party, not directly but simply in the course of casual conversation. When X's radio had been playing audibly during the afternoon siesta, or when Y neglected to sweep her section of the pavement so that litter spread to adjacent houses, the offended woman would mention it to another in passing, knowing that her views would be conveyed to the offender. If comments were disregarded and conduct was not modified, criticism might become more public and lead to a loss of reputation or to an open row. Women who did not heed indirect social comment were considered 'insensitive' (αναίσθητες), in itself a serious fault. This manner of indirect complaint through a third party was an effective way to limit quarrels. Open confrontation was avoided, the appearance of cordiality maintained, each person's pride was saved, and normal neighbourhood association could continue without disruption.

In the interest of preserving harmonious relationships some women maintained a degree of detachment from excessive involvement in neighbourhood life, an attitude expressed as 'not too many dealings' (όχι πολλές παρτίδες) and in the emphasis on 'minding your own business' (κάνοντας την δουλειά σου). These women stressed that it was 'better to have your mind at rest' (καλύτερο νά 'χεις το κεφάλι σου ήσυχο). With an evident attitude of reserve, these women were somewhat withdrawn from news circles. Although they were not the first to know what was going on, they were never uninformed. If they could escape the charge of being 'stuck up' or conceited (having a ψηλή μύτη, φαντασμένη), they could become highly regarded for their discretion. In praise it was said of such women, 'You can tell her your problem and it goes no further' (Μπορεί να της πεις τον πόνο σου και δεν πάει να τον πει αλλού).

But those women who liked to be more actively involved in the life of the neighbourhood ran the risk of being called gossips and needed to show caution and restraint. Thus they often employed pretexts in their social contacts. Sophia, typical of those who were more involved in the exchange of news, would always enter her neighbours' yards with an excuse—a small plate of food, a sweet dish, or a request to hang out laundry as the line in her own yard was full. Since this frequently occurred when something of interest was happening, people tended to regard her 'sociability' with caution. On the day that the daughter of the local dressmaker was due to give birth, Sophia was seen carrying a pile of clothes to the dressmaker's house for alteration. The neighbours laughed, 'Look at that gossip Sophia. She found today to have her clothes altered!' (Κοίτα την κοτσομπόλα — βρήκε σήμερα να φτιάξει τα ρούχα της). Once a woman concerns herself with gathering information, it is assumed that she also spreads it, whether with malicious intention or not.

Coffee-drinkers and Friends

There was no obligation to invite a neighbour into one's home, nor was access expected, except under the special circumstances of name-days and of death (see Chapter 10). A neighbour wishing to borrow an item or to ask advice would enter a yard and call to the housewife and the conversation would usually take place outside. Since access to the home entailed involvement and exposure, women usually limited this to a few trusted friends and to kin.

The initial overture to greater intimacy was expressed casually in an invitation to drink coffee or to have a sweet:

'Come inside for coffee' (Έλα μέσα για καφέ) or 'Come let me treat you' (Έλα να σε κεράσω). This first invitation was critical, for once a woman accepted hospitality in the home, she was obliged to open her own home in turn. By refusing the invitation, however, she indicated reluctance, and further overtures were unlikely to be made. This invitation was not a necessary part of everyday neighbourly exchange. Neighbours certainly did drink coffee together but they did so outside the house, in courtyards or on the pavement. To be on house-visiting terms was to share a different level of intimacy, which might be expressed either in the idiom of kinship or, in a less intense sense, as the relationship of those who 'drink coffee together' (Πίνουν καφέ μαζί). Since informal categories of intimacy grade into—and indeed out of—one another, one of the characteristic features of these friendships was their cyclical fluctuation (see below).

Access to the home therefore indicated a degree of intimacy not normally contained in the relationship between neighbours. Significantly, the 'coffee-drinking relationship' which entailed access to one another's homes developed more frequently between women from different neighbourhoods than with those living in the same vicinity. In short, intimacy tended to be inversely related to proximity (though this was not an absolute correlation since neighbours could become spiritual kin). But where little remained secret and one's reputation was formed by minute details of daily information, it was prudent to limit access to one's home to those who were geographically distant. In the neighbourhood the close, continual scrutiny of daily life created hazards which were reduced with physical distance.

House-visiting would take place either in the late morning when the housework was done, *en route* between shops and home, or in the afternoon. On these occasions refreshments were invariably offered and had to be accepted—a cup of coffee, a sweet preserve (γλυκό), or a 'morsel' (μυρωδιά), a small portion of the midday meal, if something special had been prepared. Conversations during these visits tended to centre on family problems, and difficulties experienced with respective neighbours whose biased judgements were generally deplored. Much mutual ground for sympathy existed, complaints commonly voiced being that neighbours 'speak behind your back' and that 'you cannot find an upright person' (Μιλάνε πίσω σου, δεν μπορείς να βρεις σωστόν άνθρωπο).

The coffee-drinking relationship usually implied an intermediate level of intimacy, however, and a level of reserve still existed. A woman might say, for example, 'We drink coffee together but we are not friends' (Πίνουμε καφέ μαζί, αλλά όχι φιλενάδες). Close friendships, in which serious personal and family matters were disclosed, were described significantly in terms of kinship. The special nature of this relationship was revealed in phrases such as, 'She is like my own sister,' or 'I come and go as if it were my own house' (Σαν την αδελφή μου είναι. Μπαινοβγαίνω σαν το σπίτι μου). Once one had shared in the secrets of a household, one could no longer be seen as unrelated; complete confidence was expressed through the idiom of blood ties and of the sanctity of the home.

Cyclical Fluctuations in Friendship

The question of trust was a central one in these relationships; it was the basic postulate of family life and was the point of greatest ambiguity in neighbourhood association. Intimacy between unrelated women should not violate the exclusivity of family loyalty, but the exchange of confidences itself demanded a unique and exclusive commitment to the friendship. People appeared to believe that one could not concurrently be a close friend of two people, because it is human nature to speak, intimacy implies openness, and trust could easily be violated. Consequently, friendships contained a strong element of possessiveness, revealed in frequent questions about one's whereabouts and movements, and in increasing demands for company. As the intensity of exchange inevitably increased, so did the sense of obligation. All these factors were liable to produce irritation, even boredom, as the women saw one another more and more often in a limited daily context. If one of the women attempted to withdraw, so would the other, and their friendship would lapse. Similarly the development of other friendships was seen to endanger the trust placed in the first. A woman's comments to me on the growing distance between herself and one former friend were indicative: 'She has become friends with the next-door neighbour, and so I'm keeping my distance' (Έπιασε φιλία με την διπλανή, γι'αυτό αποφεύγω).

It was extremely difficult, therefore, to maintain close friendships or 'coffee-drinking' relations in a state of equilibrium. Even if open conflict did not arise, a period of intimacy was likely to be replaced with one of distance until the women again started to keep company. Consequently such friendships tended to have a cyclical rhythm. Neighbours were usually well informed about the state of these friendships. At different stages they would observe and comment, 'They're not speaking' (Δεν μιλιούνται) or 'They've rowed' (Παρεξηγημένοι είναι) or, once the cycle of close interaction started up again, 'They've made it up' (Τα φτιάξανε πάλι) (cf. du Boulay 1974: 213–15).

Although long-term stable friendships between unrelated women tended to be rare (unless reinforced by other social bonds such as *koumbariá* or marriage between their relatives), friendship was an important social institution, with distinctive features. Its fluid character was related to the value placed on undifferentiated sociability and on reciprocal exchange in the neighbourhood. Emphasizing openness, these values directly challenged any single or exclusive relationship. Social contacts could occur easily and develop rapidly under the momentum of exchange and its concomitant obligations.

Spiritual Kinship

The institution of *koumbariá*, spiritual kinship, is contracted through sponsorship of a wedding and through baptism of a child, in ritual roles required in the Orthodox services. *Koumbariá* ties exist between the wedding sponsor and the married couple (and by extension their immediate kin) and between the godparents and natural parents of the baptized child, expressed by the reciprocal term *koumbáros*, -*a*, and *koumbároi* (pl.). It is sociologically important in allowing personal choice to strengthen and reinforce already-existing social relationships, or to create new ones through participation in a ritual event (du Boulay 1974: 162–8). In some Greek communities influential or useful individuals are specifically chosen as sponsors, the marked difference in social position making these the relationships of patron and client (see Campbell 1964: 217–24). In

Yerania, however, *koumbároi* were usually chosen from among members of the close family, particularly siblings, from among neighbours, or less commonly through friendships formed at work.

The choice of *koumbároi* from among those who are not kins-folk permits the outsider's position to be transformed into one of more permanent trust. Already-existing relationships may be reinforced through the additional tie of spiritual kinship since the mystical sanctions which inhere in the ritual relation-ship are of a higher order. Ideally, among neighbours the additional fact of being spiritual kin should create a long-term relationship based on trust and intimacy surpassing that of the coffee-drinking relationship and of close friendship. In prac-tice, however, varying degrees of intimacy existed between *koumbároi*, and conflict was by no means precluded. Rivalry between families in the neighbourhood and in business associations could disrupt the bonds of *koumbariá*. Selfless con-duct and trust is the ideal basis of spiritual kinship relation-ships just as it is between kinsfolk. Significantly, siblings were popular choices for godparents at the baptism of children. This may reflect the desire to reinforce family ties which were sub-ject to re-alignment and tended to become attenuated after marriage.

Modes of Orientation in Neighbourhood Life

Cyclical fluctuations of relationships and differing degrees of intimacy were interesting features of neighbourhood life which emerged through observation over a long period. Simi-larly, through closer examination on a daily basis another fasci-nating pattern was discerned. A noticeable contrast existed in the style, content, and orientation of social contacts depending on the time of day: morning contacts differed from those which occurred in the late afternoons. Although these patterns were undoubtedly created unconsciously, their regularity sug-gested a socially significant patterning. In short, mornings were orientated towards the home and its concerns, afternoons to the community and to sociability on a wider scale. Different patterns of sociability have been noted which related to seasonal changes (see pp. 167–8), and the correspondence with those contrasts is suggestive: the family and home orientation of the winter months and the undifferentiated sociability of the warmer months have a parallel in the domestic orientation of Yerania housewives during the mornings and the overt communal sociability of afternoon gatherings on pavements outside the home. These observations illustrate the quality of neighbourhood life on a daily basis but they also reveal the pervasive opposition between 'open' and 'closed' modes of orientation (see Chapter 10).

Mornings were to be devoted to all chores, to housework, and to the preparation of the family meal. It was the period when a woman's energies were to be fully occupied with domestic matters. People said 'Until noon a woman is a slave, after that an aristocrat' (Δούλα μέχρι μεσημέρι, κατόπιν αρχόντισσα). In fact, women did not spend all morning in the home since many occasions arose—or were created—for contacts outside it. These took place during other activities, such as hanging out the laundry, buying bread, or shopping at the local grocer. Grocery shopping, in particular, was an evident pretext, for it usually consisted of small quantities of unperishable items such as sugar or tinned goods, which could be more efficiently purchased on a weekly basis. Visits to the grocer once, even twice, a day allowed women to exchange greetings and information under the guise of housekeeping. These morning meetings had a transient and contingent appearance (cf. Bailey 1971: 1–2). Women should not be seen to loiter too long, and conversations took place while standing in the shops or on street corners. These groups changed rapidly, and were casual and open to anyone. Indeed one felt a certain compulsion to learn what was being said about others as well as to prevent anything being said about oneself. Besides greetings and discussion about health problems, conversation tended to centre on the daily round of domestic chores. Typically a woman would say 'I've been up since five, I've done the laundry', another would interrupt, 'I've turned out the house; I'm whitewashing today'. In this reiteration of routine household tasks each woman was making a public statement of commitment to her domestic role and to activities which belonged to the closed exclusive world of the house and family. It is suggestive that the orientation and the content of the morning meetings emphasized the 'house', which is a 'closed' area in the overall context of social life. The effect of this particular pattern of association was that house-wives were far from secluded or confined to their domestic commitments. In this way they combined their primary obli-gations as housewives with considerable social involvement outside the home. The idiom in which this could acceptably occur, however, indicated the domestic realm's primacy at this time of the day.

The morning period extended past noon to a break in the day marked by the midday meal, followed by the 'siesta', a legally enforceable quiet period. Afternoon gatherings started after 5 p.m. and continued through the evening, until midnight, depending on the season. These were very different in several respects. Though still informal and spontaneous, these meet-ings were longer in duration and leisurely in intent, and con-versation and topics were broader; the groups often included men, as well as residents of other neighbourhoods. Signifi-cantly, these groups were usually orientated *outwards* towards the street (Plates 7, 10, 15).

By this time of the day the housework had to be over and the woman was expected to spend time being sociable outside the house (cf. Brandes 1975: 148), either seated outside her own home or visiting in another neighbourhood. Here she would be offered a place in one of the groups seated casually in conver-sation on the pavements. When the housewife first came out-side she would bring a chair and a piece of crochet or embroidery, and sit facing her own door (inward). Soon she would be greeted by a neighbour or passer-by (Plate 13); she might then offer a chair, but this was not obligatory. If none was brought, the newcomer would move on. Thus the after-noon gatherings were those of choice and discrimination. Passers-by were observed by those seated, various stories were told, and information exchanged, but this was a two-way pro-cess. Although the street and passers-by presented the image of a theatre for the seated, in fact 'each spectator is also an actor' (Thakurdesai 1974: 101). One's company, the frequency of visits and their duration—all were noted by others and added to the fund of information which was disseminated to other parts of the residential locality.

The significance of the afternoon orientation towards the

street and the world beyond is twofold. Firstly, the social and spatial division between house and outside world was transcended. One could say that at this time of day 'the house entered the street' as its boundaries were extended outwards. Chairs and stools, among the 'essential objects' of Yerania homes (see Hirschon 1981), were brought on to the pavement and bridged the separation between the secluded inner and visible outer areas (see Plate 8). The pavement became a quasi-private area; it became an extension of the home in full, public view: the community and family commingled. Indeed, the extension of home territory beyond the limits of the prefab house was also expressed in the efforts of Yerania housewives to keep pavement and street scrupulously clean by daily sweeping and regular whitewashing. The notion of public and private space in this locality clearly overrode simple physical, spatial boundaries.

Secondly, in contrast with morning social groups whose focus was overtly domestic, the afternoon groups conveyed a commitment to public, visible sociability and to communal participation through being a neighbour along with others. Family divisions were bridged by offering a chair and company, wider issues were discussed, men and children were usually present. Even so, this was selective sociability, and social boundaries still existed. Afternoon sociability, despite its communal orientation, did not, therefore, achieve the total state of communal participation which occurred on certain ritual occasions (see Chapters 9 and 10).

The striking vitality of neighbourhood life in Kokkinia and Yerania illustrates how notions of exchange, reciprocity, and unselective participation counterbalanced the narrower obligations based on family membership. Clearly articulated precepts of neighbourly conduct thus stood in contrast to the demands of exclusive ties within the family. Tensions and ambiguities arose; some were reflected, others resolved, in various characteristic patterns of neighbourhood interaction. The ways in which neighbourhood space and the cycle of time, both daily and seasonal, were socially constructed was another marked feature of life in this urban quarter. This shows how physical space is not simply a neutral, objective plane or location but is defined, used, and experienced in accordance with cultural notions. It is socially constructed and imbued with symbolic significance. Furthermore, the daily and seasonal alternation of patterns of interaction, from wider, more inclusive sociability to a more selective domestic focus, can be related to the 'open' and 'closed' opposition expressed in verbal categories and in social action. In the next chapters, the overall context of religious values and the Orthodox world-view will be invoked to explain further these different modes of orientation.

9

RELIGIOUS LIFE AND DEATH
IN YERANIA

Character and Context

The religious dimension of life was a striking and somewhat unexpected aspect of my experience in this long-established urban locality. Its vitality was manifested not only in numerous rituals, communal as well as familial, but also in attitudes rooted in a particular philosophy of life which is identifiably part of the Eastern Orthodox Christian tradition.

Among my unexamined assumptions before setting out was that religion would probably have little importance since this was a fully urban locality inhabited by people whose origins were also primarily urban. My error lay in accepting uncritically a deeply entrenched model of urban life as secular, marked by the diminished importance of religious institutions and the dis-integration of family structure, among other things. This model, derived from the influential Chicago school of urban ecology (see Wirth 1938; critical comments by Lewis 1952, 1973; and Gold 1980: 146 ff.), is also associated with the assumed polarity of 'traditional' and 'modern' forms of social life (cf. critiques by Bendix 1967; Tipps 1973). These preconceptions were soon shaken by first-hand experience of an inescapably 'religious' and 'traditional' orientation in Kokkinia.

This realization raised other questions, however, one being the paradox of widespread support for left-wing political groups in Kokkinia together with adherence to religious prac-tice. This apparent contradiction exists elsewhere too: it has been explored in studies of Italian social life (see Kertzer 1980), and the coexistence of the Communist Party with the Catholic Church in Poland is well recognized. In the case of Kokkinia, support for the Communist Party undoubtedly reflected the grievances and desire for redress among sections of the urban refugee population which successive governments had failed to satisfy. The commitment to social justice and a doctrine of equality which is explicit in the Communist Party programme appealed to a deprived and disappointed group of people without posing any real challenge to their world-view, since in any case these ideals were contained within Christian doctrine.

Another aspect of social life which explains the apparent contradiction between support for Communism and religious adherence is the clear separation of men's and women's spheres of activity in this locality. Their complementary and separate realms, already discussed with regard to the household (Chapters 6 and 7), extended beyond the home so that men were responsible for the economic and political concerns of the family (in formal as well as informal senses) while women were responsible for its spiritual needs. This division was not absolute in practice, but it was clear and explicit. This gave a certain latitude for any severe differences which might have arisen within the family and in the life of the community. In any case, the vote was not granted to women until 1952 so that women's formal participation in politics is relatively recent.

It must be noted that the general context of religion in Greece is somewhat different from that in Western and even in other southern European countries, whether Catholic or formerly Orthodox (such as Serbia or Bulgaria). Historically there has always been and still is a close interconnection between Church and State. The establishment of the modern Greek state in the nineteenth century did not lead to the separation of religious from secular matters, so that in 1972 the institutions of civil and religious authority were not distinct as they are in many other European countries.

During the period of the military junta, as in previous periods, close administrative connections existed between State and Church. A single government department, for example the Ministry of Education and Religious Affairs, dealt with both these matters, and members of the clergy were responsible for aspects of educational policy. On all official occasions both civil and religious authorities were represented. In addition, civil marriage was not recognized and divorce could only be obtained through an ecclesiastical court. Names were conferred only through baptism, and its registration certificate was required for admission to school. (The socialist government

(PASOK) elected in 1981 instituted civil marriage and divorce, and far reaching reforms in family law in the Civil Code of 1983.)

In 1972 Greece was officially an Orthodox Christian country and over 95 per cent of its population were declared members of the Church (census figure). Several writers have noted, however, that church attendance was very low, and that statistics showed 2 per cent to 20 per cent as church-goers (see Ware 1983: 70; Campbell and Sherrard 1968: 212–13). This criterion is, however, quite misleading as an indication of religious commitment. Certainly, in Kokkinia, church attendance was by no means the chief element in religious life. Relying on this criterion one could be misled into facile conclusions regarding the demise of religious commitment since much of what constitutes religion is bound up with conventions of everyday life. The lack of separation between 'religious' or 'sacred' and 'secular' was a marked feature of life in this locality.

Despite the overall unified framework of Orthodox Christian belief and practice, there were differences in intensity and in the overt character of their religious orientation between these urban refugees and mainland Greeks. The social history of the Asia Minor Greeks provides some clues to explaining the particularly marked character of religion in the life of Kokkinia and similar urban quarters.

In the society from which the refugees came religious affiliation was the official criterion of identity (Chapters 1 and 2). It seems likely therefore that for them, Orthodox Christianity had a conscious, even pre-eminent, place in their self-image and social organization, and provided the foundation and underpinning of their culture. In this respect they probably differed from their contemporaries in the Greek nation state at the time of their flight (although rural ethnographies also note how Greek identity is equated with Christianity, e.g. du Boulay 1974: 42; Kenna 1976: 33).

During the period of the expulsion and preceding it, this awareness had probably been heightened because religious factors had been used politically to provide the ostensible reason for their removal. In addition, the hardships they experienced during the flight and afterwards undoubtedly provoked an awareness of human frailty, with consequences for their religious beliefs, As refugees, on arrival in Greece, they immediately created a church, whether in a tent or whatever temporary shelter was available. Once housing settlements were established, the first priority always was the collection of funds for the construction of a church (League of Nations 1926). The church embodied community life in social as well as in spiritual terms for the refugees. The church also provided a con-crete point of orientation where specific links with their past life could be expressed and experienced. Icons saved from par-ish churches and homes were among the most valued pos-sessions. In Kokkinia, for example, several churches contain especially venerated icons from Asia Minor which had been preserved during the hostilities or brought across in the popu-lation exchange following the 1923 Lausanne peace treaty. One church was built which even incorporated stones brought from its namesake in the town of Nicaea (now İznik, Turkey). The religious devotion of Asia Minor Greeks and their descendants is widely recognized among those who have had dealings with them. Priests who have served in old urban refugee parishes comment on the greater involvement in religious practices in these than in the urban localities settled by Greek countryfolk. I was soon forced to reassess my initial expectations and, as time passed, I gathered much information on the practices and beliefs which constituted for this group of people, their Chris-tian heritage.

In essence, this world-view can be characterized as religious for it is based on the notion of continuous interaction between the human and divine realms. Time and space were marked by religious precepts, evidenced in various aspects of social life. The year's passage, for example, was marked by the religious calendar, while stages in the individual's life cycle were defined by religious ritual (death, birth, baptism, marriage, and child-birth). This chapter examines some manifestations of the religious framework in the cycle of time, both seasonal and related to the individual.

The Cycle of the Year

Although people in this locality were involved in the capitalist economy of a modern city (albeit one in which industrialization has the special characteristics of underdevelopment: Mouzelis 1978), the routinization of the time and its mechanical measurement so integral to industrial activity (cf. Mumford 1934) appeared to have made little impression on perceptions of the year's passage. Unusual though it may seem for an urban locality, the way people marked the passing of time was based on the cycle of religious festivals.

Kokkinia's municipal area of 86,000 persons (1971 census) was divided into ten parishes each with a church and clergy. Every day throughout the district parish bells tolling for vespers marked the passage of each day into evening. Few people attended the services in the parish churches but none the less it was a moment when many would stop to cross themselves. In Yerania the wafting scent of incense (λιβάνι) would fill the streets every evening as the more devout housewives censed their homes and courtyards. In some homes the oil-lamp (kandíli) hanging in front of the icons was lit at this time every evening, in others only on Saturdays and on the eve of major festivals.

Sunday provides an obvious weekly religious focus, but its character should be noted. In Orthodox thought Sunday is not as the Sabbath, a 'day of rest'. It is the day of resurrection, one of renewal; it is the 'eighth day'—Kyriakí, the Lord's Day—and has parallel significance to that of Easter. In Yerania the pattern of everyday interaction was suspended. The day should be devoted to leisurely sociability, not to household chores. Women would endeavour to do no housework or cooking, sending the midday meal to the local bakery in large metal roasting-pans. After the church service they would engage in unhurried conversation, often after coffee, while fathers took small children for a walk to the public square. Sundays were notably leisurely, a time of unbroken sociability, when the family might go out together as a group to visit relatives or koumbároi, or to a sweet shop (ζαχαροπλαστείο) for ice-creams and pastries. In the overall context of patterns of interaction in the neighbourhood, Sunday was more 'open', contrasting as a mode of orientation with the alternating patterns of everyday social contact (Chapter 8).

In the urban context, the notion that the year starts with a new cycle in September coincides with the beginning of the

Church year, for this is also the time when the schools reopen. The summer holidays provide an opportunity for many families who own or share small summer cottages to move out of the city for two months. During the peak summer months of July and August, therefore, the whole of Kokkinia was affected by the loss of a large proportion of its population.

In early September, however, families started to return to their homes and the locality took on a new air of life and vitality; housewives cleaned their dwellings and prepared the children for a new school year, and neighbours met again. Once the schools had opened family routines were re-established and attention would turn to the end of October and the feast-day of St Dimitrios. This is the occasion for many name-day visits between relatives, friends, and *koumbároi,* and on 28 October, a day of national celebration marking Greek resistance to the Italians in the Second World War, the schools hold parades and shows attended by parents.

Early in December, the festive season starts. Popular saints' days, Saints Barbara, Savvas, Nicolas, Anna, and Spiridon, are occasions for house visits to celebrate name-days. People referred to this period of approximately one month as 'the holidays' (οι γιορτές) its high points being Christmas, St Basil's Day (New Year), and the Epiphany, a public holiday when the blessing of waters takes place in every parish. The day of St John the Baptist, 7 January, is the last widely celebrated name-day of this season. In the Orthodox year Christmas itself does not have as great an importance as Easter, but the concentration of several major festivals provides many occasions for visiting and offering hospitality. Groups of children would roam the area singing carols at front doors, on trains or buses, and wait to be offered sweets or money. The preparation of food, sweetmeats and special buns, was the housewife's principal concern. Traditional sweetmeats made at this season include syrupy *melomacaróna* (or *phoiníkia*), *kourambiédes,* well known all over Greece, and also regional foods such as *islím* pastries, nut-filled triangles, a speciality made only by women from the Asia Minor interior.

In Kokkinia a quiet period ensued, marked only by the name-days of Saints Anthony and Athanasios,(17 and 18 January) and the Presentation of Christ in the Temple (2 February). The lull was followed by the carnival season, *Apókreas*, lasting three weeks, its exact date depending on that of Easter. Formerly adults used to dress up and gallivant bawdily as befitted the season, but in the 1970s only the children donned fancy dress, and then only on Sundays during this period. Many people over forty remembered how, until very recently, *Apókreas* had been one of the most enjoyable times of the year, with spontaneous celebration throughout the community. 'Now the streets are empty', one man remarked sadly, 'We have enough of everything nowadays, but we don't have life' (*Απ' όλα έχουμε τώρα, αλλά ζωή δεν έχουμε*). This loss of spontaneous enjoyment, he explained, was a paradoxical result of the increase in affluence and living standards, an opinion echoed by others.

Two important 'Soul Saturdays' (*Ψυχοσάββατα*) occur at this time. Services for the dead were held and the families would prepare *kóllyva*, a ritual food which they shared with strangers at the cemetery and in the neighbourhood (see p. 215). Remembrance of the dead is a constant thread running through the life of the locality and the course of the year, both in these public days of commemoration and in the memorial services for the recently deceased of local families.

The *Apókreas* or carnival period ends with 'Clean Monday' (*Καθαρά Δευτέρα*), a day of fasting observed by most families, and Lent, 'the Great Forty Days' (*η Μεγάλη Σαρακοστή*) begins. In this period of preparation for Easter the rules for fasting entail abstinence from all animal products and oil, and few people manage to keep the fast for the whole period. However, for many families, the first week of Lent and Holy Week itself were times of stricter observance, while many older women fasted on Wednesdays and Fridays throughout the period. Special Friday evening services (*Χαιρετισμοί*) are dedicated to the *Panayía*, the Mother of God, and many Yerania women arranged their time in order to attend. The festival of the Annunciation, 25 March, is also the Greek National Day of Independence, a public holiday on which some families would attend the parish church; many who did not, followed the service broadcast from the Cathedral of Athens. Attention to this major festival was evident when passing down the streets in the locality, for sounds of the church service came from radios in basement rooms and houses.

With Holy Week, the atmosphere in the area was charged

with expectancy; all activities within the home were geared to this great climax of the year. Houses were thoroughly cleaned and painted in the preceding weeks, either by housewives themselves with some help from husbands, or by local workmen. Cleaning and painting the house before Easter is considered an essential preparation, paralleled by the attention to fasting, another kind of cleansing. Housewives planned meals during Holy Week so that they could provide varied meals, and observe the fast. Great Thursday was the most popular time for taking Easter Communion. Children who had fasted with their parents for the three preceding days were taken to Communion on that morning.

On Great Thursday it had become popular for Kokkinia people to attend the liturgy at the Church of the Transfiguration of Christ in Spata, a village about an hour's drive away, and a place of regular pilgrimage. By mid-morning the excursion bus returned and women could continue with important preparations for the festivities: eggs were dyed red, loaves of sweet bread (τσουρέκια) and smaller buns were made. These were carried to local bakeries where they were baked for a small charge. Great Thursday evening service is part of the growing climax of dramaturgical representations of the events of Holy Week. Local parish churches were crowded for the service of the Trial and Crucifixion of Christ. Housewives would rush to finish their chores that afternoon in order to get to church early with their neighbours for a full view of the rituals. People waited expectantly for the moment when the sound of knocking signifies nails being hammered; then the Cross, surmounted by an icon of Christ, is brought out from the sanctuary. Women said they had come 'to see the Crucified One' (. . . να δούμε τον Σταυρωμένο). They sprinkled the procession with scent and threw flowers at it, and some wept.

The solemn atmosphere of Great Friday is emphasized by the mournful tolling of church bells in every parish. Early in the morning young girls went to the church with colourful bunches of spring flowers and decorated the *Epitáphios*, the carved wooden bier where Christ's icon is laid. On this day customarily no work should be done. Pressures of urban life are nowadays overriding, however, so that many continued to work by choice or necessity, something deplored by older people. Many women would even prepare food the day before, and a widow explained to me, 'Today we have a funeral. How can I do any work? When my husband died, did I do anything? How then for the One who created us?' (*Σήμερα έχουμε κηδεία. Πώς να κάνω δουλειές; Σαν πέθανε ο άντρας μου έκανα δουλειά; Πώς γι᾽ Αυτόν που μας έπλασε;*). Church services continue throughout the day, the most popular being evening service when the *Epitáphios* is taken in solemn procession around the parish, followed by crowds of worshippers carrying candles.

Beliefs and practices regarding the souls of the dead are integral to Orthodox Easter observances. Since Easter concerns the central message of Christianity, the victory over death and resurrection to eternal life, it follows that attention turns to the deceased. On Great Friday, the cemetery remains open all day. It was a scene of busy activity: graves were tended by members of the family, marble slabs were scrubbed, fresh flowers were brought, and the oil-lamps filled and lit. The evening service in the cemetery church started at dusk and was attended by mourning families and after dark the decorated *Epitáphios* was carried in procession along the paths between the graves.

The mood changed on Great Saturday as signs of the coming festive celebration became more evident. During the course of the week the unmistakable, somewhat incongruous sound of lambs bleating could be heard from many backyards. The customary food on Great Sunday is kid or lamb, and on Great Saturday men from the neighbourhood who had some experience in the city abattoirs offered their services as slaughterers, going from house to house. Saturday was another quiet day of observing the fast. Most families rested, awaiting the climax of the midnight service.

From eleven o'clock that night vast crowds gathered at the church: whole families, young children, the old and infirm, all dressed in their best clothes and carrying long Easter candles were present. At midnight the dramatic moment occurs when all lights are extinguished and the priest emerges from the sanctuary with a single lighted candle, the Holy Light. People surged forward to light their candles until the whole church was illumined. The light was passed from one candle to another throughout the huge crowd gathered on the porch, overflowing into the square, and blocking the surrounding streets. Throughout the locality church bells pealed out and the triumphant hymn 'Christ is Risen!' (Χριστός Ανέστη!) was taken up by all. This long-awaited moment when Christ's victory over death is reaffirmed ensures the redemption and salvation of all mankind. It was a time of intense communal feeling.

Although the service continued into the early hours, the crowd gradually dispersed, people greeting one another openly and warmly. They carried their Easter candles, guarding the burning flame. It is customary before entering the home to blacken the lintel of the door with the sign of the cross, which is left there all year until it is painted out before the following Easter. The fast is broken now, usually with a plate of *mayerítsa* (Easter lamb soup), red eggs are cracked ceremoniously, and the Easter bread is divided.

The atmosphere of well-being carried through into Easter Sunday as people greeted one another in the streets and women prepared the Easter meal. Even the poorest families served lamb chops or a small roast portion. The Sunday afternoon service is called the 'Second Rising' (η Δεύτερη Ανάσταση) but it was mainly attended by older women. By this time, families with young children were more concerned with the social aspects of the day, and the evening was spent visiting relatives and *koumbároi* in other districts who until now had celebrated Easter separately.

Easter is the major festival of the Orthodox Christian calendar: 'The entire worship of the church is organised around Easter' (Schmemann 1974b: 13). But its social effects are equally important. In rural Greece, Easter is known as the period when intracommunal hostility and the tensions of hostile family relationships, of everyday suspicions and rivalry are transcended (du Boulay 1974: 58, 60–2; cf. Pina-Cabral 1986: 140). Indeed even among Sarakatsani shepherds, whose lack of conviviality between unrelated families is well described, Easter is a time of generous exchange. It is 'probably the only occasion during the year when a man penetrates into the home and receives the hospitality of another unrelated shepherd' (Campbell 1964: 350). Easter has the effect of transcending divisions and generating communal solidarity; its transcendent aspect is a key to understanding many other aspects of social life (see Chapter 10).

The period after Easter is the height of spring. Permission for marriage is seldom given during Lent, so that numerous weddings take place on the first Sunday after Easter. Thoughts turn to the countryside at this time: on 1 May, an official holiday, families customarily go into the country for the day and return with a colourful wreath of wild flowers which hangs at the front door for two months and is burnt on the mid-summer bonfires of St John's Day.

Until Ascension Day, it is believed, the souls of the dead released by Christ's victory over death, are free to circulate, but when Christ leaves the earth to take his place in Heaven, the deceased must themselves return to their places. The Saturday following Ascension Day is therefore a major Souls' Day; it is the duty of every family whether recently bereaved or not to prepare *kóllyva* called on this occasion the 'Golden *Kóllyva*' (*Χρυσοκόλλυβα*). People told me that unless the soul has a grain of this it suffers hardship and returns deprived and aggrieved (*παραπονεμένο*). In 1972, as Ascension Day approached, some of the old people talked of dreams in which the deceased in the family, a husband, mother, or child, even the long-dead, complained of neglect and reminded the living of their duty to prepare *kóllyva* for this occasion. On Ascension Day, too, many families tried to observe the tradition of taking their first sea-bathe.[1]

Two major festivals mark the next period, but the growing heat of summer began to dominate life in the city. At Pentecost, a festival celebrated over a long weekend, schools were shut, and many families spent a day or two at the seaside. In 1972 the eve of St John's Day (23 June) was the last celebration observed widely throughout the locality. Yerania children collected newspapers and wood, and piled up huge bonfires which were kept burning on street corners until nearly midnight. Adults and children alike took turns to leap over the flames. The older people sat reminiscing about this old custom (cf. Megas 1963: 135–8) and about life in their Asia Minor homes. Towards the middle of June, with the school holidays imminent, families prepared to leave for their summer cottages. Once the schools had closed, families with access to houses at the seaside began to escape the oppressive heat in the city. Social life lost its intensity as the population dispersed.

During the summer the only festival celebrated in the locality was the Dormition of the Mother of God on 15 August, which was preceded by a fasting period observed by some older women. The temporary loss of population was noticeable and local life had an incomplete quality. Many houses were shut up, while those families remaining in the area tried to find relief from the intense heat by closing the shutters of their houses during the day and making daily excursions to the seaside on privately run Pullman coaches.

With September community life was restored. Linked with the changing seasons and with the new school year, the cycle of the year began afresh.

Individual Life-markers

For members of the Orthodox Church, who comprise the vast majority of Greek citizens, there were until very recently no civil alternatives to church ritual at major points in the life cycle—naming, marriage, and burial. The Church's monopoly over these life-crisis rituals was ended only in 1983 when state legislation permitted civil marriage and divorce. Although marriage is held to be an immutable bond by the Orthodox Church, divorce is allowed under certain conditions; both partners have to agree to the divorce except in cases of adultery. Up to three marriages are allowed. For everyone some degree of religious participation was inevitable on the occasions of major life-cycle events. But while death and mourning rituals as well as name-day celebrations engendered widespread and inclusive communal involvement, celebration of marriage and of baptism was in this locality restricted to family, invited neighbours, and friends.

After a birth there is a customary period of seclusion for the mother and infant which lasts for forty days. The newly delivered mother (λεχώνα) would stay at home with the baby, waited on by relatives, since this is held to be a time of great vulnerability (cf. Hirschon 1978). Not all mothers wished to or could observe the period of seclusion: some disregarded it or modified it. (They would go shopping in the neighbourhood but would not actually enter the shops.) All mothers observed the custom of 'churching' after forty days, however, and took their infants to be blessed by the priest.

Baptism and naming usually takes place within the first year: until then a child, called *Béba*, is not a full member of the community of Christians, hence of Greek society (cf. du Boulay 1974: 42; Kenna 1976: 33). After the baptism ceremony, during which the name is conferred, the family, close relatives, and godparents celebrate a formal and festive meal. On the following three Sundays the child is taken to church for Communion by the godparent. Thereafter the mother or grandmother usually takes the child to church for Communion about three times a year at the major festivals. Thus Orthodox practice becomes closely bound up with the child's experience from infancy; it is also given systematic content through catechism classes held in the parish church on Sundays, which are attended by many children until adolescence.

Until recently proof of baptism was required for a child to register at school, reflecting the identification of the religious and civil community in the Greek state. However, in Greek thought the individual's name is not simply a matter of identity. It is related to each family's concern with life and continuity (cf. Chapter 6). Children ensure that 'the name comes out' (*να βγει το όνομα*), for in Greek society names are not chosen at random; they are usually drawn from the saints of the Church's calendar, following a recurrent pattern within the family. Thus, first names are repeated in alternate generations. This often means that sets of relatives will have the same first names, distinguished only by the second or patronymic. The emphasis on continuity in naming and its commemorative power is explicit. In some parts of Greece, the children of each sex bearing the grandparents' names are said to have 'resurrected them' (*τους ανάστησαν*) (cf. Kenna 1976; Danforth 1982: 134). If a young adult dies without offspring a sibling will name a child after the deceased lest the name 'be lost'.

The significance of naming goes even further, however. The usual response on learning a person's name is 'May you have joy of it' (*Να το χαίρεσαι. Να χαρείς τ' όνομά σου*). Indeed, names themselves are celebrated: in Greece it is one's name-day, falling on the annual festival of the relevant saint's day, and not one's birthday, which is of importance.

Name-day celebrations are a high point of family and community life. They provided occasions for widespread sociability in Kokkinia when relatives, neighbours, and friends were received in the celebrant's home. Preparations before a name-day (γιορτή) were intense, since the house had to be freely accessible to any and all callers (a most significant feature to be interpreted in the wider context of beliefs, see pp. 235–9). Customarily one did not work on one's name-day, but even those who did remained at home from the afternoon to receive well-wishers and to offer conventional hospitality. Visitors were given a customary liqueur, the *kérasma*, to greet the celebrant with the toast 'Many years!' (Χρόνιαπολλά! Πολύχρονος να 'σαι!) and were then offered chocolates, nuts, cakes, and ice-cream. No one went empty-handed and gifts were of the same kind: pastries, chocolates, or liqueurs.

The locality was transformed on the name-days of popular saints: in Kokkinia, for example, on the days of St George (23 April), Saints Constantine and Helen (21 May), St Dimitrios (26 October), and St Nicolas (6 December) houses were illumined, shutters opened wide, and callers came and went until the early hours. Similarly, festivals such as the Annunciation (25 March, with the associated names Evangelos, Evangelia) and the Dormition (15 August: Panayiotis, Panayiota, Maria) were days of widespread communal festivity.

The significance of name-days is profound. First, each occasion commemorates a particular holy person (or an event in that person's life, for example St John the Baptist may be commemorated on at least three different days). Secondly, the name-day is a joint family celebration of all relatives, both ancestors and contemporaries who share the same name, and thirdly, by extension, it is a shared celebration with all others in the wider community who have that name. A name-day celebration, therefore, includes the living, the deceased, and those unrelated to one another in a community of celebrants, past and present, by reference to a holy figure. It is a universalistic and inclusive ritual, referring to the whole community and not just to the individual: significantly, it is an occasion when the house is open to anyone. Name-days are celebrated in a manner expressing the open mode of orientation already noted. In contrast, birthdays are specific to individuals and secular, and until very recently in Greece they have not been marked by any celebration.

Rituals of Death

Of all the life-crisis rituals, those related to death were the most striking, widely observed, and inclusive. While other life-crisis events involved only family members, neighbours, and close associates, death mobilized the whole community and provoked an awareness of common human experience. At such times sentiments expressing the transient nature of life would be expressed by young and old alike: 'This world is false and deceptive', I heard people say: 'We are no more than visitors here' (Ψεύτικος ο κόσμος—μουσαφιραίοι είμαστε εδώ). Death is seen as the inevitable fate which levels the fortunes of all, eliminating social divisions. 'Death is for each one of us, rich or poor', people would say. Experienced communally, the event of death generated a unique level of participation, comparing with that of Easter. But while Easter festivities convey a joyous message of victory and redemption, death creates a total hiatus in the fabric of social relationships. Furthermore, I was forcefully struck on the occasions of death in Yerania, by the way in which the normal ordering of social relationships was disrupted. It has long been noted that death in the community provokes a marked departure from normal social patterns (cf. Hertz 1960; Needham 1973: 306 ff.). In Yerania the spatial division between 'house' and 'road' was dissolved as the neighbourhood entered the domestic realm of the bereaved family. With death the house opened, and, it seemed, the community and family merged in response.

In contrast with other religious events men were expected to attend the mourning observances and they participated in observances in the bereaved homes, attended funerals and memorial services. Children were also present on all these occasions, including the wake, and in addition regularly accompanied their mothers or grandmothers to the cemetery to care for the graves of the family's deceased, for the observance of death is an integral part of everyday life.

People from all over the city would attend the rituals of death. Indeed, a wider sense of the refugee community was generated with the deaths of older people, those in their seventies and over, the original refugees, whose memories had been the living source of communal identity and who had transmitted to their descendants a vital sense of their heritage. Feelings of grief and shock at the loss of a familiar person were amplified and therefore gave rise to a collective anxiety about their sense of identity and awareness of their bonds as 'refugees'. The loss of a direct link with their Asia Minor past showed how the continuity of this identity was being threatened. At such times people said, 'The old people are going . . . and refugeeness is ending' (*Φεύγουν οι γέροι . . . πάει και η προσφυγιά*), indicating in this the shared cultural dimension contained in their self-designation as 'refugees'.

With the death of a young person, continuity into the future is threatened. A sense of tragedy compounds the feelings of personal grief. On two such occasions during my stay in Yerania, news of sudden death created a public commotion. Crowds gathered on streets and some unrelated people wept openly. These funerals were attended by large crowds. Visits to the cemetery always included a look at new graves; those of the unmarried, marked by white ribbons, would invariably provoke sorrowful comments.

The overt expression of grief and deeply felt loss should not be misinterpreted, however, for death is not seen as a final end to the relationship which preceded it. In conversations and dreams, and in all rituals associated with death, living and dead continue to communicate, though now separated into different worlds for a time. 'The other world' (*ο άλλος κόσμος*) awaits everyone, this is one final and absolute truth. 'That's where we all go', people said (*Εκεί θα πάμε όλοι*).

The force which transcends that separation is memory (*ανάμνηση*) and its ritual enactment. Acts which commemorate the deceased have therefore an intrinsic value and are believed to confer grace. To remember is equivalent to reinstating life in some way. Thus, the recurrent rituals of commemoration through the Church's year are the institutional expression of the positive, essential contribution of individual acts of memory, and the act of remembrance itself carries a symbolic weight, not readily grasped unless seen in the context of Orthodoxy (cf. Chapter 2).

Obviously, therefore, to treat death with a clinical or impersonal attitude, as a simple biological matter, is repugnant. If death appeared to be imminent for someone in hospital, the family would arrange for their transfer home if at all possible, for only in the home could customary practices surrounding death be properly observed. Should this fail, the bereaved family would express their concern that they were unable 'to grieve over it' (να τον κλάψουμε). I also heard of conflicts between the medical authorities and the family over autopsy, an unacceptable practice since, in the people's view, it violates the body's integrity after death. Belief in resurrection of the body is part of Orthodox dogma.

In Kokkinia, adherence to the rituals surrounding death was universal and striking in its conformity. Variations in degree and detail (such as the exact period for which black is worn or for lighting the graveside oil-lamp) obviously existed but the overall level of observance of ritual was maintained by the coincidence of social and spiritual issues. Three interwoven concerns can be seen to have coexisted. First, the welfare of the deceased's soul was a direct and continuing responsibility of the living members of the family. It was their obligation to cater for the spiritual needs of the deceased. Secondly, associated with this was the belief that grace accrued to those persons who undertook tasks on behalf of the deceased (κάνουν ψυχικό). Besides these spiritual aspects to the rituals, there were clearly defined social expectations which acted as pressures to conformity. Observance of the immediate rites associated with death as well as with long-term mourning rituals were a direct response to concern with approval and prestige in the community. Analytically distinct as these three aspects are, in practice they coexisted and were interrelated.

The following detailed description of procedures surrounding death best illustrate these features.

The Process of Death

Yerania people expressed a well-defined acceptance of the inevitable: nature and God's will take their own course, and human attempts to prolong life were said to be nothing but 'patches' (μπαλώματα, as in mending a worn-out garment). This attitude reflected the belief in God's omnipotence but it did not mean that people were fatalistic. On the contrary, there was considerable interest in medical practices and people would go to great lengths and considerable expense to effect a cure. Among the older people I noted some scepticism about the power of medical treatment, but none the less they consulted doctors and took their prescribed remedies. Yet all this was tempered by a clearly stated attitude—that if these had any effect it was only because God willed it, for ultimately human intervention alone was ineffective. At times of critical ill-health, or when death loomed up before an aged person, I heard adults of all ages express the sentiment that 'Life is from God. Naturally you will do what you can for a person but beyond that it is God who decides.'[2]

The image employed most frequently for human life is that of the oil-lamp, the *kandíli* which hangs before the icons and burns only as long as it has oil. The ending of life is as natural and inevitable as the flickering out of the *kandíli* when the oil is used up. But unlike the *kandíli* cared for by human hands, the *kandíli* of life has an unknown amount of oil: the hour of death and the length of life are unknown and impossible to predict. 'When the *kandíli* has oil,' people say, 'it stays alight' (*Όταν έχει λάδι το καντήλι ανάβει*). And when the hour arrives nothing any human being can do will change the inevitable. 'Death does not regard age; whether young or old, when the hour comes . . . ' (*O θάνατος δεν κοιτάει ηλικία—μεγάλος, μικρός, όταν έρθει η ώρα σου . . .*).

Death is personified in two images, that of the Archangel Michael who comes to call the soul, and that of Charos (cf. Danforth 1982: 45). This is an interesting conflation of two traditions because in the most common stories St Michael is assisted by Charos, the pre-Christian personification of death (cf. Lawson 1910: 101). One such tale relates how Charos was sent to fetch the soul of a young woman. Her children were weeping around her, so he took pity on them and left her. He returned and the Angel asked, 'Where is the woman's soul?' Charos explained that he had felt sorry for her young husband and children and had left the woman. The Angel boxed his ears in punishment. Ever since then he has been deaf and does not hear pleas when he comes to collect the soul. This picture of an unheeding and merciless death is relieved, however, by the intimacy and familiarity with death which some people showed when they referred to it simply as 'Michael': for example, 'when Michael. comes to take me . . . ' (όταν έρθει ο Μιχάλης να με πάρει . . .).

This familiarity with death is undoubtedly a specific aspect of the refugee experience since the urban refugees in particular have experienced intense periods of social turbulence and physical deprivation. Besides the events of the war in Asia Minor and the horrors of the expulsion, they lived through the Second World War and the hardship of the German Occupation. During the winter of 1942 the port of Piraeus was blockaded and essential food supplies did not reach the city. An estimated 100,000 persons died from starvation in the city and losses in the refugee quarters were high. Throughout Kokkinia and Yerania many families experienced the deaths of relatives and neighbours, and it was common to witness death in the streets. To the older adults, therefore, death and the process of dying had become familiar, particularly for the women, who undertook most of the duties associated with it. Consequently younger people readily turned to older women in the community for guidance on how to deal with acute illness and death in the family.

I was closely involved in the deaths which occurred in three Yerania families and learned much about its management. A number of stages can be recognized when death takes a natural course; those who are in attendance should conduct themselves appropriately to aid the dying in this natural process. Before departing, the soul is believed to seek its last earthly pleasures, and so the dying should be granted any last wishes, such as puffing a cigarette or having a specially desired plate of food. Family members should be near at hand and photographs of absent relatives be produced when the dying person asks after them.

I was told that a voluntary surrender of one's consciousness makes dying easier; it facilitates the departure of the soul from the body. Since this is also one of the signs of a good and virtuous life, no obstruction should be caused by the actions of the living. People said that those who had led evil lives do not die easily, for their souls are reluctant to leave. Once buried, their bodies do not decompose. Anxiety therefore centres on the day when, three years later, the body is exhumed, lest it be found 'undissolved' (ἄλυωτο).

In the last days or hours, the sinking of the dying person into silence and a state of semi-sleep is interpreted as contact with other beings invisible to those present. The dying person is said to be 'surrounded by angels' (αγγελοφορεμένος, lit. 'wearing angels') and at this stage silence is important. Conversations interrupt the process by bringing the person's consciousness back to this world and making separation difficult. One old woman advised a younger neighbour in these terms when her father was dying: 'He has been surrounded by angels for many days. We mustn't speak to him because he realizes what is happening; he feels regret, and doesn't surrender himself' (Είναι πολλές μέρες αγγελοφορεμένος. Δεν κάνει να του μιλήσουμε. Εκείνος καταλαβαίνει και λυπάται, δεν παραδίνεται). As limbs get heavier, experienced attendants can estimate from the changing state of the body the stages of the soul's movement through the body towards the mouth, until it leaves 'like a little bird' (σαν πουλάκι).

Neighbours and the Open House

Social and practical concerns are intimately associated with the crisis of death. It is at such times that the presence of the neighbourhood becomes even more apparent. Neighbours would call frequently at the home of an ill person to enquire about progress or to leave a small gift (usually food or drink). Interest and concern was expected when illness occurred, and involvement was one of the major obligations of good neighbouring at such times.

Should the patient's condition deteriorate seriously the housewife (or nearest family relative) must make preparations for death. A bottle of wine (for preparing the corpse) and white winding cloth (σάβανα) must be laid aside. In some homes thirty-three coins were saved to be placed in the coffin, reminiscent of Charos's boat ride to the other world in pre-Christian times, but also of an early Christian folk belief in the toll-houses where the deceased's sins were remitted on passing. Dried chick-peas (στραγάλια) and rusks, customarily offered with brandy and a cup of coffee to those who come to condole must be provided, and enough small coffee-cups should also be available for the mourners. The housewife would keep the home scrupulously tidy and would clean with even greater diligence than usual. Great anxiety existed lest the house be found unprepared or poorly kept, for social competence was continually being scrutinized by others and the family's reputation should not be jeopardized by neglect or carelessness.

At the moment of death a most dramatic reaction occurs. In sharp contrast to the normal order of social life, on the occasion of death the house of the bereaved is opened and it becomes accessible to all. Neighbours, who are normally restricted from entering freely, now enter and take over the home from the family. The significance of this reversal of the usual order is multifold: the boundary between the 'house', closed to outsiders, and 'the outside world' is abolished. The community enters the home and the family is no longer separated. This opening of the house expresses the essentially communal character of responses to death. It is not an individual, nor simply a family event. Death reduces the community by the loss of a living member and so the community must react.

Preparations are made immediately death occurs. Unrelated neighbours enter, and while the relatives and close family sit weeping, they clear a room for the mourning rites and prepare the corpse. Usually two of the oldest women undress the deceased, wash the corpse with wine, wind it in the shroud and dress it in a set of best clothes. Others remove the bed and furniture from the room, cover all mirrors and pictures, sweep and arrange chairs for the all-night vigil (ολονυχτία). Meanwhile male relatives arrange the death certificate and engage an undertaker, who takes charge of funeral arrangements and delivers the coffin, flowers, and tall candles for decoration. Decisions must be taken on the number of wreaths, hired cars, and 'class' of funeral (see p. 217). Meanwhile, the bereaved women don black outfits, the coffin is prepared, and the mourning vigil begins.

The women of the family take their places on a line of chairs near the head of the coffin, where they sit for long hours without moving. The room slowly fills up with neighbours, relatives from distant areas, and others who have known the family.

People come to pay their last respects to the dead person bringing a candle and sometimes, depending upon their means, a bunch of flowers, which is added to the fragrant and colourful arrangement surrounding the corpse. The caller lights the candle, kisses the dead person farewell, venerates the icon in the coffin, and greets the family with the words 'Life to you' (Ζωή σε σας).

Neighbours expect to participate, and feel slighted if by any chance they do not learn of a death. This happened in one neighbourhood when an old man, a villager whose family had been renting a Yerania house, died. When the following day, the lid of the coffin was displayed, as is customary, neighbours who had not known of the death and missed the all-night vigil protested heatedly to the family 'But we are neighbours; if you had told us we would have helped' (Αφού είμαστε γειτόνοι . . .).

This room of the wake becomes the precinct of the women, some of whom will be present all night. Men enter the room, kiss the corpse, greet the women and then they withdraw to an adjacent room or the basement of the house. During the all-night vigil relatives and neighbours come and go at all hours. People said that to remain with the dead person all night is a spiritual act (είναι ψυχικό) and some women try to attend as many occasions as they can, where their experience and conversation enlivens the long hours. Small cups of coffee are made and served by women relatives of the deceased but the woman of the house, widow or daughter, remains at the right hand of the corpse seated until daybreak. The emphasis is on the restrained expression of grief; there are not normally laments (μοιρολόγια) in this locality and for long hours the room is silent except for a sigh or muffled weeping. Conversation takes place in the other rooms, at times enlivened by jokes, for it is said, 'You cannot have a funeral without laughter or a wedding without tears'. At dawn people return to their homes; participation in this long night of wakefulness produces a deep sense of obligation in the bereaved family who must reciprocate in future for those families who have helped them.

The funeral customarily takes place on the day following death. Notices are displayed near the home and the coffin lid stands outside so that people in the vicinity are informed. The coffin is transported in a hearse provided by the undertaker while on foot mourners follow in groups. Women usually walk together, arm in arm, but there is no formal distinction between men and women (as in some southern European communities, cf. Brandes 1981): all attend the funeral service in the parish church as well as the burial in the cemetery. As the procession passes people stand and cross themselves; the size of the crowd which follows the hearse is seen as a measure of the dead person's esteem (and that of the family). People comment on the number of mourners and of wreaths which were sent. Later, the family is proud to claim that two or three hundred coffees were served after the burial.

In the cemetery the women of the family openly express their grief, crying and calling out to the deceased at the open grave, while the men weep in a subdued fashion. Once everyone has thrown a handful of earth into the grave, all adjourn to a nearby coffee shop, where the family pays for all participants to take coffee, a small brandy, and a rusk, which they do saying 'May God forgive him/her' (*Θεός σχωρεσ' τον/την*). On leaving everyone shakes hands with the family again with the greeting, 'Life to you' (*Ζωή σε σας*). Close members of the family then return to the bereaved home for a special meal of fish soup, called the 'soup of consolation' (*σούπα της παρηγοριάς*).

Mourning Observances

The first forty days after death constitute a transition period during which the bereaved women are expected to remain secluded within the house where an oil-lamp is kept alight day and night (cf. Lawson 1910: 508–14). I was told that in the past they would do no housework and not even cook. All these tasks were undertaken by the neighbours until the normal order of life was reinstated after the fortieth-day memorial service.

On the third day after death, normally the day following the funeral, the wife or mother (nearest female relative) washes the clothes of the deceased and makes a simple form of *kóllyva*, the ritual food for the dead. On this occasion it consists of boiled wheat alone without other ingredients. On the ninth day, when the first memorial service (*εννιάμερα*) takes place at the cemetery, a more elaborate version of *kóllyva* is made and shared out.

The ninth-day memorial service is attended only by family, special friends and some close relatives. During this initial mourning period practical arrangements are made by men of the bereaved family. They organize the impending major memorial service, the construction of the tombstone and grave slab.

By the time forty days have passed news of the death has spread. The family sends out invitations to far-flung relatives and acquaintances to attend the memorial service and the crowd attending this service will be larger than at the funeral. Following a church service, prayers are said at the grave, now marked by a cross and marble tombstone with a glass-fronted compartment displaying a framed photograph of the deceased. People follow the family to a coffee shop, where they are served coffee, brandy, and rusks. *Kóllyva* is distributed to each participant in small commercially printed packets and eaten with the words 'May God forgive him/her' (Θεός σχωρέσ' τον/την). The preparation and presentation of *kóllyva* for the forty-day memorial period takes much time, care, and expenditure. It includes raisins, sugared almonds, sesame seeds, toasted flour, pomegranate seeds with the boiled wheat, all carefully moulded into a mound and elaborately decorated. Some families would order *kóllyva* from professional confectioners, adding considerably to the cost and lavishness of the display.

The oil-lamp should be lit at the grave every Wednesday and Saturday evening at least for the first three months, and some families would do this for the whole year. It is the responsibility of the adult women of the family to care for the grave for this whole period. Successive memorial services on the third, sixth, and ninth months after death are public events and take a similar form. After that they are held annually for three years. On the third anniversary of the death, the bones are disinterred. They are removed from the grave and, after prayers have been said, are added to those in the communal ossuary.

Coincident Concerns

In these rituals for the dead the coexistence of several separate but interrelated concerns can be discerned. Remembrance of the dead acts in this community as a powerful and positive force, one which has several dimensions combining both spiritual and social concerns.

Firstly, in Orthodox folk practice a belief exists that spiritual grace is gained through participating in various religious activities (for example the baptism of a child, visiting a shrine). It is also gained by those who attend to the welfare of souls of the deceased and those who at any time commemorate them. In most contexts charity is not acceptable to people in Yerania: it is seen as recognition of the family's failure to be self-sufficient and it challenges the ideal of family competence and independence. But charitable acts performed in the name of those who have passed away are acceptable. Thus, food, clothes, even money, may be given and received when accompanied by the words 'For the soul of X' (Για την ψυχή του/της).

A second concern reinforcing the observance of death rituals is a belief that the soul of the deceased itself has certain requirements and that its welfare is jeopardized when these are neglected. Bereaved women show how the expectations of the deceased are an uppermost consideration: at the graveside their characteristic cry is 'What complaint do you have? I've done everything for you' (Τί παράπονο έχεις; Όλα σου τα 'κανα). Anxiety about producing children and heirs reflects this concern since without them there is no one upon whom these responsibilities devolve. The interdependence of living and dead entailed in the performance of graveside rites is also linked to the strong attachment which Greeks have to their place of origin.

Thirdly, an entirely social concern is also apparent: the pressure of public opinion and the awareness that social expectations themselves must be filled. Since the ritual practices are standard and known to all and since death entails almost total communal participation, the bereaved family is especially conscious that any deviation from accepted procedures may provoke criticism and loss of prestige. Their personal grief compounded by the awareness of possible public denigration, therefore, charges the mourning period with acute tension.

Besides the pressure to conform, another social factor also influences mourning observances. This is the competition between families for recognition and prestige. Rising affluence together with the increasing availability of variety in commodities was leading to a form of 'conspicuous consumption' in burial practices. Undertakers were exploiting this situation by suggesting ever more elaborate and expensive arrangements. The Church had also encouraged this competitive element since funeral services, weddings, and baptisms are graded by expense and lavishness, while the cemetery is itself divided into first-, second-, and third-class grave-sites, costed accordingly.[3] Once a few local families were prepared to pay larger sums of money to bury their dead, others felt compelled to make increasingly elaborate arrangements simply to keep abreast of current standards. I was told that right into the early 1950s graves in the local cemetery were simple earth mounds surmounted only by a wooden cross. Nowadays, marble tombstones of several raised tiers are common while various styles of cross, optional marble vases, and ornate lettering are also available. Expenditure on the tombstone and grave alone may therefore be considerable, a fact deplored by all. The elderly who remember former simplicity and who are anyway removed from the inter-familial rivalries of younger adults particularly abhor this extravagance. But attention to the grave of the deceased is considered essential, and where families are engaged in rivalry for prestige, inevitably greater elaboration will occur.

Social reputation, closely bound up with mourning observances in general, is also involved in concern for the condition of the grave itself over an extended period of mourning. For the housewife therefore the grave demands continual attention just as her home does. In popular usage the grave is called 'the last residence' (η τελευταία κατοικία), the home of the deceased person for a three-year period. The cemetery is in a sense a residential locality demanding effort and upkeep as does the home area of each family (cf. Danforth 1982: 133). Here too the critical eyes of neighbours assess the competence of each family. But in Kokkinia the grave is not simply a 'domestic extension' for the housewife. Because the position of graves in the local cemetery is not related to neighbourhoods or home location, the cemetery is primarily a public and communal space. It serves a large densely populated area including several municipalities besides Kokkinia. The significance of this for women whose duty it is to serve the dead, lies in their acceptable *public* role (see Chapter 10).

Rituals associated with death take pre-eminence over the other life cycle events for local people. The conduct of bereaved families reveals the compound effect of worldly as well as metaphysical concerns. Participation in these rituals confers spiritual grace on the participants, serves the welfare of the dead in the other world, while also being involved in the struggle of those living in the present world for recognition and prestige. These rituals demonstrate how the community includes the deceased as well as its living members and how acts of commemoration promote a sense of continuity after death has ruptured the social fabric.

This chapter has dealt with the religious events integral to the passage of time over the seasons of the year, and with those which mark the individual's life cycle. Like Judaism and Islam, Orthodox Christianity is a way of life; 'sacred' and 'profane' are not dichotomized but the religious dimension pervades many aspects of life. In the next chapter, the differential involvement of women, men, the aged, and younger adults in religious activities and philosophy is examined. Finally, the key to understanding certain patterns of social life, the open and closed modes of orientation (noted previously), are explained in the wider context of indigenous thought, the Orthodox Christian world-view.

10

THE TRIUMPH OF LIFE

The description of social life in Kokkinia in 1972, with its specific attention to the smaller district of Yerania, has centred on major aspects of social organization: the inhabitants' sense of cohesion and separate identity in Greek society, their economic activities, the household, family, and neighbourhood, and the religious demarcation of time. In addition, religion adds a further dimension to social organization. Differing degrees of religious adherence and practice provide, in analytical terms, a structuring principle. In this chapter the complementarity of gender roles and age groups is demonstrated more fully (cf. Chapters 5–7). Finally, the contradictions and tensions which mark symbolic categories and social relationships in this locality are set within the overall cosmology, that of Orthodox Christianity.

Women, the Public Realm, and Social Integration

A clearly defined gender dichotomy was the basis of family organization in Kokkinia and, I would argue, on a wider scale, of all Greek social life. Adult men and women were not seen as total entities, as individuals in their own right, apart from their families. In this way of thinking, men and women are not complete in themselves; it is their relationship which creates a totality and this is one of complementarity. Furthermore, complementarity entails interdependence which is not only functional and operational, defining what men and women do, but is also symbolic and spiritual, thus relating to abstract and ideal qualities.[1] While women have a nominally inferior position in Greek society, their sphere of influence is also clearly defined and extensive, and their proclaimed subordination is contradicted by the open acknowledgement of male vulnerability and of the limitations of male power (Chapter 7).

Two archetypal images, those of Eve and Mary, are available

as models for women's identification. It is primarily through motherhood that women approach the attributes associated with Mary, the Mother of God, but numerous other ways exist in which a woman may redeem the flawed aspects of her nature, among them religious observances. These are not undertaken, though, with any self-conscious sense of piety, but through the expectations associated with the complementarity of gender roles based in the family. In many rituals in the home, church, and cemetery, women play the central role. The house itself is accorded attention—the *iconostási* is kept stocked with holy substances, the *kandíli* is lit for festivals and Sundays, the courtyard and interior is scented with incense. In these observances, the woman can be seen as a 'domestic priestess', the house manifesting its sacred dimension. In other activities, especially pilgrimages (see pp. 222–5), the woman's role parallels that of the Most Holy One, the *Panayía*, who is seen as intercessor, as Mother of God and of all the world (για όλον τον κόσμο).

Religious activity in Kokkinia also involved groups of women, neighbours as well as relatives: they would attend church together, accompany one another to the cemetery to clean tombstones and light the grave's *kandíli*. Neighbours would bring back from the Sunday liturgy a piece of blessed bread (αντίδωρο) for those too busy or ill to attend themselves, and similarly collect and share holy water (αγιασμός) from the monthly blessing of water.

Clearly, therefore, most religious activities at the informal level are undertaken by the women, a characteristic noted in many parts of southern Europe. In most interpretations their involvement is seen as an extension of the women's domestic role (e.g. the church as the house of God, cf. Brandes 1981) or as a legitimate pretext to escape from domestic seclusion and confinement (Dubisch 1983). Usually the contrast is with men in the 'public realm' of political and economic life (cf. Brandes 1981: 178), or with the male hierarchy, the priests, who monopolize all formal aspects of religious organization. This contrast is applicable to religious structures in Greece as a whole, and also to Kokkinia.[2]

However, in Kokkinia the full significance of women's informal religious activities becomes clear only when viewed in the total context of social life and as part of the overall gender division of labour. Here, the complementarity of male and female roles is again revealed. Taking an overall view, it is clear that both women and men are actively involved in the public realm, i.e. the area geographically distant from and socially unrelated to the home.[3] Through their involvement in religious pursuits, women achieve considerable mobility and have contact with strangers in public areas far removed from home and from the familiar presence of the neighbourhood.

However, for men and women, the purpose of pursuits in public areas is very different. In short, public involvement for men entails economic endeavour and political activity and emphasizes the furtherance of the family's *material* interests. For women, public involvement beyond the home and neighbourhood concerns the *spiritual* welfare of family members, both the living and the dead. The contrast, therefore, lies between the worldly, temporal concerns of the men, and the more metaphysical, transcendental interests of the women. This division of activities is generally accepted and expected: neither men nor women should get too involved in one another's designated spheres. Thus, the complementarity of male and female roles, so clearly expressed in the home environment, actually extends beyond it too, into the public arena.

The significance for women of their religious responsibilities should not be missed. First, the woman's active involvement in pursuing the spiritual needs of the family gives her a recognized and accepted public role. Secondly, these contacts mean that women become agents of communication beyond the locality. I suggest that they act as a force for social integration, since their contacts, however brief or transitory, generate an awareness of the wider society, a recognition of universal human issues, and of sentiments which transcend the exclusive bonds of family-based loyalty. Undoubtedly, men also have a part in creating networks of relationships in the wider society. I would argue, however, that the specific interests of men are likely to express a competitive drive, given the urban context, the market, and the political forces with which they must contend. In brief, therefore, the effects of men's and women's participation in the public realm are somewhat different: women's activities tend to promote a more universal awareness and to overcome narrow

and specific commitments while men's involvement in economic matters as petty traders, entrepreneurs, and wage-
earners tends to be divisive, family-based, and more geared to
rivalry and competition.

One example will suffice. The cemetery in Neapolis, north of
Kokkinia and near Yerania, serves four municipalities (several
hundred thousand people). I began to see that it had a latent
function as a meeting-place for a large section of the city's
population. Since the position of graves bore no relation to the
residential neighbourhoods of families, women who attended
the graves to arrange flowers, to clean and light the *kandíli*, were
often strangers from entirely different localities. Their common
purpose in caring for the deceased, however, allowed easy communication, and they learned of the fortunes and hardships of
others (cf. Danforth 1982: 14 ff.).

In their common confrontation with death, the fate of all,
they exchanged views and shared sentiments confronting
transcendental issues. Their attention turned away from narrower daily concerns: the partial loyalties and exclusiveness
(which characterizes neighbourhood and family life) were
replaced by the realization of mortality and transience, and by
teleological questions. At this level, contacts between women
in the cemetery centred on philosophical concerns and promoted an awareness of universality and common human
experience. Frequent excursions to religious shrines around
the country from all parts of Kokkinia have a similar effect;
again it is the women who are the links with a wider society.

Women as Pilgrims

A very popular pursuit in Kokkinia among women of all ages
was to go on excursions to religious sites throughout Greece.
Journeys might be prompted by specific promises (*τάματα*) to
particular saints, to the *Panayía*, or to Christ, or simply to take
the form of pilgrimages (*προσκυνήματα*). In Greece many shrines
and monasteries are visited as places of healing or for other miraculous events, those specifically associated with Asia Minor
being particularly favoured by people from Kokkinia. The
Church of St John the Russian (*Ο Άγιος Ιωάννης ο Ρώσσος*) in the

village of Prokopi in Euboia is one of them (see below). Refugees from Kappadokia settled there in the 1920s bringing with them the saint's relics, already renowned in the homeland (cf. Hasluck 1929: 440–1). Similarly, the shrine of the *Panayía* of Soumela in northern Greece built with contributions mainly from Asia Minor refugees is a national place of pilgrimage, the site of a miraculous icon said to have been painted by St Luke and brought from its former home near Trapezounta (Pontus region, now Trabzon, cf. ibid.: 66). At the shrines the women may take Communion, are blessed and anointed with holy oil by the priest, and collect substances imbued with spiritual power to add to the stock kept on the *iconostási*. These journeys supplement the spiritual resources of the household, bestow grace on the woman who attends and, thus, indirectly on her household.

On these excursions the women were sometimes accompanied by children but rarely by husbands. However, even those men who were mean with household money or objected to activities outside the home did not object to their wives' attendance on pilgrimages. Here the woman acts as intercessor and representative of her family, a clear parallel with the *Panayía*, the All Holy One, who supplicates on behalf of human beings.

Although these excursions around the countryside have an explicit religious purpose, they are also intrinsically recreational. Again, the absence of separation between 'sacred' and 'profane' is shown on these occasions. They are called πανηγύρια which translates both as 'patronal festival' and as 'fair'. Music, dancing, and feasting usually follow the communion service: to the participants no clear boundary exists between religious and recreational motivations. Consequently religious excursions from Kokkinia had a mixed air of religious devotion and of festive celebration.

In company (παρέα) with local women, I attended the name-day festival of St John the Russian in May 1972. On arrival in Prokopi village the party of some thirty women, several small children, and two men joined thousands of worshippers from all over Greece at the crowded church. The atmosphere was reverent as the procession of holy relics went around the village. The throng listened to an address by the local bishop attended by two visiting bishops, several archimandrites, and

many priests and monks from Mount Athos. Once the liturgical events had ended, however, the mood changed. People
crowded into coffee shops and tavernas for refreshments;
others laid out picnics under the trees. A fairground of stalls
offered fabrics, clothing, toys, and curios, while near the
church, icons, amulets, crosses, and religious booklets were put
on sale by monks and pedlars. Few returned without some
souvenir of the trip, a material sign to reinforce the act of
memory. Women treated one another to coffee or ice-cream at
the cafés near the square and the festive atmosphere of the
journey continued that evening with a stop at a seaside tavern
where most participants enjoyed a meal of fresh fish, salads,
and beer.

Everyone is aware of the recreational outlet provided by these
excursions but that does not contradict the main purpose of the
journey: to worship at the shrine of a holy personage. Participants should set out in a spirit of reverence, and they would
vehemently deny the attacks of any critics by saying simply 'We
went with faith' (Πήγαμε με πίστη). The critics were usually
younger men who, normally uninvolved in religious matters,
delighted in teasing the older women, saying that they go only
for the outing (για την βόλτα), that they sing songs on the bus
and on arrival they sit in tavernas.

This contradictory interpretation reflects an opposing view-
point based on a major structural division: the attitudes of
young adults, particularly men, whose concerns centred on
worldly achievement contrasted with those of the elderly,
especially the women, whose world-view and activities tended
to have overt metaphysical associations.

Pilgrimages to the Holy Land itself were also a strong element
in the Asia Minor tradition. Although not strictly part of Christian teaching (on the contrary, cf. Zander 1971: 5–37), pilgrimages to the Holy Places have been popular for Christians
throughout the ages. Among metropolitan Greeks, the custom
appears to have lapsed in the nineteenth century but in refugee
quarters such as Kokkinia these pilgrimages continued to be
popular. Long before cheap package tours, groups in Kokkinia
organized excursions to reduce costs. Those who returned from
the pilgrimage often added the prefix *Hadzi* to their name, for
example *Hadzianna*, *Hadziyeorgis*. This obvious parallel with the

Arabic *ḥajj* suggests that the close association of Jews and Muslims (for whom the practice of visiting these Holy Places is prescribed in religious teaching) with Christians in Asia Minor encouraged this example of 'cultural borrowing'.

For Christians the purpose of visiting the Holy Places culminates in the pilgrim's 'baptism' in the River Jordan. White robes worn on this occasion are kept to be used for the funeral shroud. Baptism is a rite of death and rebirth (Schmemann 1974a) and for the elderly pilgrim 'baptism' in the Jordan is a direct preparation for death and the other world. The most favoured time to visit the Holy Places is Easter. Shortly thereafter in 1972 word passed around Kokkinia that the groups had returned. Holy water, icons, amulets, and brocade cloth were being given away to friends, or sold to help cover the cost for some pilgrims.

Obviously these journeys to shrines and pilgrimages abroad provide opportunities for geographical mobility and a means whereby local communities are linked in a common purpose; contacts between strangers, however transitory, generate a sense of unity. Participation in ritual produces a strong awareness of the worshippers' common adherence to Christianity which overrides distinctions of class and identity based on regional origin or background, a major divisive feature in Greeks' perceptions of one another. A sense of the widest community is achieved and they can say, as one woman put it, 'We came with faith, we are all Christians, and all the world is here' (Ἤρθαμε με πίστη, είμαστε όλοι χριστιανοί και όλος ο κόσμος είναι εδώ). Together with participation in other religious rituals, pilgrimages act as a powerful integrative force (cf. Turner 1974: 166–230).

In so far as religion creates a universalistic disposition and generates sentiments of involvement in the common experience of all mankind, it is the women who convey this through their extra-domestic activities. Women are instrumental therefore in promoting social integration.

Separation of Generations: Style and Philosophy

A further distinction in men's and women's roles needs to be explored, however, for involvement in religious practices is not uniform. Although religious observance tends to be primarily the concern of women, another cleavage is apparent, for religion in its broadest sense (as world-view or popular philosophy, not only ritual practice) involves both men and women of the older generation. Their attitudes and values reflect metaphysical concerns and a consciousness of spiritual realities; their conduct has a metaphysical orientation contrasting with the more materialistic concerns of younger adults. This contrast was epitomized in the young men's ridicule of the older women returning from a day's pilgrimage: in it the structural contrast between the values and world-view of young and old, men and women, was clear.

For younger adults in the expansion phase of the family's development cycle, material success is a primary concern, for through it the family achieves recognition and prestige in the eyes of others. Success must be manifested, though, and a husband's earning power is shown by expenditure, particularly on consumer goods (electrical appliances, furnishings, clothing). Consequently external appearances become extremely important.

In Kokkinia the different stages in life were precisely marked by style and philosophy. For men, the period before marriage is usually carefree with few responsibilities. Young men associated in informal peer groups based on neighbourhood ties, on school friendships and work contracts, and on common affiliations to football teams. In the late afternoons and at weekends, they would meet at motorcycle shops where they tinkered with their small vehicles, or at lottery shops. On Sunday evenings particularly, the pavements outside lottery shops were crowded and noisy as the various groups gathered to discuss the results of the football pool combinations (Προ-Πο) and the day's matches.

As this age sexual exploits are expected to be part of a young man's experience and the more assertive aspects of masculinity are emphasized. Young men's talk is loud, they push and gesticulate, attracting as much attention as possible, and they take every opportunity to comment on the young girls who pass. In Kokkinia, these youths were fashion-conscious, spending money on clothes as well as on entertainment and cigarettes. Although earning money, they lived at home; being unmarried, they were still their parent's responsibility, and they enjoyed the conscious indulgence of their mothers.

Marriage, however, is the intended lot of every person and thus, once a young man had done his army service and was earning an income, his parents would start considering arrangements for a suitable marriage. From the man's point of view marriage is a great responsibility. Full education has seldom been possible here because of the tremendous economic pressures on families and with few qualifications to his credit, a man is expected to provide for his wife and children in a world of limited economic opportunities.

The dowry which a wife offers, therefore, takes on great importance, for it ensures certain essential material conditions for family life in the form of a dwelling and basic furnishings. Although young men of this generation were aware of the ideals of romantic love and of individual choice, nevertheless they were also aware of economic realities. They intended, therefore, to combine the advantages of the *proxenío*, the formally arranged marriage which included negotiations regarding the girl's dowry, with those of individual choice and personal sentiment. In the urban environment, girls cannot be kept secluded in their homes, and opportunities for personal acquaintance exist. Frequently a young man himself decided on a desirable match, after meeting a young woman and establishing her willingness, and then the formal approaches would be made to establish the important question of the dowry.

After marriage the young man's patterns of association would change gradually. At first he would continue to keep company with his peers, but more often inside the coffee shops than out on street corners. In his own household he assumes a position of authority, regardless of the co-residence of his wife's relatives. An important change occurs with the birth of the first child; the responsibility of parenthood makes his role as breadwinner of primary importance. At this stage, the emphasis is on his successful application to the problems of economic life, the protection of his family's interests, and on sober personal habits (the avoidance of gambling and extravagant spending in coffee shops). Men's energies are concentrated on improving their family's material position and, through this, its reputation in the community.

A man's responsibility for his children includes providing for the marriages of both girls and boys. The necessity for providing a daughter with a dowry in the form of a dwelling is a particularly acute concern since this has almost become a precondition for marriage. In addition, a man should guide his son into a correct marriage choice which will ensure a viable base on which to establish a family. In their concern for the son's future, parents fear and deplore the possibility of a love-match for their son.

Once the children are married, a father relinquishes all authority over them, his life becomes 'quiet' and his mind is at ease (ησύχασε). A remaining concern is that grandchildren will be produced, especially that his son will bear a son, so that his own name will have continuity. Although parents may be resident in the same building with their married children, their households are quite separate; they have their own budget, they cook and eat separately. There may be close contact between the women, but the father may not interfere in any way in the households of his married daughters (see 'Maro's Isolation' pp. 155–8). A father may interfere to protect his daughter only if the economic existence of the new household is threatened, if the husband is incapable of supporting it, through lack of effort or through irresponsibility (e.g. by gambling).

An older man with a pension would spend time in the coffee shops in the morning, reading the newspapers; returning home for the midday meal and siesta, he would leave again in the evening to join men of all ages, playing backgammon or cards in the coffee shops (see Plate 11). On the warm summer evenings he might accompany his wife on a stroll to the main square where they would sit on benches and chat with other couples. At this time of life, they are not concerned with the improvement of the family's position; their needs are simple, and pride is now derived from the progress of their children and grandchildren.

The stages of life for women have a similar pattern. Girls in their late teens live in a state of precarious transition, for the prime concern is to contract a successful marriage and the rest of their lives will rest on this. Their position in society and their standard of living will depend upon the men whom they marry: the plight of older women in the neighbourhood who married at earlier, more difficult periods, and had endured many hardships was used as a constant reminder of the critical importance of marriage. Many young girls undertook employment to contribute to their dowry; others learned trades which can be practised in the home, thereby earning money while at the same time avoiding the kinds of doubts which arose about working girls' reputations. Girls rarely finished high school for, as in the case of boys, economic pressures overcame the priority of education. In addition, many parents worried about the exposure to temptations at the local high school with its crowded unsupervised conditions and felt that these outweighed any advantage that education might offer. In the minds of the parents and girls employment and education served the same purpose: to improve the chances of contracting a successful marriage. Both were seen as a step on the road to the ultimate goal of marriage.

Girls were not secluded in their homes in Kokkinia, but nor was complete freedom of movement allowed. Most girls went out and many travelled daily to their work-places but seldom alone. Ideally they would be chaperoned by a member of the family, but often peers kept company for this reason. Parents had reservations about the trustworthiness of unrelated girls: relatives or the daughters of *koumbároi* were preferred. Young girls who went on errands in the neighbourhood, or just walked together often arm in arm, were always carefully dressed and neat. They were on show just as were the young men who called out to attract their attention from street corners.

In 1972, fashion dictated the appearance of many young girls, who wore sleeveless low-cut blouses, trousers, and make-up. This visible modernity should not, however, be misinterpreted, since the concern for modesty remained, daughters were kept under surveillance, and their reputations protected. Adherence to fashion was related to the notion that an attractive image is appropriate to youth; since fashion determines what is attractive, fashionable dress was acceptable, always retaining the criterion of moderation, however.

Once a woman married, a marked shift in emphasis occurred since, as a wife, she had to be entirely devoted to her home and family. The housewife spent much of the day involved in domestic chores and wore a standard garment, a buttoned housecoat (ρόμπα) over an old skirt or petticoat. Although the style was uniform, the colour and pattern of the fabric was defined by age. Younger women wore brightly-coloured designs (except when in mourning), but with increasing age, duller shades and muted designs were more appropriate; black was associated with death and reserved for mourning garb. My own housecoat in a practical dark shade provoked disapproving comments, 'You are young, you must wear a floral print' (Είσαι νέα, πρέπει να φοράς εμπριμέ).

But on formal and festive occasions, no matter how poor or busy, the housewife would take care to appear in attractive clothes. A new handbag and matching shoes were considered desirable for special occasions: an unmistakable element of competitive assessment existed in the glances of neighbours as a family appeared on formal occasions transformed by their best clothes. Great care was taken with children's appearance— even in the rough and tumble of daily life mothers worried that children should remain spotless and tidy, and would change their clothes several times a day. A good suit of clothes was also essential for a married man, since at this period in the family cycle the competitive drive is most intense and the family's prosperity would be assessed from dress and appearance among other things.

As the children grow older it is their progress which becomes the focus of attention. The emphasis would change as mothers became increasingly concerned with their marriageable daughters' clothes and appearance, less with their own. Until they were in their forties, most women would wear lipstick and have their hair done weekly (the neighbourhood hairdresser was an important focus for female social contact) but once they reached their fifties, these adornments were considered inappropriate and provoked ridicule.

While there are young children, a woman's primary obligations are to them and to the upkeep of the home; religious observances are secondary and can be neglected or undertaken by an older relative, but, once the children are married and have established separate households, there is a distinct change in orientation. At this time, religious observances become increasingly important: the older woman is free to attend services and go on excursions to shrines in the countryside. Being geographically more mobile, she has a wide range of contacts beyond the immediate locality, so that her perceptions of social life and of its significance may change. In fact, it was striking that the outlook of the older people, both men and women, becomes increasingly philosophical, abounding in references to the transient nature of life: 'We are all visitors here' (*Μουσαφιραίοι είμαστε εδώ*), 'Today we are, tomorrow we are not' (*Σήμερα είμαστε, αύριο δεν είμαστε*). The idea of transience, of God's will as the final arbiter, and of divine providence were expressed in common phrases: 'Whatever God decides . . . God abandons no one . . . God will provide' (*'Ο, τι θέλει ο Θεός . . . Ο Θεός δεν αφήνει κανένα . . . 'Εχει ο Θεός*).

Many older women would divest themselves of personal possessions, significantly, giving away whatever valuables they owned (a gold cross, pendant, bracelet) to daughters, daughters-in-law, and granddaughters. The process of stripping oneself of possessions suggests a shift of emphasis from an acquisitive drive to non-material concerns. Old people frequently used expressions deploring human insatiability and greed for property and possessions: 'What do we want these things for? After all, everything remains here' (*Τί τα θέλουμε αυτά αφού όλα εδώ θα μείνουνε;*). Being closer to death and more involved in rituals associated with it, the aged characteristically turned their attention away from the material concerns which had occupied them when they were younger; they were now little concerned with prestige, possessions, or wealth.

In Yerania even the premises they occupied had suggestive connotations: old people usually lived in basement rooms excavated under the original houses (created to provide additional living space and accommodate married daughters in the family home, see Chapters 4 and 6). Thus, while younger married couples lived at ground level, the aged were housed underground, providing a metaphorical association with death although one not explicitly mentioned.

Among the values articulated by Kokkinia people were two sets of concerns. On the one hand, the desire for prestige and family advancement was expressed in material display and the emphasis on appearance. Rivalry between families is intense during the period of expansion when parents are in their middle decades, from their twenties to their mid-forties approximately. On the other hand, a philosophical concern with the transient nature of life, commonly expressed among older adults whose children had already married, revealed notions regarding a spiritual dimension to life, the existence of divine providence, and of mankind's inefficacy before supernatural forces. The incompatibility of these two sets of ideas is accommodated by the marked separation of generations, so that both the material issues and the spiritual concerns were given full expression. The 'dialectic of the development cycle' (Turner 1969: 82) allowed the co-existence of these contradictory values. In the concern with teleological issues more appropriate to their time of life, the elderly reminded the younger people of universal human and philosophical themes which counteracted the emphasis on the materialistic struggle for family prestige.[4]

Most important, life in this locality allowed close and continual contact between young and old: co-resident households represented different stages in the developmental cycle, and neighbourhood life consisted in daily contact between people of different generations. The transmission and continuity of notions regarding metaphysical issues were thereby ensured. The coexistence and structured opposition of different sets of values provided a dialectical contrast in social life but with it, too, a sense of continuity which was far from being static (Hirschon 1983).

Social Change: Cautionary Remarks

This clear separation between the generations both in life-style and philosophy raises interesting questions regarding the nature and process of social change. Given common assumptions about urban life and modernity, it would be easy to impute these differences between aged and young adults to the decline of traditional values, the in-roads of consumerism, and an increasing preoccupation with materialistic and secular issues.

This is particularly tempting in the study of urban life where Western expectations about the nature of urban phenomena are deeply influenced by the presumed inevitability of social change (cf. Nisbet 1969), by ideal-type polarities such as 'traditional/modern' (cf. Bendix 1967), by the urban–rural dichotomy in sociology (associated with Tönnies, Durkheim) and the folk–urban continuum in anthropology (Redfield's construct challenged, for example, by Lewis 1973). These concepts, developed by distinguished thinkers, have been influential but have often been misapplied. Despite critical assessments published over at least two decades, and growing awareness of ethnocentrism, the assumptions bound up with these ideal-type constructs continue to inform approaches to the analysis of urban life.[5]

Anthropological analysis in Greece has frequently not avoided these pitfalls. Consequently, studies set in 'rural Greece' allow its specialists to treat this as a world separate, even divorced from urban life. In Greece, the folk–urban continuum has too often been applied as the folk–urban divide. In this rural emphasis, what constitutes posited 'tradition' is implicitly located in the countryside, the city being seen as the locus of inevitable, radical, and rapid social change where any 'traditional' practices are only curious remnants, soon to pass into oblivion.

The significance of the ethnographic observations regarding generational differences in Kokkinia is that these assumptions regarding social change, whether in country or in urban settings, must be questioned. For Greek society, the separation of generations is a major structural feature. The different emphasis in life-style and values of age categories in Kokkinia is a feature also observed among Sarakatsani shepherds.[6] Its primary implication, one which must be considered wherever generational differences provide the basis for structural distinctions, is that a process of 'cyclical' (or spiral) rather than 'linear' change may be the pattern.[7] This accommodates the co-existence of a wide range of values and precepts, all aspects of a complex cosmology. In the life of an integrated community such as Kokkinia daily contact between all age groups gives expression to contrasting perceptions of life. The separation of generations based on a dialectical opposition of philosophical concerns provides cultural continuity as one social category passes into another stage of life where different expectations apply. Consequently, facile and simplistic conclusions regarding the existence of change should be avoided.

Without denying that considerable forces which promote

radical change do exist, it remains clear that the study of social change can be effective only if firmly grounded in long-term empirical research. The questions which need to be asked refer both to the existence and to the nature of change.

A cautionary note needs to be sounded regarding a possible source of confusion: 'change' should not be confused with differences of a stylistic kind, or those of internal processes (an established distinction in social anthropology, see e.g. Leach 1954: 5; Radcliffe-Brown 1957: 87; Firth 1964: 57). Stylistic differences are those which reflect a different environmental setting. In Kokkinia in 1972 the observer was struck by the visible differences in conduct and appearance of urbanites in contrast with villagers. Young people's clothes were fashionable; they appeared to have unlimited freedom of association; many women were engaged in the work-force and earned money; people lived in areas with dense traffic; many houses had modern conveniences: there were telephones, refrigerators, and washing machines. These impressions reinforce the in-built tendency to anticipate a radically different social order from that which exists in the countryside. Although the observation of external differences is important, I suggest that these are ones of style which 'do not necessarily alter the basic forms' (Firth 1964: 57). The expression of masculine honour and feminine worth, for example, in the urban setting of Kokkinia as compared with the transhumant shepherds of Epirus (Campbell 1964) is undoubtedly different; the stark and absolute gender dichotomy in the pastoral community does not apply as clearly in the city. None the less, in Kokkinia social life revolves around the division of the sexes and their complementary roles, while family reputation and prestige were principal concerns. All are features described as central to other rural Greek communities. I conclude that many differences which do exist constitute response to a different environment but are not necessarily associated with social and cultural change.

While it is obvious that changes do occur in society, the point is to ascertain that the phenomena studied really have been subject to change, that they are different in essence as well as in appearance. Once it is clear that differences in social life are not of a stylistic or external order, but entail reorganization of a more fundamental kind, further questions need to be asked.

The analysis of change requires a rigorous examination of conceptual categories as well as of the phenomena studied. Above all, changes in one area of social life need not imply changes in other aspects, for some features are more resistant to modification than others. One possible approach allows a degree of independence between different aspects of social life, analytically distinguished, for example, into economic, demographic, social, and cultural dimensions. Cultural values and ways of thinking may not submit to change as readily as patterns of conduct; modernization may occur in one dimension without affecting others. Many examples can be quoted to illustrate how innovations may be adopted—and adapted—in culturally different and unexpected ways.[8] The analysis of urban social life, as of social life in rural localities, must be informed by an awareness of these issues, of the need for examining presuppositions, and for rigorous conceptual clarification.

Open and Closed Modes of Orientation

The contrasting philosophies of aged and younger adults have been discussed in terms of social change and of the structuring of social relationships. Their coexistence has other implications, however, in the whole set of ideas which constitute the worldview or cosmology. In this section, certain ambiguities and tensions in the patterns of social interaction will be interpreted.

Among these the opposition between 'open' and 'closed' is central; it is verbally explicit and expressed in numerous metaphors. The idiom of 'opening' carries positive connotations while that of 'closing' is negatively connoted. Thus marriage and childbearing are 'open' states. Unmarried girls are frequently urged to get married and 'open a house' (άνοιξε το σπίτι σου). Childbirth is said to 'open' the body (ανοίγει το σώμα) and the annual renewal of natural life in the season of spring (άνοιξη) similarly connotes 'opening'. The association of life and creation with the state of being 'open' is clear. In other contexts—relating to 'luck', which opens (ανοίγει η τύχη), to light (ανοίγω/κλείνω το φως, lit. 'open/close the light', not 'turn on/off the light'), to prayer or communication with divine beings when 'the heavens open' (άνοιξε ο ουρανός), to joy when the heart is open (άνοιξε η καρδιά), as well as to the approved 'open' personality—the fortunate and positive connotations of opening are evident.

Conversely, the 'closed' and the 'confined' are negative states, associated with misfortune, death, sin, isolation (as in the κλεισούρα of houses on an inner courtyard), the negative power of sorcery, expressed as 'binding' (δέσιμο).[9] The Greek word for worry, vexation, or depression, *stenachória*, is derived from a narrow, tight place (στενός χώρος), and to have a 'closed character' (κλειστός χαρακτήρας) is not desirable. The death of sons or the absence of men is said to 'close the house' (έκλεισε το σπίτι). Thus, 'closing' and the 'closed' convey states of limitation and restriction; they all refer to a condition of misfortune, and are unsocial.

I suggest that these verbal metaphors have also an observable social dimension, for the ethnographic data suggest that social interaction was patterned in different ways. These patterns can be identified as reflecting a more open, communal orientation, or a more selective, inward-looking, and closed orientation. This contrast at the analytical level is variously associated with distinctions at the social level between family and neighbourhood organization, between 'house' and 'road', and with variations in seasonal and daily routines.

The two modes of ordering relationships may be presented summarily. The 'open' emphasizes life and continuity, the unity of all people with one another, of the living with the dead, and the communion of the divine with the human. It asserts the universal community which is egalitarian, undivided, and integrated, comprising all members, past and present, dead and alive. It also conveys the dimensions of eternal realities, transcending all boundaries. In Yerania, the communal, open mode of orientation characterized key ritual events: Easter, name-day celebrations, the immediate period following death, and also the atmosphere of Sundays. These occasions tended to emphasize universal bonds, generated a spirit of unity and solidarity, and required communal participation. Death and mourning rituals and the annual commemorative days (Soul Saturdays, Ψυχοσάββατα) had a related effect. They provided occasions for public commemoration and united the deceased and the living in a continuing relationship.[10] The values which informed interaction between neighbours showed interesting similarities. Neighbourhood values were inclusive, egalitarian, co-operative, and undifferentiated, and contradicted the inevitably divisive consequences of family- and household-based loyalties.

The other mode of orientation may be called 'closed', for it is selective, is directed inwards, and creates boundaries. Characteristic of family- and household-based relationships, this orientation reflects exclusive loyalties, generates a competitive disposition and implies notions of social hierarchy. The family/household has boundaries, it is the elementary locus of 'us/them' distinctions, secrecy is maintained within it, suspicion and even hostility without; as an institution it segments and structures. The closed mode of orientation differentiates between persons, it is selective, and excludes some of them. Consequently it segments the community and its effect is one of fragmentation, not unity.

These patterns of interaction characterized different occasions. Also most striking is the contrast apparent in people's use of space. In Kokkinia social life was marked by the division between the 'house' and those who belong to it, and the 'road', neighbourhood, or outside world. The appropriate location for gender and age categories and for particular activities was defined by this spatial and conceptual division. Women and children were best associated with the house, which provided a protective environment where integrity and purity could be maintained. In contrast the 'road' representing the 'outside world' was seen as treacherous territory where disaster could befall those whose vulnerability required protection (especially unmarried women and children). A woman 'of the road'(του δρόμου) and a child who is 'learning the side-streets' (μαθαίνει σοκκάκια) exemplify how purity may be corrupted. The contrast between 'house' and 'road', therefore, suggests that between a state of perfection and pristine values, of Paradise before the Fall, and that of the fallen world where evil forces are rampant and human action is subject to corruption. Attitudes to small children also suggested this, for they were kept at home by preference and were not encouraged to mix with others. Influences from outside the home were felt to be potentially harmful. Crèches, playgroups, and nurseries were disapproved of by mothers and fathers alike: the general view was that the longer children could be kept at home the better. In everyday life, the house was treated as a sanctuary, an area of limited access with boundaries which could be crossed on a selective basis.

An interesting question arises, therefore, from the division of 'house' and 'road', for this metaphor also denotes the social division between family and neighbourhood relations. These two essential social institutions are associated with different sets of values which are often directly contradictory with the result that many double-bind situations arise in practice. For example, the good neighbour who should be sociable, co-operative, and open has also to preserve family secrets and conserve its resources (Chapter 8).

The juxtaposition of these social contexts with the two modes of orienting social relationships requires further explanation. In verbal metaphorical usage the 'open' state carries positive connotations, while the 'closed' state is negative. The correspondence of a 'closed' mode of orientation with the social contexts of family and house in everyday activity, and of an 'open' mode of orientation with the neighbourhood or outside world is thus somewhat puzzling. However, this is not an absolute correlation: the importance of context in dealing with symbolic oppositions is critical (cf. Needham 1973: xxv). Strikingly then, on certain occasions the house does become an open area, expressing the communal mode of orientation. These occasions include the traumatic occurrence of death as well as the festive, auspicious event of name-days; thus the puzzle intensifies.

The premise underlying my interpretation is that a people's world-view has an explanatory role: it provides an interpretation for these contradictory patterns which, after all, exist at different levels of analysis—verbal expressions, social observation and activity, and analytically-defined patterns. In taking account of the world-view or cosmology of the people a unifying framework for understanding these contradictions is provided. In terms of Dumont's notion of hierarchy and levels, the contradictions and paradoxes of the social and metaphorical juxtaposition are transcended.[11] This is not surprising since religion is a central aspect of their tradition and heritage; it provides a framework, not only for ritual practices but also for the values and perceptions which underlie social action.

Redemption and the Fallen World

Early in my acquaintance with people in this locality a common phrase which struck me was 'the deceptive world' (ψεύτικος ο κόσμος), often accompanied by remarks on the transience of life and of material wealth. Elderly people would reflect that this world is one of misplaced certainties since 'everything remains here' and 'we are only visitors' ('Ολα εδώ θα μείνουνε· μουσαφιράιοι είμαστε εμείς). In similar vein another characteristic phrase was 'Today we are, tomorrow we are not' (Σήμερα είμαστε, αύριο δεν είμαστε). These popular expressions reflect the notion that the world is transient and has become a place of deceptive realities, while others express the view that human nature is flawed and fallible. In the overall context of the cosmology of this society, these phrases take on a wider significance, for the world-view is based on Christianity, a universalistic religion with an explicit body of doctrine.

In my view, two fundamental tenets of Orthodox Christian doctrine have sociological significance, the Fall and the Resurrection. Associated with the first is the notion that the phenomenal world and human beings exist in a fallen state, separated from divine reality and a pristine condition of purity. Human nature, though redeemable, is inherently weak and imperfect, susceptible to corruption. These notions are contained in the phrases quoted, and were summed up cryptically when people would say, 'What can you do? We are only human' (Τί να κανεις; Ανθρώποι είμαστε). Used to excuse conduct when mistakes were acknowledged or when help was offered, the statement clearly implied that human capacities are limited and tend to fall short of their mark. I was often told, 'Don't hesitate to call us if you ever need anything—after all we are only human'. At first I failed to recognize its implications, but once I became familiar with people's views on autonomy and obligation, I realized that any such call would not cause one loss of face nor fear of a rebuff.[12] Essentially an acknowledgement of human frailty, this notion of human fallibility in a fallen world has several social consequences.

Firstly, people's dependence on one another is recognized and allowed expression. This notion tempers the values of self-regard (εγωισμός) and independence characteristic of Greek life, which would otherwise take on an absolute character. The strength of neighbourhood expectations in the locality is undoubtedly also related to this recognition of human limitations and need.

Secondly, because of the imperfections inherent in fallen human nature, failure to live up to expectations can be understood and excused. Allowances for inadequate performance can be made and less pressure is felt to achieve externally-set goals. Consequently, feelings of personal guilt and inadequacy do not arise as easily as, say, in a society with a Protestant heritage of personal responsibility for salvation. Possibly too, the quality of moral judgements tends to be conditional and contextual, rather than absolute.

Another aspect of this conviction is the acceptance that human existence in this world is compromised, rarely achieving the harmony and fulfilment promised in the other. This world in which the force of evil operates insidiously is seen as being full of potential hazards, and no-one is immune to its threat. Though people may have good intentions, their susceptibility to corruption is ever-present; consequently, trust in others must be tempered by prudent scepticism. 'You can't have trust/confidence', people would say (Δεν μπορείς να 'χεις εμπιστοσύνη), often followed by the significant statement *o kósmos einai kakós*. Since *kósmos* is both social and physical, meaning people and the world, the statement contains a revealing ambiguity. 'The world/people are bad/evil' explains why caution is required in dealings with others.

However, the Greek word *kakós* is loaded differently from its English equivalent 'bad'; it is not unequivocal. Indeed, it is important to realize that notions of good and evil are less than absolute moral categories in Greek thought. This was established early in the Eastern Orthodox Christian tradition. Thus, St Maximus the Confessor states that 'What is simply called evil is not altogether evil, but evil in one way and not another', and the same applies to what is called good (quoted in Yannaras 1984: 37). Interestingly, too, this ambiguity is reflected in folk usage, for example in the designation of the sexual act as evil (η κακή πράξη), and in the equivocal connotations of the word for 'cunning' or 'shrewdness' (πονηριά), as well as pride (περηφάνεια), characteristics seen as assets in adult men's public dealings, yet which are also deplored and are subject to open criticism.

None the less, the 'evil of the world/people' is a frequent warning to children and adolescents. It conveys the separation between the sanctuary of the home environment—the house, and the hazards of the outside world—the road. Furthermore, this opposition alludes to the separation between the divine realm, the eternal world where an ideal state of being is located, and the phenomenal world, transient and compromised. Under conditions associated with the Fall, ideals are rarely attainable since human motives and actions, however noble, are in some way warped. Because of human frailty, the threat of corruption, and the dangers inherent in life, protection must be provided for the vulnerable. The domestic realm, therefore, must be kept bounded in everyday life, divided from its surroundings. I suggest that this set of notions regarding the fallen world is associated with the boundaries, selectivity, and distance which structures relationships based on family and household membership. This may help to explain the paradoxical situation of the new bride and of the newly delivered mother (λεχώνα), who both remained secluded in the home at their time of auspicious 'opening' (the metaphor for procreative sexuality and life). At such times when life-giving forces predominate, the house is even more cut off from the outside world. In an ideal world the open mode of orientation could be freely manifested and would predominate, but, given the fallen condition of life, when a woman is most open and vulnerable the house must provide a sanctuary from the dangers of the outside world.

Intimately bound up with this concept of the fallen world is the Christian interpretation of death and the Resurrection. The biblical story of Adam, Eve, and the Serpent in the Garden is common to the Judaeo-Christian and Islamic traditions, but the interpretation of this story differs considerably, even within branches of Christianity. 'The significance of the sin of Adam and its consequences for mankind is understood along quite different lines', as Meyendorff notes for the Catholic and Orthodox traditions (1974: 143). In Orthodox thought, guilt and mortality are viewed in a different light; the notion of sin has a personal character while the Latin idea of a 'sin of nature' is absent, as is that of inherited guilt (ibid.).

Orthodox Christian doctrine identifies the Fall, the result of the transgression in the Garden, with the condition of mortality rather than with that of sinfulness. The heritage of the Fall afflicting all generations of mankind is death and not inherited guilt.[13] For St Maximus the Confessor and other early Church fathers, 'the wrong choice made by Adam brought in passion, corruption, and mortality' but not inherited guilt (quoted ibid.: 145) and it is death which makes sin inevitable (cf. Yannaras 1984: 35–40).

In the Orthodox interpretation of humankind's fallen condition, the centrality of death gives added emphasis to the second fundamental tenet in this world-view, the belief in Christ's Resurrection. Here again, the particular character of Eastern Christian doctrine must be noted. The Orthodox are categorical that 'there was a genuine resurrection from the dead in the sense that Christ's human body was reunited to his human soul, and that the tomb was found to be empty' (Ware 1979: 111).

The redemption offered by Christ's death on the Cross 'was not primarily a justification, but a victory over death . . . not to satisfy a legal requirement, but to vanquish the frightful cosmic reality of death' (Meyendorff 1974: 161). Christ's death is seen as a voluntary sacrifice, and it was a real death in physical as well as in spiritual terms. (Orthodox views countenance no dichotomy between material and spiritual dimensions.) Christ though God took a human form: fully God he became fully man. As a son of Adam he was subjected to mortality but being God he alone could vanquish death. His voluntary surrender became a total victory, bringing redemption to the world and humankind.

The Resurrection is the total victory over the fallen condition of mankind. It is celebrated in the Easter services through the hymn, *Christós Anésti*:

> Christ is risen from the dead,
> trampling down death by death,
> and to those in the tomb,
> he bestows life.

Repeated many times not just at Easter but throughout the forty-day period following it, the message is clear and can escape no one. Death is vanquished, mortality is overcome. God is shown as the victorious conqueror in another Easter verse, 'Let God arise and let his enemies be scattered.'

Death no longer has the finality it had; its transitional nature was emphasized by the early Church fathers:

It is true we still die as before but we do not remain in death, and this is not to die . . . this is no longer death but a falling asleep. (St John Chrysostom)

Henceforth we are dissolved for a time only, according to our bodies' mortal nature, in order the better to receive resurrection; like seeds cast in the earth we do not perish but sown in the earth we shall rise again since death has been brought to nought by the grace of the Saviour. (St Athanasius)

This set of beliefs offers an interpretation for a number of social and ritual actions. The immediate response to death is that the house opens, it becomes accessible to all, and this correspondence with other rituals of a festive kind (name-days, Sundays, Easter) seems puzzling. The open mode of orientation which characterizes all these occasions suggests a positive, auspicious message even though death clearly is a sad and traumatic event. But in the celebration of Easter the solution is provided, for Easter is primarily and essentially a reaffirmation of life.

Easter, the centre of Orthodox worship, is an explosion of joy . . . at the triumph of life after the overwhelming sorrow over death . . . All things are now filled with the certainty of life, whereas before all had been moving steadily towards death . . . Orthodoxy emphasises with special insistence the faith of Christianity in the triumph of life. (Fr. Dumitru Staniloae, quoted in Ware 1979: 166)

The particular emphasis of the Orthodox Christian tradition is on the redemptive power of Christ's death and with it the end of the tyranny of mortality. Seen in this light, the rituals immediately following death assert the positive message of salvation, the promise of eternal life, central to a Christian worldview.

In human terms, of course, the experience of bereavement is actively painful. The mourners are given the chance to express their grief and to come to terms with loss over a period during which ritual observances guide their actions. At one level the rupturing effect of death is recognized in the responses of sorrow and grief which present it as a traumatic, inauspicious event.

But another aspect is also evident: the symbolic actions and patterns convey a different message. The open house, the unstructured time between death and burial, full communal participation in that period, the oil-lamp kept lit for forty days in the house; all are expressions of the open mode of orientation. These expressive aspects of the rituals reveal the promise of life's continuation, of the 'triumph of life' over death.

By taking account of the emphasis on the Resurrection in the Orthodox tradition, the approach to death is related in a meaningful way to festive ritual events whose atmosphere of joy and open participation is very different. Common to all these occasions is the open mode of ordering relationships, that of communality and participation. Furthermore, it is associated with the divine realm which contains the notion of an undivided body of believers united in Christ. The open mode of orientation contrasts with the structured divisions of everyday interaction where, I suggest, notions related to the fallen world pertain. In the fallen condition, the state of openness and unity cannot be wholly realized; it is inevitably warped and altered by negative forces. For this reason, boundaries and divisions must be maintained in normal life. On certain occasions and at times during the year, however, the assertion of an ideal state, of the eternal community, is made.

Certain theological tenets have provided a context for interpreting these modes of orientation (open/closed), their associated verbal metaphors, and the contradictions arising out of opposing social expectations based on family (house) and neighbourhood (road). They also enlighten our understanding of the pervasive symbolic dimension in local life. In Orthodox thought, the fallen condition does not constitute a final or hopeless state of condemnation. Christ's Incarnation, Death, and Resurrection offer redemption to all. A new life and attainment of the divine world is possible. But Orthodox understanding of the relationship between God and human beings clearly specifies the notion of free will and the freedom to exercise it (Ware 1979: 65, 75–6). Without human effort, God's action cannot be effective; it depends on the free participation of human beings.

Since Orthodox thought does not accept any duality of the material and the spiritual and these elements are intermingled in all aspects of life, participation with the divine can take many forms. Furthermore this present existence and the divine realm are not separated in a temporal sense (e.g., this world/the next world) but are coexistent. Thus people referred to 'the other world' (ο άλλος κόσμος), implying its coexistence, but never to the 'next world'. Contact and communication between these two realms is always possible, therefore, and in infinite ways.

But the further significance of this set of notions at the social level is that a symbolic dimension is invested in most activities, even in material objects which appear familiar and mundane. The sacramental qualities of household furnishings have been discussed: tables, beds, and chairs have more than a practical function and represent the values of commensality, of conjugal unity, and of hospitality. The tangible world can be seen as imbued with spiritual values, expressed through people's everyday actions, both overtly and in unconscious ways.

I am not suggesting that Kokkinia residents have especial theological expertise. Consistent with Orthodox Christianity as a way of life, wholly integrated, for historical reasons in a long cultural tradition, participation in ritual and religious observances forms a normal part of everyone's socialization, from childhood attendance at wakes, to Sunday catechism, seasonal and life cycle rituals, and the annual celebration of Easter. Through this integrated experience, formal doctrinal precepts are existentially woven into people's understanding; they become part of a repertoire of standard philosophical phrases and adages. Though not consciously articulated, formal doctrine is clearly reflected at the popular level of religious life and, further, is expressed even in non-ritual contexts.

The Refugee Lesson

An elderly neighbour, puzzled for several months by my interest in everyday life and ideas in Kokkinia, finally concluded that I had come to study 'the lesson of refugeeness' (το μάθημα της προσφυγιάς, see Preface). Her remark prompts me to ponder what this lesson is.

The settlement of Kokkinia in the 1920s by an uprooted,

traumatized group of people who had lost their homeland, almost all their material goods, as well as their family and community ties, provides an instructive long-term case-study of a refugee situation. Over the decades, people adjusted to their conditions in this locality, responding with remarkable resilience to a chronic situation of acute hardship, political neglect, and economic marginality. Their place in metropolitan Greek society was the combined result of several interacting forces. On the one hand, their sense of grievance and neglect at the hands of successive governments led many to have a vested interest in their status as refugees. The unfulfilled promises of compensation were remembered into the 1970s, a direct result of inept policies regarding housing and refugee ownership rights. For many, their situation became one of being refugees for over fifty years.

This political and structural feature, recognized in many studies of ethnicity and identity, does not, however, fully explain the situation in Kokkinia. Indeed the people indicated this by their own self-designation: they would call themselves both *prósphyges* ('refugees') and '*Mikrasiátes*' interchangeably. The latter term, denoting place of origin, was used specifically to indicate their cultural heritage and tradition in contrast to that of metropolitan Greeks. For the outsider, these distinctions were hardly significant, seeing that Asia Minor Greeks shared with mainlanders and islanders a common religion and language and close similarity in most aspects of culture and tradition. For the newcomers to the Greek nation-state, however, a crucial part of the process of adjustment was the establishment of their identity. This consciousness of a separate identity was part of their heritage itself, for these people had been subjects of the Ottoman Empire whose many ethnic groups were administered in the *millet* system. Curiously then the notion of a separate identity was one among many facets of their culture reestablished in the new environment by emphasizing minutiae of detail, of differences of degree rather than kind. In this sense the Asia Minor Greeks, in relation to the host society with which they shared so much, constitute a limiting case of ethnicity (where objective grounds for distinction are minimal).

The continuity of culture and tradition, the structural replication of their position in Greek society, their emphasis on family and neighbourhood and on the complementarity of age and gender—all were striking aspects of a way of life which was highly integrated, though beset by internally contradictory norms. The process of reconstituting this way of life was achieved through the conscious application of memory, itself culturally valued and institutionalized, and by the sure conviction of the value of their way of doing things.

This, then, was the lesson gleaned from these refugees. In the face of extreme material loss and deprivation, the invisible and intangible aspects of culture provided sustenance. Through the tenacity of their traditions and their preference for re-establishing familiar patterns, maintaining continuity with the past, they found a way of overcoming the personal alienation and social disintegration into which, both as individuals and as a group, they might otherwise so easily have sunk.

The extent of their success was revealed in some events in the autumn of 1972 when the fiftieth anniversary of the Asia Minor catastrophe (η Μικρασιατική Καταστροφή) was commemorated. In several areas of the city events were organized at an official level by the municipal authorities and the 'homeland associations' (πατριωτικοί σύλλογοι). In Kokkinia these included some parades and tableaux by schoolchildren, three talks by slightly known writers, and a commemorative liturgy in the church of St Nicolas. With the exception of the last, which more closely expressed the tragic personal aspects of that period, the atmosphere at these events was spiritless and attendances were small. Talks bore sentimental titles such as 'Lyrical Recollections of Smyrna' (Λυρικές Αναμνήσεις της Σμύρνης) and 'Lost Homelands' (Χαμένες Πατρίδες).

Near Yerania the official inauguration of a building to house the Smyrna Association (Σύλλογος Σμυρναίων) provoked a revealing incident. The programme included several tableaux presented by some pupils of the high school, as well as poems and a talk by a minor writer. Families of the children who were involved sat expectantly in the audience, as well as residents of the prefabricated dwellings of nearby Yerania. Owing to a late start, the talk and poetry went on until 11 o'clock. Suddenly an official announced that the tableaux were cancelled. The dignitaries arose, leaving the hall amidst angry murmurings. One woman from Smyrna, in her late sixties, called out angrily, 'We came here to see our grandchildren perform not to hear the words of intellectuals' (*Για τα παιδιά μας ήρθαμε, όχι για τους φιλόλογους*). She was cheered by those around her. As the audience reluctantly dispersed, people exchanged comments, 'They forgot us for so many years. Now what do they want of us?' (*Τόσα χρόνια μας ξεχάσανε·τί γυρεύουν τώρα από μας;*).

The building itself provoked similar remarks over the following weeks. Local residents said, 'For years they've been promising to build this for the Smyrnaians . . . what do they want it for *now*—now that the refugees are disappearing?' (*Τόσα χρόνια το 'κτίζανε αυτό . . . Τί να το κάνουν τώρα—τώρα που φεύγουν οι πρόσφυγες;*). These exasperated comments reflect the frustration caused by long years of neglect by the central government: now it was neither necessary nor relevant to the situation, and indeed these reminders of Asia Minor and the past were unwelcome and painful. Old people were now involved in their families and were far more interested in seeing their grandchildrens' performances than hearing prettily phrased descriptions of places whose painful associations can never be erased.

Partly as a result of changes in the wider society, and partly through the ever-widening timescale between the younger people and the carefully preserved heritage of their place of origin, the refugee world (*ο προσφυγικός κόσμος*) was disappearing. A woman in her seventies expressed it thus: 'Our "refugee-ness" is disappearing, the old people are dying and whatever one might describe, it is only like a small patch of cloth. We experienced it, but it's like a fairy story to our children' (*Πάει η προσφυγιά, φεύγουν οι γέροι. Ό, τι κι αν πεις σαν μπάλωμα είναι. Εμείς κάτι ξέραμε αλλά για τα παιδιά μας σαν παραμύθι είναι*).

APPENDIX I

CONFLICT IN CLOSE QUARTERS
The Legal Tangle

The legal aspect of housing in Yerania is best illustrated by the situation in some typical cases of co-residence.

Extreme hostility existed in one crowded dwelling shared by two unrelated families (see Fig. 6): the front part was occupied by Sophia, a widow from Smyrna, and her two married daughters, Maria and Anna and their families, while the back portion was the residence of Zoe and her family. Sophia claimed that the dwelling was granted to her and her husband in 1928. Zoe claimed that her deceased mother, a refugee from Pontus, had been the original occupant, and that Sophia had been given shelter in the front room some years later but had never left.

In 1972 the front room of the original dwelling housed one family: Sophia's younger daughter Anna, her husband, and two small children. Under it a basement room excavated years before to increase living space now housed five persons: the elder daughter Maria, her husband and their two teenage children, and old Sophia herself. It comprised a living/sleeping room and two alcoves extending out into the pavement area. A double bed and large refrigerator (important storage space under such crowded conditions) took up over two-thirds of the main basement room. The two children slept on camp-beds which were folded up during the day while old Sophia slept on a narrow bed fitted into an alcove in the wall. Both sisters cooked separately for their families in the small kitchen alcove (2.5 sq. m.) excavated under the pavement. This constituted the only example of shared cooking facilities known to me in Yerania, but even so, each woman had her own utensils and meals were prepared separately.

The back portion of the dwelling, enlarged by the addition of two rooms, was slightly less cramped, and housed a family of five: Zoe, her husband, and their three children, an 18-year-old daughter, a 19-year-old son, and a 21-year-old daughter who was ready for marriage and required part of the dwelling for her dowry. They occupied the second original room of the dwelling, its original kitchen which had become a bedroom, an excavated basement room of 12 sq. m., and a room built in the courtyard.

Although the residents of the back and front of the dwelling were

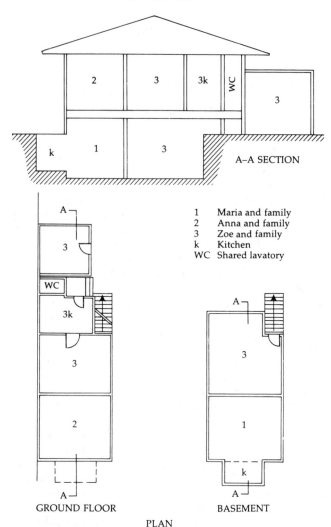

FIG. 6. Conflict in Close Quarters

not on speaking terms and tried to avoid contact, the fact that the only lavatory (in Zoe's section of the house) was shared by all fourteen occupants made this unavoidable. It is interesting to note that these families were far from being poor. Indeed, Maria's family was among those with the highest household income in Yerania: her husband had a well-paid job as a senior dockworker and her son and daughter both worked at skilled trades (metalworking and dressmaking respectively). Sophia earned her keep as a nurse by giving injections in the neighbourhood. Household income was over 9,000 drs. per month, almost twice the average in the locality, sufficient for them to have rented a whole house in Yerania. Similarly Anna's family had an adequate income as her husband was a well-known professional wrestler. Despite the relative affluence of these families, they were unwilling to relinquish their 'refugee' claims, for which they had endured considerable discomfort over the years. Their attitude was expressed in a defiant retort, 'Why should we leave? We have rights here—should we lose them?' (Γιατί να φύγουμε; Έχουμε τα δικαιώματα μας εδώ—να τα χάσουμε;).

Similarly, Zoe's husband was a taxi-driver who also earned above the average wage, and their household income was supplemented by the older children: the son was a metalworker and the elder daughter was an office-clerk earning a regular monthly salary. The younger girl in her final year at the high school further indicated the family's relative affluence, since full education for girls was generally considered somewhat superfluous.

These conflicting claims to ownership were under review by the Ministry of Social Welfare during the latter part of 1972. Maria's husband, a conservative man from the Mani, was openly optimistic about the outcome. 'Don't worry, we have influence', he would say (Έχουμε μέσο, μη στεναχωριέσαι), referring to contacts through his brother, a police officer (a position of some power during the junta period). He proved right; the tribunal decided to grant the house to Sophia, and Zoe's family were granted a new three-roomed flat in Piraeus.

Bitter conflict was not avoided even where close kinship ties existed, as the following case shows: Mr and Mrs Roulis were refugees from Smyrna. As a young couple with children in 1928 they were given a whole dwelling unit on a corner plot. Mr Roulis's younger sister and her husband remained unhoused so she asked her brother to accommodate them until government compensation was made. Believing this would be temporary, Roulis agreed. After some time the couple was offered a grant of land, but they did not have the money to build so they decided to stay where they were. Years passed, the sister remained in residence, had a daughter, and increased the living quarters by excavating a basement room under the front room. She continued to ignore her brother's suggestions that they move out. Once the 1946 tenancy 'moratorium', came into effect, though, Roulis discovered that her family could not be removed and their relationship became openly hostile. His niece Effie grew up; when she married in 1954, the ground-floor room became her dowry and her parents moved into the basement room—the typical Yerania pattern. Roulis's family of four children were growing up in the back part of the dwelling but living space could not be expanded much because this was a small corner plot. They excavated a basement room, however, and enlarged the original kitchen. In the 1950s their only daughter was given one room on her marriage. Mr and Mrs Roulis then moved into the basement room, and excavated a small kitchen alcove for themselves. After their three sons moved out on marriage, the daughter took over the ground-floor rooms for her growing family.

After the sister's death, the bitter quarrel continued, now between the families of uncle and niece: three separate households of close kin were living in a single dwelling but were not on speaking terms. Mr Roulis wished to pay for the concession but was prevented from doing so because Effie contested his claim. He, therefore, welcomed the Ministry's arbitration in his case. After lengthy investigations, a decision was taken: Mr Roulis was granted the whole house by paying 4,000 drs. for the concession. Effie's family was to be rehoused in a two-roomed flat in a new state housing project near Piraeus harbour. She declared to all that she was delighted because a new flat was worth far more than an old shack. The neighbours remarked amongst themselves, however, that she was trying to save face after years of adamant refusal to accept a voluntary move.

Both the Roulises and their daughter were equally happy with the decision, since the old couple suffered from the infirmities of old age, and had been finding life in the basement increasingly difficult. For years they had been unable to move to better premises in case they jeopardized their rights to the 'concession'. They decided to take over the front quarters which the niece would be vacating, and to give their basement rooms to their married daughter who needed the extra room for her teenage children.

Some co-resident families did manage to agree on a voluntary course of action without recourse to arbitration although this was not common. Despite hostile relations, this occurred in the dwelling unit of Rosa, an elderly widow refugee from the Pontus. After the bombing of Piraeus harbour during the war she had offered shelter to a childless couple from her home area ($\pi\alpha\tau\varrho\ell\delta\alpha$) in the back room of her house. Since they were homeless and fell under the terms of the 1946 tenancy 'moratorium', they remained living there for the next twenty-five years, disregarding the problems caused to their benefactors. Rosa had to bring up her three children in the front part of the house, where a basement was excavated. Later, her only daughter Eleni took the main ground-floor room as her dowry on marriage. Eleni's husband built a small room in the courtyard for Rosa, and when the sons moved out to their own wives' dowry residences, Eleni took over the front basement room which she needed for her three children.

In view of the Ministry's imminent arbitration, the co-resident families reached an agreement in 1971: the elderly couple applied for
rehousing in a new block of flats. Since they had no heirs or other relatives to benefit from the property, their decision was easier. But a long
delay ensued. Later in 1972, Rosa and Eleni's family were still awaiting
the transfer of the other family with some impatience, so that they
could pay the Ministry for the concession. They did not wish to live in
the house any longer, but required the concession to dispose of the
property before they could move away into a new dwelling.

Other difficulties encountered by the legal situation of refugees and
their property rights are further evidenced by the case of Yota, a
middle-aged woman, whose mother, Vasso, was a refugee from Aidini.
She expended considerable time and effort in establishing their sole
claim to ownership of their Yerania dwelling. Vasso, a widow in her
seventies, had moved into the dwelling in 1928 with her mother-in-
law, the original occupant, who had died five years later. For some
years the house was jointly occupied by Vasso's family and her husband's unmarried siblings who had never considered paying for the
concession and who finally left Yerania. In 1972 Yota had to produce
evidence on behalf of her mother, that the original occupant's other
heirs (i.e. Vasso's deceased husband's siblings and their children) had
no claim to the dwelling. Yota had difficulty in tracing her cousins
whom they had not seen for years and whose position in life had
improved considerably. Hearing of her efforts to gain the title to the
refugee property, some of them tried to contest her claim. Yota had
then to prove to the Ministry that they had left the Yerania dwelling
many years before, and that they owned property elsewhere (in the
middle-class suburb of Nea Smyrni).

After nearly nine months Vasso's family's sole claim was established, the necessary sum was paid, and the concession granted to
Vasso. The family noted that the problems would have been infinitely
more complex and the cost four times higher had the old woman died
before this issue was settled. As a reminder of the complication, their
next-door neighbour Afro was negotiating with the Ministry at this
time about a payment of 60,000 drs. for the concession to her dwelling.
She had 'inherited' it from her mother's sister, who had been childless
and had 'endowered' Afro on her marriage. The aunt had died without
obtaining the titles, and in this case the cost of the concession was
twelve times higher.

APPENDIX II

RESULTS OF HOUSEHOLD SURVEY IN YERANIA, 1972

Number of houses in survey	42
Number of households in survey	62
Number of shared houses[1]	37
Shared houses as percentage of total	88%
Number of persons in survey	208

SIZE OF HOUSEHOLD

Survey average	3.4
Overall Yerania average (1971 census)	3.2
Overall Athens average[2]	3.3

ORIGIN OF ADULTS

Number of persons over 26 years	124
Number of persons who identified themselves as 'refugees'	105
'Refugees' as percentage of adult population	85%

CHARACTERISTICS OF WORKING POPULATION

Employed persons

Total number	83
As percentage of total population	40%
Overall Athens average	35%

Employed women

Total number	19
As percentage of working population	23%
Overall Athens average	27%

Employed persons under 21 years

Total number	27
As percentage of working population	33%
Overall Athens average	11%

[1] More than one household.

[2] All figures for Athens are taken from the 1971 census.

Employed women under 21 years
    As percentage of working population   15%
    Overall Athens average   11%
    As percentage of female working population   60%

PENSIONERS

Total number   9
As percentage of total population   4%
Overall Athens average   7%

Pensioner households
    Total number   9
    As percentage of total households   15%

APPENDIX III

CATEGORIES OF OCCUPATION IN YERANIA, 1972

	No.	% of working population
Unskilled and semi-skilled (εργάτες)[1]	35	42
Artisans (τεχνίτες)[2]	16	19
Commerce (εμπόροι)[3]	10	12
Transport services[4]	11	13
Employees (υπάλληλοι)[5]	6	7
Professional	2	2
Seamen	3	4
TOTAL	83	

Note: Incomes estimated on basis of average earnings per job category; estimated average monthly income per head = 1,800 drs. (Average monthly per head in Greece = 2,720 drs. OECD 1972.)

[1] e.g. labourers, factory workers, building construction-workers.
[2] e.g. carpenters, metalworkers, shoemakers.
[3] Private traders.
[4] Private haulage, taxi-, and unspecified drivers.
[5] Mainly low-grade municipal jobs.

NOTES

1. Rural settlement was given priority, particularly after the exchange of populations. Many villages were re-established and whole communities reconstituted as entities, unlike the situation for most urban settlements (see League of Nations 1926; Ladas 1932; Pentzopoulos 1962).

2. People in Kokkinia seldom used the word *Romaios, -oi* for themselves or for Greek identity, although this term is directly related to the Greeks' inclusion in the *Rum millet* within the Ottoman system of administration (see p. 10 and Chapter 2), reflecting continuity from the eastern Roman Empire through the Byzantine Empire. The hostility towards 'Hellenism' as a pagan and polytheistic culture which characterized much of that period (see Campbell and Sherrard 1968: 20–30) may possibly be part of the connotations of the term *Ellenes* as used by people of Asia Minor origin for local Greeks. For some other aspects of the Romaic/Hellenic distinctions, see Herzfeld 1982.

3. 'Greek identity' is not a simple issue, however, since regional affiliation (τοπικισμός) is marked and enduring (see e.g. Dimen and Friedl 1976). At the same time, identity and the insider–outsider distinction shifts by social context in a segmentary fashion (see Herzfeld 1985).

4. The presupposition that 'traditionality' and 'modernity' are mutually exclusive polarities continues to inform many sociological analyses of southern European and Greek society. Although challenged powerfully by Bendix (1967), and Tipps (1973), indeed even earlier by Lewis (1952), this inadequate conceptual framework particularly continues to influence the approach taken to urban studies in this region.

5. The seven Ecumenical Councils (AD 325–780), which met in Constantinople, Nicaea, Ephesus, and Chalcedon, laid down fundamental tenets of Christian doctrine. Contemporary reports describe a high level of informed public debate on theological issues (e.g. St Gregory of Nyssa on the Second Council held at Constantinople in AD 381, quoted in Ware 1964: 43–4).

6. Considerable controversy centres on the existence and reliability of statistical records in the late Ottoman period. McCarthy (1980) has rejected as fraudulent official census results widely used in the literature. The figure of 1.5 million Greeks in Asia Minor, recently published by Kitromilides and Alexandris (1984–5), is lower than

that quoted by Greek propagandists writing after the First World War (e.g. Soteriades 1918). It is based on archival records proving the existence of a detailed census taken between 1910 and 1912 by Greek consular authorities in collaboration with Greek Orthodox ecclesiastical authorities in Asia Minor and Thrace (ibid.: 21–30).

7. The history of the Asia Minor Greek communities and their uprooting must be set in the context of international relations and the policy for a 'Greater Greece', the *Megáli Idéa*, whereby Greece sought to regain the territories to which it had historical claims (Pentzopoulos 1962: 25 ff.; Llewellyn Smith 1973). For a useful bibliography see Clogg 1979: 227.

CHAPTER 2

1. Kitromilides (pers. comm.) has alerted me to the evidence for idealization of the refugees' past. Data available at the centre for Asia Minor Studies, Athens, show that conditions were often worse than the refugees claimed.

2. This was of course Ottoman Turkish, considerably different from modern Turkish owing to the reforms in language made in the past fifty years. A fascinating study of the retention of this form of Turkish could have been made but has not been, to my knowledge.

3. The Armenian Church has a doctrinal formulation regarding the nature of the Incarnation which differs from the definition set by the Ecumenical Council of Chalcedon (AD 451). Furthermore, the Armenians celebrate both the Epiphany and the Nativity on 6 January, thereby retaining the original practice of the Eastern Christian Church (S. Brock, pers. comm.).

CHAPTER 3

1. Prior to this, Greece and Bulgaria had conducted an exchange of minority populations, but on a voluntary basis and fewer persons were involved (Ladas 1932).

2. Despite its limitations as a policy, the emphasis on rural settlement characterizes most internationally funded relief programmes right up to the present day (see Harrell-Bond 1986).

3. One result of the events of 1922–3 was that Greece itself became ethnically homogeneous, particularly in the contested area of Macedonia (Pentzopoulos 1962: 125 ff.; Clogg 1979: 121). The success of this rural settlement policy in the North went further, though, for 'The whole region served as a laboratory for the development of practical methods of settling and uplifting the morale of a war-torn and expatriated people'; it was visited by officials from

Egypt, the Sudan, India, China, Burma, and South Africa (Pentzo-poulos 1962: 111).

4. For a thorough analysis of Greek political structures and conduct in this period see Mavrogordatos 1982.

5. Pentzopoulos deals fully with the proceedings of the seventh Pan-Refugee Congress. Although his analysis of 'refugee conscious-ness' stresses the refugees' claims for compensation as the basis for maintaining their identity, he notes that 'more profound and less utilitarian' reasons also existed, grounded in a common back-ground and experience (1962: 204). My argument emphasizes the combined effect of two sets of factors, the cultural and the political/economic, in promoting the sense of 'separate identity' in this group of Asia Minor urban refugees.

6. The Communist Party was restored to legality some forty years later with the return of parliamentary democracy to Greece in 1974.

7. These figures, derived from a preliminary analysis of local electoral returns, are indicative but provide only an approximate picture of political affinities. A full interpretation of voting returns and their significance must account for historical influences and other changing factors, e.g. tactical voting, reordered party alliances, adjustment of electoral boundaries, etc.

8. Different historical influences played a critical role in forming the identity of those born in Greece of refugee parents. This was clearly shown in a discussion between two brothers: one was born in 1928, the second child of four, while the youngest was born in 1941. 'I am a refugee,' the older man said, 'Since my father is, so am I, it's inherited; after all, I lived as a refugee' (Είμαι πρόσφυγας· εφόσον είναι ο πατέρας μου, είμαι και 'γώ. Τό' χουμε κληρονομικό. Και εγώ έχω ζήσει την προσφυγιά). The younger man disagreed, saying that he would first say that he was a Greek, and then that he was a refugee (Πρώτα λέγω ότι είμαι Έλληνας και μετά ότι είμαι πρόσφυγας). But he explained that life had been easier for him than for his brothers: by the time he was growing up, the family had a house, money was being earned regularly and he went through school.

9. This reconstruction of the history of Kokkinia is based mainly on first-hand accounts of the older inhabitants. I am especially grate-ful to Mr and Mrs Kapayiannides who provided detailed infor-mation. He was employed from 1920 to 1930 first by the Greek government and then by the RSC in various capacities, including the survey and allocation of housing in Kokkinia. She served on various local committees and the municipal council for a number of years.

10. Information on education was provided by Inspector Phytanides of the Third Educational Division, Piraeus, by the municipality of Nikaia, and by the headmaster of the primary school of Yerania; I gratefully acknowledge their co-operation.

CHAPTER 5

1. It is possible that political conditions of the time—the oppressive regime of the colonels, a military dictatorship seen to be imposed by 'local Greeks'—heightened the sense of refugee solidarity in Kokkinia and similar areas.
2. In a society where the house is the centre of social, symbolic, and personal significance, being 'mistress of the house' confers self-esteem and prestige on a woman. The nuances of the Greek *noikokyrá* are not conveyed by the usual English translation, 'housewife'.
3. In Greek society, *symphéron* is better understood as 'family interest' since individuals do not act outside the family context.

CHAPTER 6

1. The Greek Civil Code was extensively revised in 1983. The previous Family Law had specified a parental duty to provide dowry at marriage. This is no longer a legal stipulation, but customary expectations cannot be eliminated by the legislative pen. Dowry continues to be part of marriage strategies, and current legislation provides for a reduced rate of transfer tax from parents to children, whether at the time of marriage or afterwards (γονική παροχή now replaces the προίκα).
2. Loizos has argued that Greek Cypriot dowry has changed over the past fifty years in response to the relative shortage of men in the appropriate age groups, in this case owing to emigration (1975b). The same situation undoubtedly has obtained in post-war Greece.

CHAPTER 7

1. Monks and nuns take up the monastic vocation as celibates but always as part of a community. Called an *adelphótis*, from the etymological root denoting sibling bonds, the monastic community can be seen as a family with the abbot or abbess as parent (K. Ware, pers. comm.).
2. Το σερνικό πουλί φέρνει, το θηλυκό κτίζει. Το σερνικό φέρνει χόρτα και κλαριά και το θηλυκό φτιάχνει την φωλιά.
3. Χωρίς γυναίκα σπίτι δεν γίνεται. Η γυναίκα ζεσταίνει το σπίτι, είναι το χρυσό πάπλωμα, το σκεπάζει και ζεσταίνεται. Είναι απαραίτητη

στο σπίτι. Ο άντρας είναι επίσης απαραίτητος. Είναι ο στύλος του σπιτιού, είναι και η βάση.

CHAPTER 8

1. This definition of neighbourhood, an emic one, is based on people's use of the term *yeitonía*, on their use of the locality, and on my own observations and interaction with neighbours.
2. A culture cannot be derived from its proverbs, but differing degrees of sensitivity to public opinion are suggested by contrasting the English: 'Sticks and stones may break my bones but names can never hurt me', with the Greek: 'The tongue has no bones but it can break bones' (*Η γλώσσα κόκκαλα δεν έχει, αλλά κόκκαλα τσακίζει*).

CHAPTER 9

1. An interesting symbolic correspondence associates water with two points in Christ's ministry. The Epiphany, the celebration of his baptism, is also called the Theophany, (*Θεοφάνια*), the manifestation or revelation of God, a point marking the start of his ministry. Blessing of the waters takes place throughout the Orthodox world; in Greece it is a widespread custom, at sea-, lake-, or riverside settlements, for the priest to throw the Cross into deep waters, from where it is retrieved by young men who dive for this honour. Ascension Day, the end of Christ's earthly appearances, is celebrated in folk practice by the first seabathe: the custom is to pass through forty waves 'to be cleansed' (Megas 1963: 126–7).
2. Typical statements included: 'The years are from God. You do whatever you can for your loved one—you don't sit with arms crossed. But after that, it's whatever God says. When your hour arrives . . .' (*Τα χρόνια είναι απ' τον Θεό. Ό, τι μπορείς θα κάνεις για τον άνθρωπό σου. Δεν θα κάτσεις με σταυρωμένα χέρια. Πέρα απο 'κει, όμως, ό, τι πει ο Θεός. Όταν έρθει η ώρα σου . . .*).
3. Grave sites may be purchased; an advertisement in an Athenian newspaper is revealing: 'For sale at the 3rd Cemetery, Athens, a grave with marble tombstone, in a very good position (1st Section), telephone . . . '.

CHAPTER 10

1. Male attributes for a mountain village in Euboia are described by du Boulay (1974: 101 ff.). Campbell discusses the Sarakatsani attachment to St George and St Dimitrios, who are warrior-saints and have attributes which accord with pastoral life (1964: 343).

2. In the official hierarchy of the Church, men have the sole right to hold positions. The main Church Committee (Επιτροπή) which handles the revenue from collections and candles is composed of men. Women deal with charitable matters on the Friends of the Poor Committee (Φιλόπτωχο) and the Welfare Committee (Πρόνοια) under the leadership of the parish priest. The Scripture Circle (Αγιογραφικό Κύκλο), a formally organized group which meets to discuss readings from the Bible, is composed of women again led by a priest.

3. The public/private dichotomy, commonly employed in gender analysis, may simply refer to spatial or geographical distinctions but it usually carries political and economic overtones, appropriate to the situation in Western industrial society. The question of relative power and status (where male : public : power is opposed to female : private : dependence) should not be assumed, however. The cultural evaluation of gender roles is an empirical question, and the ways in which power and relative status relate to public/private spheres are analytically a separate issue (cf. Hirschon 1984: 19).

4. It is worth noting that in Jung's psychological theory people have a 'natural religious function' which tends to be expressed in the individuation process more characteristic of the second half of life.

5. Some early criticisms include: 'The folk–urban and the urban–rural dichotomies may be regarded as ideal-type constructs which are the products of Western writers but these have not been used in accordance with Weber's injunctions on the use of ideal-type constructs . . . .' (Hauser and Schnore 1965: 514). Furthermore, 'many of the extant generalisations about urbanisation either as dependent or independent variables do not have adequate empirical justification; . . . what is known is . . . based essentially on limited observations over time and space mainly in Western culture' (ibid.: vi). Also, Gulick concluded clearly, 'So far, anthropological findings indicate that urbanisation *per se* does not necessarily destroy traditional cultures' (1965: 52).

6. Among Sarakatsani shepherds, 'A family needs at least one man in the role of unmarried brother whose unreflecting courage guards its honour, and one man in the role of married leader whose prudence and self-control secures its material strength' (Campbell 1964: 317–18).

7. Lison-Tolosana's distinction between 'structural time' and 'generational time' has similar implications. The former indicates the 'recurrent temporal divisions into which the biological age of an individual is subdivided', but, 'each new situation is seen and experienced from a different angle by the contemporaneous gener-

ations.' While 'structural time' implies stability, permanence, enduring qualities, 'generational time' is accompanied by innovation and change' (1966: 200–1).

8. Nakane's cogent study of modern Japan, for example, made this point clearly, 'In the course of modernisation Japan imported many western cultural elements, but these were and are always partial and segmentary and are never in the form of an operating system. It is like a language with its basic indigenous structure or grammar which has accumulated a heavy overlay of borrowed vocabulary; while the outlook of Japanese society has suffered drastic changes over the past hundred years, the basic social grammar has hardly been affected. Here is an example of industrialisation and the importation of western culture not effecting changes in the basic cultural structure' (1970: 149).

9. In a biblical reference to the forgiveness of sin incorporated in the Orthodox funeral service (Danforth 1982: 51–2) the terms used, 'loosing' for forgiveness and 'binding' for non-forgiveness, have similar connotations.

10. The notion of an eternal community is fundamental among Orthodox theological concepts (Yannaras 1984: 41), and its everyday expression, I suggest, was evident in this 'open' orientation in Kokkinia's social life.

11. The notion of different levels developed in my analysis without reference to Dumont's idea of hierarchy and value (1982). His idea of transcendence and distinctions of levels could well be applied to this material.

12. The most commonly used prayer, recited three times and known to everyone, is the *Trisáyion*: 'Holy God, Holy and Strong, Holy and Immortal, have mercy upon us' (Άγιος ο Θεός, Άγιος Ισχυρός, Άγιος Αθάνατος, ελέησον ημάς). It addresses God in terms of characteristics which human beings implicitly do not have.

13. 'The inheritance of the Fall [is] an inheritance essentially of mortality rather than of sinfulness, sinfulness being merely a consequence of mortality' (Meyendorff 1974: 145).

REFERENCES

ALLEN, P. S. (1976). 'Aspida: A Depopulated Maniat Community', in M. Dimen and E. Friedl (eds.), *Regional Variation in Modern Greece and Cyprus* (New York: New York Academy of Sciences), pp. 168–98.

BAILEY, F. G., ed. (1971). *Gifts and Poison: The Politics of Reputation* (Oxford: Blackwell).

BARTH, F., ed. (1969). *Ethnic Groups and Boundaries: The Social Organization of Culture Difference* (Oslo and London: Allen and Unwin).

BENDIX, R. (1967). 'Tradition and Modernity Reconsidered', *Comparative Studies in Society and History*, 9 (3), pp. 292–346.

BERNARD, H. R. (1976). 'Kalymnos: The Island of Sponge Fishermen', in M. Dimen and E. Friedl (eds.), *Regional Variation in Modern Greece and Cyprus* (New York: New York Academy of Sciences), pp. 291–307.

BLOCH, M., ed. (1975). *Language and Oratory in Traditional Societies* (London: Academic Press).

BRANDES, S. H. (1975). *Migration, Kinship and Community: Tradition and Transition in a Spanish Village* (New York: Academy Press).

—— (1981). 'Gender Distinctions in Monteros Mortuary Ritual', *Ethnology*, 20, pp. 177–90.

CAMPBELL, J. K. (1964). *Honour, Family and Patronage* (Oxford: Clarendon Press).

—— and SHERRARD, P. (1968). *Modern Greece* (London: Benn Ltd.).

CENTRE FOR ASIA MINOR STUDIES (1980, 1982). Έξοδος (Athens).

CHRISTIAN, W. A. (1972). *Person and God in a Spanish Valley* (London: Seminar Press).

CLOGG, R. (1979). *A Short History of Modern Greece* (Cambridge: Cambridge University Press).

CUTILEIRO, J. (1971). *A Portuguese Rural Society* (Oxford: Clarendon Press).

DANFORTH, L. M. (1982). *The Death Rituals of Rural Greece* (New Jersey: Princeton University Press).

DAVIS, J. (1973). *Land and Family in Pisticci* (London: The Athlone Press).

DIMEN, M., and FRIEDL, E., eds. (1976). *Regional Variation in Modern Greece and Cyprus: Towards a Comparative Perspective on the Ethnography of Greece* (New York: New York Academy of Sciences).

DORE, R. P. (1958). *City Life in Japan: A Study of a Tokyo Ward* (Berkeley and Los Angeles: University of California Press).

DOUGLASS, W. A. (1969). *Death in Murelaga* (Seattle: Washington University Press).

DUBISCH, J. (1983). 'Greek Women: Sacred or Profane', *Journal of Modern Greek Studies* 1 (1), pp. 185–202.

DU BOULAY, J. (1974). *Portrait of a Greek Mountain Village*. (Oxford: Clarendon Press).

—— (1976). 'Lies, Mockery and Family Integrity', in J. G. Peristiany (ed.), *Mediterranean Family Structures* (Cambridge: Cambridge University Press), pp. 389–406.

DUMONT, L. (1982). 'On Value', Radcliffe-Brown Memorial Lecture 1980, *Proceedings of the British Academy*, 66 (Oxford: Oxford University Press).

ECONOMIST INTELLIGENCE UNIT (1975). *Greece* (London: The Economist Annual Supplement).

ELIADE, M. (1959). *The Sacred and the Profane* (New York: Harcourt, Brace and World, Inc.).

FINNEGAN, R. (1973). 'Literacy versus Non-Literacy: The Great Divide', in R. Finnegan and R. Horton (eds.), *Modes of Thought* (London: Faber).

FIRTH, R. (1964). 'Social Organisation and Social Change', in *Essays on Social Organisation and Values* (London: The Athlone Press).

FRIEDL, E. (1962). *Vasilika: A Village in Modern Greece* (New York: Holt, Rinehart and Winston).

—— (1976). 'Kinship, Class and Selective Migration', in J. G. Peristiany (ed.), *Mediterranean Family Structures* (Cambridge: Cambridge University Press), pp. 363–87.

GIBB, H. A. R., and BOWEN, H. (1950, 1957). *Islamic Society and the West*, Parts 1 and 2 (Oxford: Oxford University Press).

GILMORE, D. D. (1978). 'Varieties of Gossip in a Spanish Rural Community', *Ethnology*, 17 (1), pp. 89–99.

GOLD, J. R. (1980). *An Introduction to Behavioural Geography* (Oxford: Oxford University Press).

GOODY, J., ed. (1968). *Literacy in Traditional Societies* (Cambridge: Cambridge University Press).

—— (1977). *The Domestication of the Savage Mind* (Cambridge: Cambridge University Press).

GULICK, J. (1965). 'Old Values and New Institutions in a Lebanese Arab City', *Human Organisation*, 24 (1), pp. 49–52.

HADJINICOLAOU-MARAVA, A. (1953). *O Ἅγιος Μάμας* (Athens: Institut français d'Athènes, Centre for Asia Minor Studies).

HARRELL-BOND, B. E. (1986). *Imposing Aid: Emergency Assistance to Refugees* (Oxford: Oxford University Press).

HASLUCK, F. W. (1929). *Christianity and Islam under the Sultans*, 2 vols. (Oxford: Oxford University Press).

HAUSER, P. M., and SCHNORE, L. F., eds. (1965). *The Study of Urbanisation* (New York: Wiley and Sons).

HERTZ, R. (1960). *Death and the Right Hand*, trans. R. and C. Needham (London: Cohen and West).

HERZFELD, M. (1980). 'Honour and Shame: Problems in the Comparative Analysis of Moral Systems, *Man*, NS 15 (2), pp. 339–51.

—— (1982). *Ours Once More: Folklore, Ideology and the Making of Modern Greece* (Austin: University of Texas Press).

—— (1985). *The Poetics of Manhood: Contest and Identity in a Cretan Mountain Village* (Princeton: Princeton University Press).

HIRSCHON, R. (1978). 'Open Body/Closed Space: The Transformation of Female Sexuality', in S. Ardener (ed.), *Defining Females: The Nature of Woman in Society* (London: Croom Helm), pp. 66–88.

—— (1981). 'Essential Objects and the Sacred: Interior and Exterior Space in an Urban Greek Locality', in S. Ardener (ed.) *Woman and Space* (London: Croom Helm), pp. 72–88.

—— (1983). 'Women, the Aged and Religious Activity: Oppositions and Complementarity in an Urban Locality', in P. Allen and L. Mackrakis (eds.), *Women and Men in Greece* (*Journal of Modern Greek Studies*, 1 (1); Baltimore), pp. 113–29.

—— (1984). 'Property, Power and Gender Relations', in R. Hirschon (ed.), *Women and Property, Women as Property* (London: Croom Helm), pp. 1–22.

—— (1985). 'The Woman–Environment Relationship: Greek Cultural Values in an Urban Community', *Women and Space in Human Settlements* (special issue), *Ekistics*, 52 (310), pp. 15–21.

—— and GOLD, J. R. (1982). 'Territoriality and the Home Environment in a Greek Urban Community', *Anthropological Quarterly*, 55 (2), pp. 63–73.

—— and THAKURDESAI, S. (1970). 'Society, Culture and Spatial Organisation: An Athens community', *Ekistics*, 30 (178), pp. 187–96.

HOUSEPIAN, M. (1966). *The Smyrna Affair* (New York: Harcourt, Brace, Jovanovich; repr. London, 1972).

İNALCIK, H. (1978). *The Ottoman Empire: Conquest, Organization and Economy* (London).

KARAYEORGAS, D. (1974). 'Οι οικονομικές συνέπειες της στρατιωτικής δικτατορίας', *Anti*, 1 (1), pp. 41–6.

KAYSER, B., and THOMPSON, K. (1964). *Social and Economic Atlas of Greece* (Athens: Social Science Centre).

KENNA, M. (1976). 'Houses, Fields and Graves: Property and Ritual Obligations on a Greek Island', *Ethnology*, 15 (1), pp. 21–34.

KERTZER, D. I. (1980). *Comrades and Christians: Religion and Political Struggle in Communist Italy* (Cambridge: Cambridge University Press).

KITROMILIDES, P., and ALEXANDRIS, A. (1984–5). 'Ethnic Survival,

268 REFERENCES

Nationalism and Forced Migration: The Historical Demography of the Greek Community of Asia Minor at the Close of the Ottoman Era', *Bulletin of the Centre for Asia Minor Studies*, 5 (Athens: Centre for Asia Minor Studies), pp. 9–44.

LADAS, S. P. (1932). *The Exchanges of Minorities—Bulgaria, Greece and Turkey* (New York: The Macmillan Co.).

LAMBIRI, I. (1968). 'The Impact of Industrial Employment on the Position of Women in a Greek Country Town', in J. G. Peristiany (ed.), *Contributions to Mediterranean Sociology* (Paris and The Hague: Mouton and Co.), pp. 261–8.

LAWSON, J. C. (1910). *Modern Greek Folklore and Ancient Greek Religion* (Cambridge: Cambridge University Press).

LEACH, E. (1954). *Political Systems of Highland Burma* (London: Bell).

LEAGUE OF NATIONS (1926). *Greek Refugee Settlement* (Geneva).

LEGG, K. R. (1969). *Politics in Modern Greece* (Stanford: Stanford University Press).

LEWIS, B. (1963). 'Faith and Learning', in *Istanbul and the Civilization of the Ottoman Empire*, repr. in L. E. Sweet (ed.), *Peoples and Cultures of of the Middle East* (New York: The Natural History Press, 1970), pp. 102–13.

—— (1968). *The Emergence of Modern Turkey*, 2nd edn. (London: Oxford University Press).

LEWIS, O. (1952). 'Urbanisation without Breakdown: A Case Study', *Scientific Monthly* 75, pp. 31–41.

—— (1973). 'Some Perspectives on Urbanization with Special Reference to Mexico City', in A. Southall (ed.), *Urban Anthropology: Cross-cultural Studies of Urbanization* (New York: Oxford University Press), pp. 125–38.

LISON-TOLOSANA, C. (1966). *Belmonte de los Caballeros: A Sociological Study of a Spanish Town* (Oxford: Clarendon Press).

LLEWELLYN SMITH, M. (1973). *Ionian Vision: Greece in Asia Minor 1919–1922* (London: Allen Lane).

LOIZOS, P. (1975a). *The Greek Gift: Politics in a Cypriot Village* (Oxford: Blackwell).

—— (1975b). 'Changes in Property Transfer among Greek Cypriot Villagers', *Man*, NS 10 (4), pp. 503–23.

—— (1981). *The Heart Grown Bitter: A Chronicle of Cypriot War Refugees* (Cambridge: Cambridge University Press).

LYNCH, K. (1960). *The Image of the City* (Cambridge, Mass.: MIT Press).

McCARTHY, J. (1980). 'Greek Statistics on Ottoman Greek Population', *International Journal of Turkish Studies*, 1 (2), pp. 66–76.

MAUSS, M. (1969). *The Gift*, trans. I. Cunnison (London: Cohen and West).

MAVROGORDATOS, G. T. (1982). *Social Coalitions and Party Strategies in Greece, 1922–36* (Berkeley: University of California Press).

MEGAS, G. A. (1963). *Greek Calendar Customs* (Athens).

MERLIER, O. (1974). *Ο τελευταίος ελληνισμός της Μικράς Ασίας* (Athens: Centre for Asia Minor Studies).

MEYENDORFF, J. (1974). *Byzantine Theology: Historical Trends and Doctrinal Themes*, (Fordham University Press; London and Oxford: Mowbray, 1975).

MOUZELIS, N. P. (1978). *Modern Greece: Facets of Underdevelopment* (London: Macmillan).

MUMFORD, L. (1934). *Technics and Civilization* (London: Secker and Warburg).

NAKANE, C. (1970). *Japanese Society* (London: Weidenfield and Nicolson).

NEEDHAM, R., ed. (1973). *Right and Left: Essays on Dual Symbolic Classification* (London: University of Chicago Press).

NISBET, R. (1969). *Social Change and History: Aspects of the Western Theory of Development* (New York: Oxford University Press).

OECD [Organisation for Economic Co-operation and Development] (1972, 1975). *Greece* (Paris: OECD, Annual Economic Surveys).

OKELY, J. (1975). 'Gypsy Women: Models in Conflict', in S. Ardener (ed.), *Perceiving Women* (New York: Wiley), pp. 55–86.

ONG, W. (1982). *Orality and Literacy: The Technologizing of the Word* (London and New York: Methuen).

OTT, S. (1981). *The Circle of Mountains: A Basque Shepherding Community* (Oxford: Clarendon Press).

PENTZOPOULOS, D. (1962). *The Balkan Exchange of Minorities and its Impact upon Greece* (Paris and The Hague: Moulton and Co.).

PESMAZOGLU, J. (1972). 'The Greek Economy since 1967', in R. Clogg and G. Yannopoulos (eds.), *Greece under Military Rule* (London: Secker and Warburg).

PINA-CABRAL, J. DE (1986). *Sons of Adam, Daughters of Eve: The Peasant Worldview of the Alto Minho* (Oxford: Clarendon Press).

RADCLIFFE-BROWN, A. R. (1957). *A Natural Science of Society* (New York: Free Press).

RAGLAN, Lord (1964). *The Temple and the House* (London: Routledge and Kegan Paul).

RAMSAY, W. M. (1917). *The Intermixture of Races in Asia Minor* (London: British Academy).

RELPH, E. (1976). *Place and Placelessness* (London: Pion Ltd.).

SCHMEMANN, A. (1974a). *Of Water and the Spirit: A Liturgical Study of Baptism* (New York: St Vladimir's Seminary Press).

—— (1974b). *Great Lent*, rev. edn. (New York: St Vladimir's Seminary Press).

SCIAMA, L. (1981). 'The Problem of Privacy in Mediterranean Anthropology', in S. Ardener (ed.), *Women and Space* (London: Croom Helm), pp. 89–111.

SHAW, S. J., and SHAW, K. E. (1976–7). *History of the Ottoman Empire and Modern Turkey*, 2 vols. (Cambridge: Cambridge University Press).

SOTERIADES, G. (1918). *An Ethnological Map Illustrating Hellenism in the Balkan Peninsula and Asia Minor* (London: E. Stanford and Co.).

SOTIRIOU, D. (1963). Ματωμένα χώματα (Athens: Themelio).

STANIFORTH, M., trans. (1968). *Early Christian Writings: The Apostolic Fathers* (Harmondsworth: Penguin Classics).

STREET, B. (1984). *Literacy in Theory and Practice* (Cambridge: Cambridge University Press).

THAKURDESAI, S. G. (1974). ' "Sense of Place" in Greek Anonymous Architecture', in D. and M. Kennedy (eds.), *The Inner City*, Architects Yearbook, 14 (London: Paul Elek), pp. 94–102.

TIPPS, D. C. (1973). 'Modernisation Theory and the Study of National Societies: A Critical Perspective', *Comparative Studies in Society and History*, 15, pp. 199–226.

TUAN, Y. F. (1974). *Topophilia: A Study of Environmental Perception, Attitudes and Values* (Englewood Cliffs, N J: Prentice Hall).

TURNER, V. (1969). *The Ritual Process* (London: Routledge and Kegan Paul).

—— (1974). 'Pilgrimages as Social Processes', in *Dramas, Fields and Metaphors* (Ithaca and London: Cornell University Press).

VASILIOU, I. (1944). Η λαϊκή κατοικία (Athens).

VENEZIS, E. (1931). Το νούμερο (Athens: Kollarou).

VEREMIS, T. (1977). Οι επεμβάσεις του στρατού στην ελληνική πολιτική (1916–36) (Athens: Exandas).

WARE, K. (1964). *The Orthodox Church*, rev. edn. (Harmondsworth: Penguin).

—— (1973). 'Notes and Comments', *Eastern Church Review*, 5 (1), p. 70.

—— (1979). *The Orthodox Way* (London: Mowbray).

—— (1983). 'The Church: A Time of Transition', in. R. Clogg (ed.), *Greece in the 1980s* (Basingstoke: Macmillan), pp. 208–30.

WARNER, M. (1976). *Alone of All Her Sex* (London: Weidenfeld and Nicolson).

WIRTH, L. (1938). 'Urbanism as a Way of Life', *American Journal of Sociology*, 44, pp. 1–24.

WRIGHT, S. (1981). 'Place and Face: Of Women in Doshmar Ziari, Iran', in S. Ardener (ed.), *Women and Space* (London: Croom Helm), pp. 136–57.

YANNARAS, C. (1984). *The Freedom of Morality* (New York: St Vladimir's Seminary Press).

YATES, F. (1966). *The Art of Memory* (London: Routledge and Kegan Paul).

ZANDER, W. (1971). *Israel and the Holy Places of Christendom* (London: Weidenfeld and Nicolson).

INDEX

Virgin Mary, *see* Mother of God
virginity 121, 138, 152

War(s):
  Balkan 12, 41
  Civil 47, 48, 53
  First World 7, 41
  of Independence 10, 11
  Second World 47
  see also German Occupation
water 140, 202, 220, 261
widows 38, 108, 220
work, *see* economic; employment;
    occupation

world-view 104–5, 193, 195, 226, 235,
    238–43
  of elderly 222, 226, 231, 232, 239

Yerania:
  hardships; handicaps 59–60, 68–70,
    171, 210
  history of settlement 50, 59–60
  household number; size 64, 78
  housing provisions 60–2
  population 61, 63, 74–5
  population density 63
  survey (1930) 24–5, 60, 68, 69
  survey (1972) 65, 71, 79, 254–6
Yunanistan 7